Perjury for Pay

*An Exposé of the Methods and Criminal
Cunning of the Modern Malingerer*

*A Legal History of Personal Injury Court Cases
vs. Railroad Companies in the 1800s*

By Dr. Willis P. King

PANTIANOS
CLASSICS

Published by Pantianos Classics

ISBN-13: 978-1-78987-099-2

First published in 1906

Contents

Dedication

To those rare individuals, the honest litigants in personal injury litigation — the men and women who do not want something for nothing; who, though, perhaps, seriously injured, are willing to go upon the witness stand and swear to the truth concerning it — adding nothing and nothing concealing — this book is admiringly dedicated.

The Author.

Preface

IN the preface to my first and only book before this — "Stories of a Country Doctor"— I stated that I scarcely knew why I had written the book; but, I cannot say the same thing of this one and speak the truth. I know very well why I have written this work, I wish that the reasons that impelled me to the task did not exist. I wish, for the sake of my countrymen and country women, for the sake of Christian civilization and morality, that those reasons did not exist — that I might be able to truthfully say that the whole thing is untrue and that I might conscientiously submit the manuscript to the flames.

But, alas, and alas, the reasons do exist and, unfortunately, instead of growing better the conditions of which I write, are growing worse every day. More and more people are becoming willing to act a part to malinger, to go upon the witness stand and perjure themselves for the sake of a little money.

Our so-called, "modern society" is in a large measure to blame for this. The concentration of the wealth of the country in the hands of the few, and the gaudy display that this few makes of it, is to blame. Those who are poorer see all this display, they become envious and desire to purchase fine things, to buy all the comforts of this life and to remain in comparative idleness while others toil.

When thoughts of this kind enter the heads of poor, weak mortals many of them begin at once to think of and to concoct schemes by which they may get something for nothing, by which they may secure a large amount of money without earning it, and this, amongst all the dishonest schemes, seems to them the easiest and the best. Of course, a great majority of those people do get hurt, more or less, and the dishonest schemes to make money out of the accident come to them afterward; but, if we could know the truth about the number who go to work and deliberately *create the accident*, if the reader will pardon the bull, he would be astonished more than ever.

I know precisely why I wrote the book, and so, I owe no apologies, and have none to make, to anyone for having written it.

I hope that it may cause many people to think, that it may influence them in the direction of honest and right living, and that it may influence others against lending their aid to this robbery for the sake of a small pittance of the spoils, or simply even for the sake of kinship or of friendship.

The conditions treated of in this book are even worse in the East than in the West, for there the conditions which bring about such desires have existed much longer than in the West — the rich are richer and the poor are poorer — hence, wealth makes a greater and more vulgar display and treads more often upon the toes of poverty and poverty is, therefore, more often made jealous and envious.

I sincerely hope that the book may do good. If it shall, then the motives which impelled me to the task of writing it will have been gratified.

Willis P. King, M. D.
Kansas City, Ma, March, 1906.

Introduction

IN the early part of the year, 1875, I received the appointment of local surgeon of the Missouri Pacific railroad company, at Sedalia, Missouri, where I then resided.

This position I held and discharged the duties of until 1881, when I was appointed consulting surgeon to the company hospital, at Sedalia, which had been removed to that place from Washington, Missouri.

During the period from 1875 until 1881 I discharged the duties of local surgeon— caring for all injured employees and sending them to the hospital at Washington.

To me, a young and aspiring surgeon, the experience was most valuable. I was often called out at midnight; in fact, I was called at all hours, both day and night, to go to some hotel or boarding house, there to find some poor switchman or brakeman — more often, however, it was a switchman — mangled and torn and would then, for an hour or two, give myself to the task of patching him up, or amputating a leg or an arm.

I did not amputate often, I am proud to say, for I soon found that any butcher could chop off a leg or an arm, but that it took a surgeon to save the member.

I knew then, as I know now, that many men acquired reputations, on both sides of the conflict in our Civil War, whose almost whole experience had been in cutting off legs and arms; and, I fear, often when they could and should have been saved.

I wish right here, to pay a deserved tribute to railroad men and, more especially, to trainmen, for their endurance, their courage and their stoicism at such times. I never expect to meet or see any braver set of men than I found in the Missouri Pacific train service.

For twenty-five years I continued to care for those men, and my experience never varied, so far as their exhibition of courage in the most painful and trying circumstances was concerned.

If our United States Army could be recruited wholly from the railroad train service of this country we would have the noblest and bravest army that ever did or ever will put on a uniform or shoulder a gun in its country's service.

In 1881, as said before, I received the appointment to the position of consulting surgeon to the hospital. I did not do so much operating as before, for the injured employees were operated upon and cared for at the hospital.

I was, however, nearly always called to assist at such times and this experience was still more valuable to me, for here I had the opportunity to watch and assist in the treatment of the case to the end; and, as the practice of surgery was, at that time, making great advances, I had an opportunity to hear, see and take part in the adoption of the new and better methods, which have since brought the practice of surgery to such a high plane of perfection and to have established it so firmly in the confidence of intelligent people.

On February 2, 1885, after a change of chief surgeons, I was appointed by my friend and classmate. Dr. W. B. Outten, to the position of assistant chief surgeon, in charge of the hospital at Sedalia, and of the then Sedalia Division (which embraced all lines West, Southwest and Northwest of Jefferson City) which position I held without change, except change of location, for about fifteen years.

The hospital was in the old Missouri, Kansas and Texas General Offices Headquarters building — the Missouri Pacific having acquired the M., K. & T. road, by lease, for a long period of years; and as soon as it did so, the M., K. & T. General Offices were taken to St Louis.

The capacity of the hospital was from sixty to ninety per day — the capacity being greater in Summer than in Winter; as in Summer time, we could put in cots and care for many more men than in Winter.

During the fifteen years that I had charge of the hospital we cared for and treated thousands of sick and hundreds of wounded employees.

The character of the injuries was every kind of wound, from a mere abrasion of the finger up to injuries requiring the amputation of a leg, thigh or an arm, to trephining the skull, and even returning extruded intestines and other viscera and closing up and treating the wound by which they made their exit. In addition to the above we had often to reduce dislocations and set fractures and, in fact, we did everything required of surgeons situated as we were and having the duties to perform that we had.

The character of the sickness of those treated was such diseases as prevail in the Missouri and Mississippi valleys, and upon the high prairies of Missouri, Kansas and Nebraska, together with the degenerative diseases of the brain and spinal cord and the nervous system and diseases of nutrition, which do not depend upon locality or climate.

The reader will be surprised, no doubt, when I say that, out of all of the numerous injured employees treated, I met six of them in Court — six who had failed to adjust their claims against the company on account of their injuries and had, therefore, brought suit against the company, in order to force a settlement in that way; and, of these six, four were settled before they came to trial, so that I went on the witness stand and testified in only two of the cases of the men whose injuries I had treated in the hospital. Of course, there were other suits, but they were of employees who had lost an arm or a leg; and in such cases, they do not need the services of a physician, as it is a question of liability, and for the jury to say how much should be assessed against the company for inflicting those injuries.

I wish here to commend the policy of the Missouri Pacific management in settling such cases. The management does not like to fight its injured employees in Court, and the claim department would go to any length and even pay more than it should in settlement, rather than have suit brought. This, however, was not often the case; for as a rule, I found the employees reasonable in their demands and their motto seemed to be, "I would rather make a reasonable settlement and retain my position than to have a lawsuit and no position."

During the twenty-five years of my service with the Missouri Pacific Railroad Company, I examined, by order of the chief surgeon, or by request of the general claim agent, or some of his assistants, or of the company's attorneys, more than two hundred injured citizens and passengers or persons who assumed to have been injured; and of these, I assisted at the trial of about fifty cases.

It is humiliating, and a disgrace to humanity; and, especially to American manhood and womanhood, for me to be obliged to say, in justice to the truth in the matter, that I found only six or seven of these more than two hundred, to have been permanently injured as claimed by them. So that about two hundred or more of these persons— citizens, passengers and others — were attempting to sustain their cases; and, if possible, win them and, thereby get a verdict for a large amount of money, solely by malingering, fraud and perjury on their part and by perjury of their relatives or friends, or both.

I insist that this is a humiliating confession for me to make, after this long service and this vast experience.

Before I began this service I had graduated, first in a first-class St. Louis medical college and had gone to New York later and, after about six months' instruction, had the degree *ad eundum* conferred on me by the Faculty of Bellevue Hospital Medical College, New York; and, during the time of this service I spent most or all of four terms in taking Post Graduate and Polyclinic instruction in New York. I do not make this statement to boast, but to show that I made every effort in my power to equip myself, so as to intelligently deal with and care for the sick and wounded employees placed in my charge; and, in addition, so as to properly examine and correctly diagnosticate the ailments of those who made claims or brought suit against the company. I feel that I have a right to state the facts in the matter, as well as to feel proud and gratified of the fact that I honestly tried to do my duty by all.

If I had been a man of only ordinary ability, or who had carelessly neglected to do my duty in this regard, there might be some chance of my having been mistaken in many of these cases; but, as it is, I am sure that all fair-minded persons who read this will say that it was next to impossible. Now this brings me to the object of this book. Why did I write it? Many will be ready to answer, I fear, "You wrote it at the behest of the railroad companies; they hired you to do it!" In reply to this I wish to say that not one person connected with the management of any railroad knew or knows that I have written, or that I even contemplated writing such a book; and if they had, they could not hire me to do it, nor could anybody hire me not to do it, or anything else, which I regard as being a great moral duty.

I beg to say, therefore, that I wrote the book at the behest of my own conscience, and for the benefit, if possible, of American manhood and womanhood, and of even tender and innocent childhood.

There seems to be a wave of fraud, of malingering and perjury sweeping over the land. The effort to gain something for nothing, to get the money of others by false acting and false swearing is absolutely degrading men, women and children all over the country; and, if I can add just a little toward any effort that may be made to stop it, I shall feel that this book has not been written in vain.

I know the fate of reformers, as a rule. They and their reforms fail. But, I shall not fail. Nothing beneath the heavens can check the exposures I make and that others will make, and I know that the small amount of good I hope to do will be done. I have not a twinge of fear on that point

I grew to almost middle manhood before I ever heard of a lawsuit for damages on account of personal injuries. When I was a boy; and, as I grew into young manhood, I knew of three suits being brought and vigorously prosecuted on account of slander; and, when two of these had received verdicts — one of them for quite a large sum and the other in a sum that was by no means insignificant in those days, both of them refused to permit their attorneys to make an effort to collect the result of the verdicts, but said they did not want it, did not bring suit for that purpose but to vindicate their characters; and that, should the defendant offer to pay them, they would throw the money in his face.

Just think of it, reader! Think of it and then compare such action with what you and I witness or read about every day. Does it not seem as if somebody should hold up a hand and cry, "halt."

Why, in our larger cities and towns, where many railroads enter; and, where there are street car systems, the civil dockets of the Courts are almost taken up with suits of this kind, especially of this and the divorce suits.

I confess that, when I entered the service of the Missouri Pacific Railroad Company, I was prejudiced against corporations in this regard. I had imbibed the idea — I don't know how or for what reason — that railroads hurt people and then kicked them aside and passed on, paying no further attention to them; and that, if the injured person should bring suit, the corporations went into the courts, and through their agents and attorneys suborned witnesses and bought juries — finding this cheaper and easier than to settle by compromise.

But, oh, what an awakening, when I came face to face with the facts in the case! I found the company with which I was associated always ready and willing to make settlement, and that upon terms that were more than fair to the injured party. In truth I don't think I ever witnessed a settlement of this kind with citizens or passengers where the injured person was not paid more than he was entitled to under a fair consideration of the matter.

The fact is that railroad companies are even anxious to settle and to settle early, for experience has taught them that so long as these cases remain unsettled just so long will the injured parties continue to swell their claims, and that they always get the worst of it when the case is submitted to the jury.

In fact I found the fraud and rascality all on the ether side— except in the very few cases I have named; and these cases were so exceptional that, before this book is finished, I shall either refer to these few cases by name, or in such a way that all of their friends and acquaintances may know that they are meant, in order that no injustice may be done to fair and honest people.

The juries that are called upon to try these cases seem to be imbued with about the same ideas that I was before I entered the service of a railroad and I could therefore excuse them were it not for the fact that they will not permit their prejudices to be removed, or even modified by testimony, and they will not, on any account, believe one word that anybody in the employment of the railroad company swears to.

I state this as a rule which, of course, has its few exceptions. They seem to think, and I believe they do think, that all witnesses who testify for the company are paid for their testimony; or, in case of employees, that they are afraid to testify against the company — fearing that they may lose their jobs.

In my twenty-five years' experience in this matter I have witnessed the rendering of some of the most outrageous verdicts which, look at them as you might, could not be regarded in any other light than as open, flagrant, daylight robbery.

I believe that all cases of suits for damages, for injury to the person, should be tried before a jury of intelligent physicians. There should be in every Circuit Court a commission of physicians — consisting of either three or five, appointed either by the Court or the Governor of the State, and that they should sit and hear all testimony, and that they should be permitted to even take part in the examinations of plaintiffs made by other physicians by order of the Court.

With such juries something like justice would be meted out to both plaintiff and defendant, and justice should be the end to be attained in all such suits. Nobody except an intelligent physician is capable of understanding the medical testimony in such cases.

The French have a very excellent system, but not so good as the one I suggest. They have a commission of three physicians in certain districts. When a person is injured by a corporation they go at once and examine such person. Their examinations are most painstaking and elaborate. They examine every excretion of the body, chemically and microscopically. They take the temperature, pulse and respiration and make a record of same, and they examine carefully and critically every organ in the body and record its condition.

If the injured person is confined to his bed, they make visits to him at stated intervals; and, at such visits, again examine him, noting any changes that may have occurred since the last examination.

After they are through with the injured party they make a most elaborate report to the Court, with their opinions and conclusions, based on their frequent examinations, carefully noted therein, and, when the case comes up for trial, the report of this commission and its opinions and conclusions play no unimportant part in the final verdict.

There are some things in our code of practice which must have come down to us from the dark ages.

The greatest piece of injustice, the most outrageous piece of nonsense that I have ever encountered, is that of not permitting the family or attending physician, or any physician, for that matter, who has so much as looked at the injured person; and especially, if he has expressed an opinion as to the condition of the injured party, to testify in the case.

The physician may be possessed of facts, which, if told to the jury, would defeat the plaintiff, and thereby prevent his collecting an unjust verdict; but, no, he is the attending physician. But, not so with his testimony in behalf of the plaintiff. If he is in possession of a single fact which may assist the plaintiff in his highway robbery, he is permitted to tell it to the jury. Now this rule should be changed just this far, and we cannot lay claim to being entirely free from the hereditary influences that have come down to us from our great ancestors — the cave dwellers — until it is changed.

The family or attending physician or any physician should be permitted to testify to any facts, which help to elucidate the case, and which do not tend to disgrace plaintiff or to bring him into disrepute.

The attending physician or any physician, who has been in consultation in the case, or who has seen the case with the attending physician, should not be permitted to testify to the fact that plaintiff has been or is afflicted with a loathsome disease; or, in case of a female plaintiff, to the birth of a child out of wedlock, as such testimony would tend to injure plaintiff in the estimation of his or her friends and acquaintances. But, he should be permitted and even made to testify in regard to any physical fact; and, especially as to anything that he may have seen or heard, which would tend to throw light on the case, and which would go to show that plaintiff was preparing to perpetrate a fraud.

The law should not lend itself to the perpetration of a fraud, nor to the assistance of any kind of dishonesty. Nor should a physician be expected or permitted to do so.

Not long since I witnessed the rendering of a most unjust verdict, against a corporation for five thousand dollars, largely because not one of a half dozen physicians was permitted to testify that he had seen the plaintiff's knee. Each one who had seen it had said to the attending physician something like this: "That is a tuberculous joint," or "That looks like a tuberculous knee joint," as

"The Courts had held that the statement of an opinion was equivalent to making a prescription" and so the tuberculous knee — tuberculous long before the assumed injury, went to the jury as an injury inflicted, through carelessness, of the defendant.

The leg had been amputated and, unfortunately the knee joint thrown away.

I must not close this introduction without referring briefly to "Erichson's Railroad Spine."

Prof. Erichson, a quite distinguished English surgeon in his day, but a credulous old granny, several years ago, described what he named the "Railroad Spine" which has done more to injure corporations and to help rogues and perjurers to rob railroad companies than all that has ever been written on the subject of injuries to the spine, before or since.

He described a condition like this: He said that in two, three or four days after a serious railroad wreck, individuals who had been in the wreck, and who had boasted just after coming out of it that they had come out without a scratch, would call on a surgeon and describe and complain of a group of symptoms — such as confusion of mind, tingling sensations running down one or both legs, pain in lumbar region, etc., etc., (I give the symptoms from memory, but think they are fairly correct), all cases being much alike, and he held that there was an injury to the spinal cord from the shock or concussion, (when any physician or surgeon knows that, when an injury is inflicted on the spinal cord, the symptoms coming from that injury are felt at once) — and that the symptoms coming from that injury, or shock he called it, do not develop or become apparent for several days; and, when they do develop, are almost identical in all cases.

The truth is that, when persons come out of a wreck unhurt they are usually jubilant about it at the time and are disposed to boast of their good luck; but, after the lapse of several days, during which they have had time to hear of the fabulous sums that have been paid to others, begin to "kick themselves," to use a slang phrase, for being such fools, and for not making complaint of injury and putting in a claims for damages. They feel as if they had lost their pocket book, which contained a large sum of money.

Now, when a person with a speculative turn of mind begins to see where he might have made some money under such circumstances, he at once repairs to a surgeon and describes his symptoms. This may be the last and only time he will call upon the doctor; for, one of the strangest points against those malingerers is that, though claiming the most serious injuries, they rarely ever take treatment.

When one of those speculative persons makes up his mind that he is going to "make a stake" in a case of this kind the surgeon is, as a rule, the first person he wants to see. It is not treatment that he wants, but the surgeon's opinion, based on his statement of his assumed symptoms; for, he feels that, if he can deceive this man, there will be no trouble about deceiving a jury.

Prof. Erichson, being an honest, innocent and credulous old man, accepted these statements as being true. From his standpoint he could not conceive of any person lying about such a thing and assuming a lot of symptoms which he did not feel.

The reader will naturally ask, "how is it that so many people describe their symptoms so much alike, if they are malingering?"

If the reader will carefully peruse the following pages he will find things unfolded — some things of much greater peculiarity than this. The truth is there is a sort of "chimney corner medicine" among the laity and they all seem to have the same idea as to what symptoms should follow an injury to the spinal cord; and, while the symptoms they described are false and do not belong to symptoms coming from an injured cord, yet they have their own ideas as to what such symptoms should be; and unfortunately for the defense the jury is apt to have the same ideas.

The puzzle is that physicians, and especially, such a person as Prof. Erichson, should accept such stories.

Every lawyer who makes it a business to hunt up cases and sue corporations either has a volume of Erichson's Surgery, or the weak doctor whom he employs to do the swearing for his clients has one which is easily accessible to the lawyer and, in either case, you will find the chapter on "Railroad Spine" well thumbed.

Some of those anti-corporation lawyers employ a person who has been called a "snitch" whose business it is to watch the papers for the names of persons who have recently been hurt, or to get the information in any way he can, and he then repairs, in haste, to the place to which the injured person has gone or has been taken; and he seeks an interview, presents the injured person with the card of the lawyer, and then, if permitted to do so, he expatiates upon the wonderful ability of the lawyer. He fills the injured person full of stories about the large verdicts the lawyer has obtained and the immense sums of money he has collected from corporations.

This "snitch" is also employed I believe to work up, find and manufacture evidence in each particular case and to harmonize this evidence by frequent interviews with the family and friends of the injured party.

I shall m the coming chapters speak of the different classes of injuries, or assumed injuries, for which suit is usually brought, in the order of the frequency of their assumed inflictions, and I shall describe the real injury and the symptoms which should follow its infliction and also, of the false or assumed symptoms.

I shall treat of how to detect and expose them and will then give a few cases under each class— cases at the trial of which — in nearly all of those narrated — I have been present and have assisted the corporation attorneys in defending, by lending my aid to the task of bringing out the medical evidence, and its presentation to the jury.

To give them according to their assumed frequency the spinal cord stands pre-eminently at the head of the list.

Next comes fractures, dislocations and injuries to joints.

Then, perhaps, assumed injuries to the female organs of generation; and following close upon the latter, we will find local paralysis, and these will be grouped and everything else simply treated of under the heading of "Other Injuries."

I shall give nothing but the plain unvarnished truth, and I hope that this plain narrative and the experience I have had may be of benefit to physicians who have not had the opportunity to study the subject. I believe that physicians are honest, as a rule, and that they want to do right; but, not being acquainted with the technical facts in such cases as they rarely ever see them, they take their patient's word for his symptoms, believing him to be honest, and then go upon the stand and, unfortunately, testify to a state of facts which do not exist. Not being competent to correctly interpret real symptoms it is net to be expected that they will be able to detect and expose false ones. They are honest, but they make mistakes. I desire this book to be an educator for all such honest and earnest but mistaken men of my profession.

Chapter One - The Spinal Cord

IT is a fact easy of demonstration that there are, perhaps, more claims against corporations based upon assumed injuries to the spinal cord than upon any other single cause. This is the case, no doubt, because the layman knows that, to the ordinary, half educated physician, diseases of or injury to this organ is a great mystery and one that he rarely ever solves to his own satisfaction.

It is a well-established fact, anatomists and others competent to give an opinion say, that the spinal cord is, by far, the best protected organ in the animal body. This protection is due no doubt to the high and important functions it is called upon to perform; for, in addition to its function of presiding over and governing sensation and motion of the body, it has been established by the very highest scientific authority that it is the seat of the subjective mind and of all educated, automatic actions of the body. For instance, when a young girl begins to learn to play the piano, the teacher places the pupil's fingers and thumbs on certain keys. She then tells her to strike the keys, tells her "that is A" and so on through the letters up to G. The little girl practices these different chords until she is finally permitted to play "exercises." From "exercises" she goes on to playing tunes, and she practices those tunes until she becomes so perfect, through her educated spinal cord, that she can play a tune and, at the same time, talk to another person.

She talks with her objective or brain mind, and plays the tune with her subjective mind or the mind of the spinal cord. This is called "automatic action" and yet it is the action of a mind which is a distinct entity, an entity which is endowed with the most prodigious memory, which rarely forgets.

In the vertebrate fishes, before the brain was developed this is all the mind that the animal possessed. It is yet our subjective mind. It is our dream mind and it is the mind that never sleeps.

We learn to walk, to play the violin and to perform all of those complex actions and movements of the hands and the body of which the subjective mind only is capable.

In the vertebrate fishes, before there was a brain and hence before there was an objective mind the animal from the moneron and the amaeba up to the fishes possessed this mind. This imperfect animal was capable, not only of caring for self, by seeking its food, and returning to its habitat, but it was capable of altruistic sentiments and feelings, as is evidenced by the propagation of its species and its care for its young.

Now, an organ which is called upon in the animal economy, to perform such high functions must, of necessity, receive the greatest protection.

16

To this end nature has thrown around this organ such protection as to make it almost impossible to inflict injury upon it, and this can be done only by fracturing and displacing the bony envelopment by which it is surrounded. This is true with the one exception that sometimes there is a dislocation in the cervical region, a dislocation in which a fracture does not occur.

Let us study this organ and its wonderful mechanism of protection for a moment. I have been in the habit of comparing the brain and spinal cord, in their relations to each other, to a woman's hair, plaited and hanging down her back — the hair upon the head representing the brain and the plait the spinal cord. The cord is, in reality, a mere extension of the brain downward. It comes off from the brain at the posterior part and leaves the skull through the *foramen magnum*. It then traverses the seven cervical, the twelve dorsal and two of the lumbar vertebrae.

These vertebrae do not differ materially in man from the same bones in the lower animals — being composed of a body, spines and lateral processes, and bound to each other by the most powerful ligaments, composed of strong fibrous tissue, and there is interposed between them a "chink" of elastic inter-articular cartilage, which makes it still more difficult to injure the cord.

In the descent of the cord through this opening in the vertebrae it is followed and invested by the *dura mater* — the thick and tenacious membrane which lines the inside of the skull. This thick and tough fibrous membrane invests the cord all the way down. Inside of the *dura mater* of the cord is a fluid, called the cerebro-spinal fluid, in which the cord floats and which serves to further protect it. There are also hundreds of little "guy ropes" which are attached to the cord and which reach out and are attached to the *dura mater*. This prevents the cord from "whip lashing" in case of sudden upward transmitted force.

At the termination of the cord it is divided up, or split in such a way as to resemble a horse's tail, and hence, it is called the *"cauda equina."*

In addition to all this the spinal column, or bony structure through which the cord passes, is made in curves which resemble an ox yoke — with one end smaller than the other and any upward transmitted force which has not been dissipated, or thrown off already, as hereafter described, is thrown off at those curves. The manner in which a transmitted upward force is dissipated or thrown off, before it reaches the spinal cord, may be illustrated as follows:

Let a boy jump from the barn shed, a hay stack, or a high fence and note how he alights. He first alights on the balls of his feet behind the toes; then, as the heels go down, the knees project forward, the hips backward and the body forward. Now, the transmitted upward force is thrown off at all those angles, at the ankles, knees and hips, and, if not entirely thrown off at those angles, whatever of the transmitted force that remains is thrown off at the curves of the spinal column. So that it is altogether impossible to injure the cord by falling from a height and alighting on the feet. It may be done by alighting on the buttocks, or upon the back and then only when the spinal column is fractured and a displaced vertebra is readily detected by both sight and touch, and there is immediate total paralysis of both motion and sensation in all parts below the injury, or in case of a mere pressure interence with both motion and sensation, which is apparent to anyone, by the attitude and gait of the injured person.

In fifteen years' experience in the Missouri Pacific Hospital, we had five cases of fracture of the spinal column, and consequent total paralysis of both motion and sensation in all parts below the site of injury. Three of these cases we denominated "hand car accidents," one was caused by a fireman jumping from a derailed engine, as it was entering a bridge — he striking upon the stone abutment and then alighting on his back twenty or more feet below, and the fifth case was caused by a painter falling from a bridge and alighting on his back some twenty-five feet below. In all of these cases there was total paralysis of both motion and sensation in all points below the point of injury, and all of the injured persons died in from three months to two years. There is no middle ground in those cases, and there is no such thing as "shock" or "concussion" in such cases; these cases of so-called "shock" or "concussion" being nothing more than a bruise or an injury to the nerves, after they have emerged from between the vertebrae.

Several years ago Dr. B. A. Watson, of Jersey City, N. J., took fifty dogs and experimented with them, as follows:

He carried some of them up to the fifth story of a building and dropped them on a stone or granatoid pavement, and others he struck at the base of the spine with a sledge hammer. In every instance where he had total paralysis he found, on *post mortem*, a fracture of a vertabra, with displacement of a fractured fragment, which completely severed the cord; and, in cases where there were symptoms of an alteration of sensation, or slight interference with motion, he found a fracture of a vertebrae, with slight displacement of a fragment, and this fragment pressing upon or against the cord, but not severing it Where there was no paralysis and no evidence of alteration of sensation (anaesthesia, hyperesthesia, etc.), and no interference with motion the autopsy showed that there was no fracture, no displacement, and, hence no pressure on the cord.

In discussing the question of spinal injuries, or assumed spinal injuries, I shall hereafter speak of the assumed injured person as "the plaintiff." This will aid me very much as I can thereby avoid the constant repetition of such phrases as "the so-called injured person," "the assumed injured person," etc., etc.

Now, we come to the examination, detection and exposure of the malingerer. One peculiarity of the malingering plaintiff is that he is nearly always talking about his injury and his helpless and hopeless condition. He tells his friends and even strangers, if they will listen to his story, all about his symptoms and he wants you to put your hand on the assumed painful point, and will say, "Now there! right there! right where your hand is, only a little higher up! Ouch! oh, my! don't press on it so hard for, I tell you, she hurts to kill." He will also invariably get off this kind of talk. "I don't know whether the jury will give me anything or not; but, if I could be back where I was before I got hurt, I wouldn't be hurt as I am now for all old Jay Gould is worth," or, "for all such and such a railroad would bring, if it was sold tomorrow."

Look out for the fellow with the above characteristics. He is a fraud and malingerer and is getting ready to perjure himself, as sure as you live.

In examining the malingering plaintiff there is nothing to be ascertained except what he tells you, and, as he tells you nothing but falsehoods you ascertain nothing. But there are means by which he may be detected and his false pretenses exposed. These means are three, viz.:

The electrical test for "reaction of degeneration," the test with the aesthesiometer and by espionage.

The making of a correct diagnosis or, rather, the exposure of the malingerer by electricity, in a test for "re-action of degeneration" is as follows:

When the malingerer will consent, or where the Court orders it, the plaintiff is laid upon a firm table. Then, with a Faradic current the negative pole is placed on the lower part of the spine and the positive pole is placed over some re-action center on the thigh. Now the requisite number of cells is turned on — about two on a re-action center. You will here get a response in rapid muscular contractions of a certain degree. Now, change your poles — placing the positive pole on the spine and the negative on the same point on the thigh. If the patient be really partially paralyzed and too long a period of time has not elapsed, a certain degree of degeneration of the nerve trunk has already taken place. In such case you will get a markedly exaggerated reaction on changing the poles; but, if there is no paralysis, and hence, no degeneration, then there will be a marked lessening of the muscular reaction on changing the poles. The test is absolutely good, and a malingerer can do nothing to prevent the reactions — in fact he can do nothing, except to refuse to permit the test. The malingering plaintiff is always more or less afraid of such tests, because he knows that something is going to be done which he cannot control, and it is often the case that such a plaintiff will affect to have great fears of the battery — is afraid you are going to hurt him and will, therefore, refuse such a test until ordered to permit it by the Court, or by his too confiding counsel. The test with the aesthesiometer is a good one. It is an instrument used to test the degree of sensibility of the surface. As its name indicates, it is a measure of sensation. A small pair of sharp pointed scissors will do, but Dr. Chas. H. Hughes, an eminent neurologist of St. Louis, Missouri, has invented a small instrument, which is very valuable to a specialist, who does a great deal of examining of this kind. The instrument is simply an oblong piece of steel with a slit in it from which projects two teeth or short points. One of these is stationary and the other is movable. By the movable point the two sharp points may be placed at any distance required from each other. The instrument is placed on the surface — the two sharp points slightly pricking the surface. The plaintiff is asked, "How many points do you feel?" Then the instrument may be changed and the plaintiff again asked, "Now, how many points do you feel?" One point and then two, and two again and then one may be placed on several times. All this time the plaintiff is not permitted to see the number of points touching him, nor the changes that are made in number, or the distance of the sharp points from each other. He is puzzled. He don't know what to do, and so decides on the very worst thing that he can do.

He decides to answer wrong each time. That is the nearest to deceiving you that he can do in his bewildered condition. So, when you place one point against him and ask, "How many points are touching you now?" he will hesitate a moment and then answer, "two!" You change it and place two points against him, and ask, "Now, how many?" and he will hesitate again and then answer "one!" He thinks that he is deceiving you but he is not, for it is apparent to even a layman that, if his sensibility is so altered that he calls two points one, then he certainly would not feel two points, when only one is used. It is very evident that he is lying.

The test of espionage is one of doubtful utility. You may place a detective, or a company "special officer" to watch the plaintiff. The plaintiff and his friends may claim that he is confined to his room, or even to his bed, and the detective may find him plowing corn or splitting rails, or chopping cord wood; yet the jury, as a rule, will give no heed to the detective's testimony, and will go right on and give a big verdict to the malingering plaintiff, anyway.

There is a very strong prejudice in the mind of the average juryman against detectives, and it is a rare thing when the corporation can use such testimony to advantage.

The plaintiff will detail his case to his friend, or to anyone who will listen about as follows: "I didn't know that there was anything the matter with me for three or four days, and then I begun to have a tingling sensation running down my leg" — (sometimes both but usually only one) "and then I have a pain, all the time, right in the small of my back — right here, give me your hand — right there, yes, oh! Ouch! that hurts — and sometimes it shoots up my spine and lands right in the back of my head, and then it goes over my head above my right (or left) ear. I can't remember anything any more; my eyesight's got so I can hardly read and I'm so weak I can't work. When I try to work I get that weak, trembly feeling and I have to quit."

If the case is prolonged by juries disagreeing, appeals and reversals, he will often add one or both of the following: "A few hours after the accident I had an awful haemorrhage from my bowels; and now, in the last year, I have been having some kind of spells — the doctor says it's epilepsy; I just go off out of my head, and my folks say I look sort of foolish and jerk all over; and, when I come out I feel awful weak. Oh, I tell you, if I could be back where I was before I was hurt, I wouldn't be in this fix again for all old Jay Gould is worth."

Oh, how often I have heard that lying story! And yet, another plaintiff a thousand miles away will give almost identically the same story and symptoms. This is why it is apparent that the laity have a sort of "chimney corner medicine" and pathology of their own, and will give a history and symptoms which they think ought to belong to an injured spinal cord; and this is the way they deceived' poor, credulous, honest old Prof. Erickson, and caused him, in his innocent credulity, to give forth a work which has been and will continue to be an injury to corporations and a help to dishonest, malingering plaintiffs for many, many years to come.

The plaintiff will go on the stand and, under oath, detail all of this stuff and will then brazenly admit that he has not paid out a dollar for medicine, or treatment of any kind. Sometimes he don't know why he has not received treatment, but often he gets around it in this way, "Well, from the way I felt, and what the doctor said" (this is the doctor he consulted when he decided to bring suit) "I just thought that nothing could be done, and I didn't see any use in throwing away money and get no benefit."

The detection of the malingerer is an easy task. It is strange that such dishonest persons do impose on fairly good men in the medical profession; and, if they can impose upon physicians, is it any wonder that they impose upon juries? and, I believe that, in many instances, they impose on their own attorneys. I have no doubt that it is true that the attorney often knows that his client is a fraud, and that he coaches him and cautions him as to how he shall act and talk, and as to how he shall answer questions when on the witness stand. And I fear that, in some cases, a physician is taken into this compact and lends his professional aid to the malingerer in his efforts to rob a corporation.

In such cases I feel quite sure that the physician lends himself to this task for money. He does not get much but he arranges for a contingent fee. In case the plaintiff gets a verdict for three thousand dollars we will say, the doctor is to get one hundred dollars; and the plaintiff and the attorney divide the balance; or, in case the verdict is for a larger amount, the doctor gets more.

I am glad to say that I do not believe that this thing is done very often, for I do not believe that many men who belong to the medical profession would or do lend themselves to such dishonest and swindling schemes, but, they do it in some cases. I am sure that I have been in cases with the corporation attorneys where the doctor was *particeps criminis*, for no sort of argument upon my part would move him from the advocacy of the most absurd and untenable theories; and yet, I have been in other cases where the plaintiff's expert was holding to the most absurd ideas; but, when shown the unreasonableness of his position, he would at once admit that he was wrong and that it was his lack of knowledge and experience that had misled him.

In such a case I felt sure that the doctor was honest, and that he had not entered into any scheme to assist in a fraud and to receive pay for his part in it under such circumstances. In such a case I would not regard the doctor's testimony as being perjured. It was simply testimony given with a misunderstanding of the facts in the case. But, when a doctor was made to see his error, and yet, when he went on the witness stand and then still held to and promulgated his false theories and thereby influenced the minds of the jury — many of whom were his personal friends — I cannot regard his testimony as being anything else than the rankest and blackest perjury, and for which the perjurer should be made to suffer the penalties of the law, in such cases made and provided.

The doctor, who has been educated to treat the sick, to prolong life, and to make that life more comfortable and bearable, and to bind up the wounds, to straighten the broken limbs and broken bodies of his fellow men, who lends himself to schemes of swindling and robbery, by the side of which train robbery is most respectable, has a very poor and a very low conception of his duties as a physician. Such men should be exposed and then incontinently kicked out of all medical societies to which they may belong, and all association with respectable and reputable medical men should be denied them. For, the connection of such men is not calculated to have an uplifting and an ennobling influence. The truth is that such men should not be allowed to practice medicine and surgery at all, for a man who will lend his aid to the consummation of a robbery and a swindle for a part of the booty would not hesitate very long at a suggestion of quiet murder, if by such a murder he might be the gainer financially.

I have seen a few such men, and, to me, they had "robber," "swindler" and "murderer" written in bold and unmistakable characters all over their inhuman and distorted faces.

How anybody lean make mistakes about such scoundrels is to me an unsolved and unsolvable mystery.

Chapter Two - Assumed Spinal Cord Injuries

I SHALL now proceed to give a detailed history of a number of cases of assumed spinal cord injuries, in which I examined the plaintiffs' and assisted the company's attorney in bringing out the medical testimony.

Case I. Mr. Fairman was a gripman on the Fifth street cable line of the Metropolitan Street Railway. He was fifty years old and either a bachelor or a widower. In taking his train from Kansas City, Missouri, to Kansas City, Kansas, he had to pass Armour's Packing House. The Missouri Pacific had built a spur track, crossing the Fifth street line, and into the packing house, which it used in shoving in cars to be loaded with the products of the packing house and pulling them out again. Mr. Fairman was caught by a train that was being shoved in, and the grip car was crushed, and the box-like structure, in which the gripman stands, was crushed and Mr. Fairman was caught and squeezed somewhat, but not really injured at all.

He saw his opportunity, however, and quit his position and assumed that his spinal cord was injured. After investigating his case the company refused to settle at his figures and so the result was, a suit for damages — set at ten or twenty thousand dollars, I forget which.

When the case came to trial I had never seen the plaintiff; as, for some reason, I had not been called upon to examine him, at time of attempt at settlement.

I said to our attorney, "As this fellow is claiming injured spinal cord and partial paralysis, I presume that, as usual, he is malingering?" "No, I think not When you see him and see him walk I think you will say that he is pretty badly paralyzed," said our attorney.

We were in Court in the forenoon waiting for our case to come up, and, when adjournment was taken for the noon hour, I asked the attorney to point the plaintiff out to me. "There he is," said he; and, as we left the Court room and were going in the same general direction, I dropped in behind the plaintiff and followed in his wake for some three or four blocks. His attitude and gait were so unique that they were amusing. He assumed partial paralysis in both lower extremities and, hence used two canes. He stooped forward so that his body was at almost a right angle to his legs. He carried a cane in each hand, and, when walking, he would place, say, his right foot forward and land on the ball of the foot behind the toes; then, when bringing forward the left foot, he would jiggle the right heel up and down, then, landing his left as the right had been, he would jiggle the left up and down, while bringing the right foot forward again. He walked quite briskly, and his gait and motions were absolutely amusing; so much so that I could not repress a hearty laugh.

"What do you think of him?" asked the attorney, as we left the street upon which the plaintiff was doing his jiggle act

"Why, he is no more paralyzed than you or I," I answered. "Now, you noted his attitude and gait. The attitude and gait of a man partially paralyzed on one side is this — he leans back a little beyond the perpendicular; and, with his cane in the hand on that side, places it a little behind him, so as to keep the center of gravity within the perpendicular of the base. He then brings the foot on the partially paralyzed side forward with' a swing and a flop — using the rotary muscles of the hip in doing so. The foot is planted flat on the ground, while he brings forward the other foot. Now, if a man were partially paralyzed on both sides, I presume that he would, naturally, use crutches, but he would not assume the attitude and gait this man does. Note the way he places his feet on the ground — never permitting the heel to touch the sidewalk. Why, were he partially paralyzed he could not keep that heel off the ground for the life of him, for it takes power and an effort to walk as he does.

It is really tiresome to him and requires an effort on his part to walk as he does."

The case came on in the afternoon and the Court appointed Dr. Geo. Halley, an able and eminent surgeon and myself to examine him. We made a thorough examination — using the tests for reaction of degeneration, and the aesthesiometer. We found his legs to be larger, harder and firmer than they should be naturally in a man of his age. "His attitude and gait have been a gymnasium to his legs," said Dr. Halley, in testifying in the case, "and I venture the assertion that he has larger, firmer and more athletic legs than any other man of his age in this court room. He is not paralyzed at all in any degree and has not been," continued the witness.

My testimony coincided exactly with Dr. Halley's. When the plaintiff was put on the stand and was hard pressed, on cross-examination, he broke down and bawled like a calf — and the jury gave him one thousand dollars. The money was paid — the case not being appealed, and, in one week, I learned that Mr. Fairman had discarded both canes and was walking about the streets of Kansas City, Kansas, minus the jiggle.

I said to our attorney, "Why don't you send one or two good special men over there and have them get Fairman and others of his chums and go out and have a night of it. Let them fill him up with good things to eat and drink and then let him show how strong and athletic he is. He is a big enough fool to boast of how he took the Missouri Pacific in and made them pay one thousand dollars to a man who was not disabled in the least. I think he would, also, in order to show how smart he has been, do a few stunts — such as leaping over chairs, standing on his head, etc. Then have him indicted for perjury, and have him tried for it and sent to the penitentiary, as he deserves to be?"

"Why," said he, "where would you find a jury to convict him? You couldn't get twelve men, of the kind that usually constitute our juries, who would ever find him guilty. There might be, and no doubt would be, a man on the jury occasionally, who would wish to punish this fellow for his perjury, but you would find that, in the end, we would have to pay the costs as the prosecuting witness, and this fellow would go scot free, and would then have something else to boast of, as to how he had again beaten a railroad company; and, if possible, to bring suit and make the railroad company pay for false imprisonment, he would do it; and you would see that a jury would be eager and quick to give him damages against the railroad company; and, furthermore, a majority of the people of that fellows class would regard his indictment, arrest and trial for perjury, as an outrage against the rights of the citizen, and our newspapers would, no doubt, take the matter up and animadvert severely upon the dangers that threaten us through the railroads imprisoning and trying our best and most reputable citizens for perjury, after first severely injuring them!"

And, unfortunately, I am afraid that the attorney's ideas about the matter are only too true. Such a condition of things is to be regretted; but, we cannot progress very rapidly in public morals, until good citizens are willing to take such matters up and make the perjurer feel the strong hand of the law.

Cases II and III. In the year 1888 I was ordered by the chief surgeon to go to a small village in Kansas, which I shall call Lauraville, to see and examine Mrs. Henshaw and Mrs. Morton, both of whom claimed to have received an injury to the spinal cord on our road sometime previously.

I proceeded to Lauraville — arriving there on a dry, hot day, and examined Mrs. Henshaw, who lived in town, first

The history of their cases was as follows: Some time previously they had both attended the annual assembly of the denomination of Dunkards, which was that year held at Ottawa. In order to get there they had to take the V. V. I. & W. line to Osawatomie and then take the Colorado main line in order to reach Ottawa. They had spent several days at the meeting — staying with an old mutual friend, while doing so. When they were ready to go home they took the main line back to Osawatomie, and then bought tickets to Lauraville. They took the "Cannon Ball," the fast train, to Lauraville.

When the conductor came around to take up their tickets he said, "Why, these tickets are for the accommodation train. The 'Cannon Ball' does not stop at Lauraville." They knew this, but they haggled with the conductor for sometime, and then asked if he could put them off at Podunk — which was within five miles of Lauraville. He could, as the "Cannon Ball" stopped at Podunk, regularly. But, in the confusion of taking up tickets on a crowded train, he put them off at Grisley, eighteen miles from Lauraville. They got off and walked up town on a prairie road street which was as level as a plank floor.

They proceeded to inquire and search for a Mrs. Shriggles, another mutual friend, with whom they expected to stop. They could not hear of Mrs. Shriggles anywhere. It finally began to rain and they stopped in at a house where there were five sick children in bed. They again inquired for Mrs. Shriggles. The lady answered that no such person lived in the town. They insisted that she did. "What town do you think you are in?" asked the lady.

"Why, we are in Podunk," answered the bewildered wayfarers, "Why, this is Grisley, Podunk is thirteen miles from here," said she. Not being able to procure a bed they were permitted to sit in chairs until morning. They then proceeded to take the accommodation train for Lauraville. Arriving there they went in and abused the agent awhile, on account of the conductor's mistake, and then went on home. Within a short time both brought suit for ten thousand dollars damages and both claimed a permanent injury to the spinal cord. I examined Mrs. Henshaw with the aid of the family physician and found her to be a very sick woman. She was suffering from the consequences of an accident of child birth. She had a serious laceration, inflammation, prolapsus, etc. The family physician informed me that she had been suffering in this way for years — her troubles being aggravated each month, and he saw no difference in her condition now from what it was before she made the trip to Ottawa. I found that there was no livery stable in the little village, but learned that a widow lady owned two very pious old horses and an old buggy, and could, no doubt, send me out to the country three miles to see Mrs. Morton, if I would call upon her. I did so and she sent to the baseball grounds on the commons for her thirteen years old son, who was to act as my Jehu on this trip. He came and hitched up the religious looking old horse to the old shack of a buggy and we started. I found the boy to be a character. He was thirteen years old, had a wad of tobacco, the size of my thumb, in his right jaw, which gave him the appearance of a marsupial carrying its young, his pants were rolled up to the knees and his legs were liberally streaked with dried mud. He sat with his elbows on his knees and would occasionally urge the pious old horse along with a stick which he carried, and would raise up now and then and squirt an ounce or so of tobacco juice over the right front wheel.

"You are the railroad doctor, ain't you?" he asked after we had got fairly under way. I answered that I was, but cautioned him to not mention that fact when we got to the Morton's and to not talk while there, but to let me do the talking.

We arrived in due time, and walked up to the country residence between two beautiful rows of grape vines. I found Mr. Morton sitting in the shade of their best room and Mrs. Morton was out the back way busily engaged in making grape jelly. She was fifty, and had been married only a short time. She was gray haired and very much tanned and was a little wiry, nervous creature and seemed to possess more surplus nervous energy than the ordinary person.

I asked for a drink of water and the old gentleman called on her to get it. I could not help being amused at the energy she put into the turning of the crank of the pump in drawing the water. She bobbed up and down like a half sled in a stumpy field.

The old gentleman and I exhausted the subjects of the weather, the crops and the drought, and then I gave him my name and told him my business there. He called to Mrs. Morton, "Mother, come in here." She came in. "Mother, this is Dr. King, the railroad doctor, and he's come to examine you." I watched Mrs. Morton very closely. She put on a rueful countenance and placed both hands to her back. "Oh, my!" said she, "I've never seen a well day since I took that trip. My back never quits hurting me; and, every once in a while a pain shoots up to the back of my head and just blinds me, and I can't sleep any more," etc., etc. The old story.

There was a bed in the room and she walked over and flopped down on it and began moaning; The boy hunched me with his knee and I hunched back — indicating that I wanted him to keep quiet.

She admitted that there had been no bruises; so, I made a simple examination of the heart and pulse — both of which I found to be normal, and then departed.

As we walked down between the two rows of grape vines the boy slipped up beside me and pinched me on the thigh and said, "Dang her old hide; if we'd a stayed there another half hour I believe she'd 'a' died!"

We returned to the village and I returned home and made my report, which was in accordance with the facts above stated. Both cases were set for the October term of Court at Burlington. When the time came one case was tried. Both of those women went on the stand and stated under oath that they had never been free from pain since the night they were put off the train at Grisley and never expected to be again.

The attorney for the company asked, "To what do you attribute your injury and your pain?"

"Why, to sitting upon that chair all night."

"Had you ever sat up with sick relatives and friends?"

"Yes," was the answer.

"Did that give you backache and headache?"

"No."

"Then how do you account for the fact that sitting up all night at Grisley produced your backache and headache?"

"I attribute it to the mental anxiety," was the answer of both.

They had both been well coached.

The jury hung and we gave them one hundred and fifty dollars each to quit.

Most any reasonable and unprejudiced person would say that any one ought to see that there could have been no injury in such a case, and that those women could not and should not recover damages for anything unless it should be for the short time lost in not getting home that night; but the jury does not look at it in that way.

Notwithstanding that they are sworn to try the case fairly and to render a verdict in accordance with the law and the evidence, they forget their oaths and say something like this, "Well, I guess the old ladies were not hurt much, but that conductor had no business to put them off where he did. Why didn't he take them on to their own town anyway? It would take only a few minutes to stop there and let them off." The jurymen forget that it would have been worth the conductor's position for him to have done so; that railroad managements have cast iron rules touching such matters, from which there must be no deviation, and that such rules are made and enforced strictly, because, to depart from them may mean the loss of many precious human lives and hundreds of thousands of dollars' worth of property; for, in loose methods accidents occur; and, in accidents lives are lost and property destroyed.

Case IV. In the year 1890 I was called upon to assist the company's attorney in the trial of what was regarded as being a very dangerous case, at Warrensburg, Mo.

A year previous to that time there lived at Pleasant Hill, in Cass County, a young married man, a Kentuckian, who had a wife and two children, the youngest a babe six weeks old. They had decided to move back to Kentucky, and the wife, with the babe, and a maiden sister of the husband, with the three-year-old child, started on the journey. They left Pleasant Hill on the morning train; and, when they arrived at Kirkwood, near St. Louis, that evening, they learned that there was a freight wreck on the main line, between Kirkwood and St. Louis. The train proceeded, however; and, when they arrived at the wreck, they found that there was a relief train on the other side of the wreck. The conductor assisted Mrs. McElroy (that will do for a name) from the coach and, taking the babe in his arms, and she taking his arm, he held an umbrella over her, as it was sprinkling rain, and they proceeded. They walked beside the wreck to the relief train for about three hundred yards when they reached it without accident, or trouble of any kind. When they reached St. Louis they found that all Eastern connecting trains had gone; so they sat up in the union station all night. Mrs. McElroy had a severe chill during the night; and, when they took the eastbound train for Cincinnati the next morning she was quite sick. They arrived at Stamford, Kentucky, after night fall, and Mrs. McElroy was taken in a carriage to the home of relatives a few miles in the country where she lay, quite sick, for six weeks. After her convalescence suit was brought against the Missouri Pacific road for twenty thousand dollars, for injury to the spinal cord.

As before stated, I was called upon to assist the attorney in the trial of the case. I found the trial in progress and the plaintiff's counsel almost ready to rest when I arrived there. The plaintiff's physician, who had been with her when her babe was born, was on the stand. I had the attorney ask him if any accident occurred at this last labor and if he had examined her since. He stated that no accident occurred; and, while he had not examined her since, he knew that she was sound and healthy in that regard. The lady came into the court room and was pointed out to me by the attorney; and, as Court adjourned for dinner just then, I noted her attitude and gait as she left the court room. Her physician was walking out beside me and I said to him, "Doctor, I will make you a small wager that this woman has a bad laceration of the *ceroix uteri,* that she has enlargement of the body of the uterus, with retroflexion of that organ, and enlargement and prolapse of both ovaries." He would not wager, but he said he knew that she had no troubles of that nature.

On reassembling the Court appointed four of us — two for each side — to examine the plaintiff. I had noted this in the plaintiff's posture and gait: she stooped forward and walked as if she thought something hurtful to her was going to happen. Now, a healthy woman is sway backed, and there is an inward curve in the lumbar region. In this case the plaintiff's spinal column curved the other way.

A full and thorough examination was permitted and I was put forward to make it. I drew the uterine sound through a double laceration — up to the vault of the vagina — and through a bad laceration in the anterior lip — the whole constituting what we call a "stellate laceration" and I put the sound up to the fundus of the uterus — showing that it was retroflexed and much deeper than normal, which indicated its enlargement, and I had each man feel of the prolapsed and enlarged ovaries.

The plaintiff's physician went back on the stand and testified to all of these facts; for he was an honest gentleman; but, when asked if this condition caused the plaintiff's disability, he answered that he thought not. Every physician who made the examination for the Court, testified to the same facts, and all stated that the injuries — inflammation, enlargement and displacement of the uterus and ovaries, were the cause of all her trouble, except her family physician.

In the face of all this, the jury gave her a verdict for ten thousand dollars. The Supreme Court reversed and remanded the case, I believe; any way, the case was compromised out of Court for twenty-five hundred dollars.

Case V. In 1897 I received telegraphic information of the supposed to be serious injury of a young woman at what I shall call Rapid City, Kansas. Within a few days I received a report made by the attending physician, on a blank I had sent him. The facts in the case, as he gave them, were as follows:

This young lady, who lived at Irvington, five miles from Rapid City, had come down to the latter place on the day before Christmas to visit her young friend, Ellen Bayne, and to make some purchases for Christmas. She and her friend had gone about the little town and the plaintiff, Ella Pleasants, had made her purchases and, late in the afternoon, they repaired to the depot, where Miss Pleasants was to take the train for Irvington, She sat in the depot and permitted the passenger train to go by, as she wished to ride on the accommodation freight — the conductor of that train being a friend and always carrying her free. When the accommodation freight came in she went down to the caboose, accompanied by her friend, Ellen Bayne, and went into the caboose and deposited her purchases on a seat and came out on the caboose platform again. At least, this was the testimony of a number of reliable witnesses, while she testified that she only came as far as the caboose door, from which point she was thrown as will be hereafter described. She fell between the caboose and next car, and, in attempting to save herself, fell across the rail and her jacket was caught and she was held until released by parties present. A physician was called and examined and cared for her and accompanied her to Irvington.

As before stated, he made a report to me, in which he stated that two of plaintiff's ribs were torn loose from their connection with the spinal column. I wrote him and told him that the condition he described was an impossible one, and asked him to look the matter up in his anatomy, and then note the perfect and powerful attachment of the ribs to the spinal column in connection with the lateral processes, and calling his attention to the fact that butchers did not attempt to sever this connection, except with the butchers cleaver; and saying to him, very kindly, that he surely did not wish to go on record as testifying to such a monstrous impossibility, as the case would, no doubt, be tried in Court. He then wrote and modified his first report by saying that the ribs were fractured near the spine, but, as I had stated to him that, to tear two ribs loose from the spine as he had reported, you would have to make a wound in the back that you could run your fist in, and as there was scarcely a mark on the young lady's back, he was disposed to be less tenacious with regard to his first report.

After much correspondence and effort to settle the case it finally came to a suit, at Marysville, Kansas.

The suit was, I believe, for twenty thousand dollars and permanent injury to the spinal cord was the allegation in the petition.

I was present to assist the company's attorney, Hon. James M. Orr of Atchison.

By agreement of the attorneys the Court appointed a commission of physicians to examine plaintiff. I was not of the commission, but was permitted to be present. The plaintiff was stripped, so as to show her back, and a careful examination was made. I don't think I ever saw a more perfect spine. Plaintiff was sixteen years of age, and weighed about one hundred and fifty pounds. She had a beautiful head of hair and a magnificent head well poised on splendid shoulders; she had an Evangeline forehead, a classical nose, a Cupid's bow mouth, a dimpled chin, large blue eyes and a fair complexion and was, in all respects, as beautiful as Venus when she arose from the foam of the sea. I do not believe that I ever saw a more perfect form or a better nourished body. She was coached by her mother, a grass widow, and a chronic litigant.

When the case came to trial the testimony was mainly as follows:

Miss Pleasants went into the caboose and deposited her purchases and came out on the caboose platform to talk to her friend, Ellen Bayne. The train hands had unloaded one car — the car being in front of the door of the freight part of the depot As there was a part of another car to be unloaded the conductor signalled the engineer to "slack ahead." The train, which was standing on a slight upward incline, moved up one car length and stopped. Naturally, when the train stopped the rear cars and the caboose moved up and then the slack was taken out of the cars. The process began at the car next the engine. As the process of taking out the slack came back toward the caboose it finally reached that point. When it did so the jar to the caboose was considerable. Miss Pleasants who was either standing on the platform, or sitting on the iron railing, was thrown over, her head striking the next car and her body falling between this car and the caboose. She plunged toward the depot and fell across the rail — the back wheel of the car catching her jacket and pinning her to the rail. The conductor ran in and pulled the pin of the caboose; then jumping on the depot platform, signalled the engineer to "slack ahead," which he did, thus releasing the plaintiff.

The conductor and others promptly carried her into the depot and the doctor was sent for. He stripped her waist, so as to expose her back. The physician's testimony was that there was a red streak diagonally across her back made by the car wheel, but the preponderance of testimony of the bystanders was that there was not a mark on her. She was placed on the caboose and taken to her home in Irvington. A hay buyer who was sitting on a load of hay, waiting for the train to move, testified that he saw plaintiff dancing around on the caboose platform, and he said to the driver, "There is a girl who is preparing to get hurt."

A number of disinterested witnesses swore that plaintiff was on the caboose platform when the jar which threw her off the caboose came, but plaintiff and her friend, Ellen Bayne, both testified that plaintiff, after depositing her bundles in the caboose, came to the door; and, when the jar came, she was thrown through the iron railing — the chain which usually protects the opening, not being fastened.

The mother, who had the typical female litigant's face testified to plaintiff's disability. She was not able to help her mother in the conduct of a small boarding house, and would awake at night, screaming and talking about the cars. Persons who boarded with plaintiff's mother testified that plaintiff took part in waiting on the table and in the house work, and they never heard the matter of her injury or disability mentioned, nor did they hear her scream at night. The company showed that plaintiff went to Omaha, during the Exposition and worked in her aunt's boarding house in that city, for wages, that she attended dances and also rode on the "Shoot the Chutes" on the Exposition grounds. When plaintiff's mother was asked why she sent plaintiff to Omaha she answered, "to get her out of the excitement of home and the town of Irvington."

When asked if she did not think that Omaha, at the time, with the great crowds, the playing of bands and the marching of parades, did not offer more excitement than the little town of Irvington, she answered, "It was the change of scene I wanted her to have."

The plaintiff was in Court all the time, with her hands frequently pressed against the side and back, and her physician frequently administered to her small doses of medicine in the presence of the jury. The mother never left her for a moment, for it was apparent that the plaintiff, with her great excess of vitality and animal spirits, was difficult to hold down.

The jury gave her three thousand dollars. A motion for a new trial was made; but, before it could be argued, the judge fell dead on the street. It is the law in Kansas that, when a motion for a new trial is made, if anything occurs by which the sitting judge cannot hear it, then the incoming judge must grant the new trial, without argument. So a new trial was granted in this case.

In due time the case came to trial again. Plaintiff was on hand, as beautiful and healthy looking as ever. The testimony was the same as in the former trial, except that the company had gathered a great deal of testimony against the plaintiff. Amongst other things it proved by several young men of Irvington that plaintiff made a wager with a young man that she could leave him, where he was standing, run to the end of a string of cars, climb the first car, run along the running board on top of the car and jump from car to car over five cars, climb down at the far end and run back to where the young man stood, in so many minutes. She beat the time and the young man bought the candy.

Her mother came in with additional evidence for the plaintiff. Plaintiff had bled from the bowels for several days after the injury — a fact she had heretofore forgotten; and, recently, plaintiff was having "fits" or "spells," in which she would fall, her limbs would jerk, and she would be unconscious for an indefinite time; and, on coming out of the fit, she would moan and scream and talk about the cars.

Plaintiff's friend, Ellen Bayne, made a complete summersault and testified that, when plaintiff was thrown from the platform or rather, when the jar came, plaintiff was standing on the caboose platform and had been for sometime. When asked why she had testified as she did before, she said that she wanted to help her friend out and help her make some money, but had come to the conclusion that it was wrong and she was going to tell the truth and not testify that way any more.

However, to use a sporting phrase, we had her "beaten to a stand still" and, except for a most magnificent *coup de etat*, would, no doubt, have obtained a verdict in our favor.

Right at the time when they seemed to have lost hope, the plaintiff arose in front of the clerk's desk and, in plain view of the jury, fell to the floor and went through a series of contortions and gyrations which would have done credit to a finished actress. The jury gave her a verdict for five thousand dollars. The "fit" did it

The case was appealed and I have not heard, since I left the service of the company, what disposition has been made of it.

The Supreme Court of Kansas, may affirm the case, or they may have reversed it before this; but, the case shows what the average jury will do in such cases. The reversal of her testimony by Miss Ellen Bayne alone should have caused the jury to find for the defendant. But they, no doubt, took the view that the company, through its agents, had tampered with this young girl and perhaps promised her money to make the complete summersault which she did.

I presume that I was the only employee of the company who ever spoke to Miss Ellen Bayne about her testimony. After the first trial she and I sat in the same seat in the coach on our return home, she to Rapid City and I to Kansas City.

In talking about the case I found her to be a most sweet and agreeable little lady. I say "little lady" for she was very *petite* in size. But, in her mental make up, she was a perfect little girl. She was agreeable and I could see that she had a great desire to be helpful to her friends.

I said to her, "Miss Bayne, I am an old man, and I have children — amongst them a daughter. It would hurt me infinitely, to know that she had wilfully done an injury to her own character, by wronging others — even in the fulfilment of a desire to help friends. I am afraid that those people desire to use you to accomplish their own purposes. Now, let me advise you to not permit them to do this. If you do you will regret it when you are older and your mind is more mature. I believe you to be an honest and a most sweet and good little lady; and, although you are not of kin to me, I should feel hurt if I knew that you had done yourself a lasting hurt, by joining in a scheme to wrong others, although those 'others' may be a hated and despised railroad company. A young lady, like you, cannot do a wrong without feeling it and regretting it at some period of your life, and I think it best for all of us that we should have as few things to regret as possible.

"Just remember what I have said to you, my dear young friend, and remember that I talk to you as I would like for any good old man to talk to my daughter under similar circumstances."

I do not know whether this talk was what caused Miss Ellen Bayne to change her testimony or not, but I am inclined to believe that it had its influence.

Case VI. Sometime before the last trial of the case of Ella Pleasants, at Marysville, Kansas, I received a letter from the Mayor of a noted County seat in the State of Illinois, which said in substance: "We have what we regard as a dangerous lawsuit against our town, for damages for personal injuries. The plaintiff claims to have been injured on account of a bad street. We have searched far and wide to find a physician who knows how to assist an attorney in bringing out the medical evidence. We have learned that the Missouri Pacific Railway Company has the best organized corps of physicians in the country, in that line, and that you are their main reliance. I write as Mayor of our town, to ascertain if you can come and assist us; and, if so, what your charges will be."

I answered that I could come and gave him my charges. I then added: "If your plaintiff is a malingerer and a fraud, and seeks to defraud your city by perjury, I think I can give you his symptoms as he presents them to his friends: He claims injury to the spinal cord and complains that he has tingling sensations which run down either one or both legs — usually one — and that his leg feels as it does when it "goes to sleep"; that he has a severe pain in the 'small of his back,' which frequently shoots up and lands in the back of his head, and then passes over one or both sides — usually one — of his head,

33

that his memory is failing, his eyesight is getting so that he can scarcely read, and that he suffers from insomnia, and is so weak and nervous that he cannot perform any kind of labor; and, if he is a very bold and dangerous liar, he probably tells that he had a severe haemorrhage from his bowels a few hours after the injury, which recurred a number of times within the next few days; and, if it has been some time since he claims to have been hurt, he claims that he has some kind of 'spells' or 'fits' in which he falls down and jerks and becomes unconscious; and, after coming out of the 'fit,' he is dull and stupid for several hours. He may not give all the symptoms I have detailed, but, if he is a malingerer, I will guarantee that he complains of most of them."

By return mail I received the following: "In the name of heaven, if you have seen no one who has told you of this case, or have not heard the details in some other way, tell me how you know what this man complains of. You gave every symptom that he complains of, without leaving out a single one. If you have not received this information from some one, then we want you more than ever, for we feel that you must be an expert in this kind of work."

I replied that I had never heard of the case until he wrote me, and that his letter contained no details, and that I knew no more of it than what had been written me, that "plaintiff complains of having been injured on account of our bad streets."

About two weeks after the trial of the Marysville case, in which plaintiff won her case by having a "fit" in the court room, I received a letter notifying me to be ready; and, two days after, a telegraphic message, to come. I went and was met at the depot by the Mayor. He escorted me to their best hotel, where I was introduced to the city attorney, the attorney from Centralia, who was to be leading counsel in the case, the physician who had been acting and advising on the part of the city; and, after I had had a lunch, I had a private conference with these gentlemen and the Mayor, in which I was given the following facts regarding the case: Lee Webber (this will do for a name) was then past his twenty-third birthday. He was an only child. His father had owned, previous to his death, a very fine farm, which joined the corporation of the town. He had left a will, by the terms of which Lee was to have five thousand dollars on his twenty-first birthday. This money had been paid; and, within the next two years, Lee had strutted through it and had, by means not strictly honest nor moral, overdrawn his mother's bank account to the extent of fifteen hundred dollars — without her knowledge or consent — and had also spent that. At the time he claimed to have been injured he was known to be hard up financially and was straining every point to "raise the wind."

That he was given to elocution; was fond of private theatricals; that he had been sent away to school, before he attained his majority, and had come home Christmas, with his face all covered with adhesive plaster and had stated that he received his injuries in a football contest in which he had carried off the honors and saved the day for his eleven, but had been almost killed in doing so; that, a few days afterward, another boy came home and told the astonished public that Lee had not received any injuries in a football game; that, in fact, he did not even belong to the college eleven, and that he, the other student, had placed this adhesive plaster on Lee's face with his own hands.

This went to show Lee's vanity and that, like calamity's wife he was "skittish and unreliable."

I was also told that Lee had been sent away from the school because he would not study and had then been sent to a college belonging to a religious denomination in Missouri, of which church his parents were members, and that he had been sent home from this college, because he was indolent, negligent and would not study. All this was told to me in order to give me an insight into the young man's character.

This was the story of his supposed injury: At the time he claimed to have been injured, the little town was engaged in improving its streets. To this end they were putting in tiling across the streets. At the street where plaintiff claimed to have received his injury they had dug a ditch, a little more than one foot deep and the same in width; but, as they did not receive their tiling in time, they had left this ditch without a guard or a red light. On the night Lee claimed to have been injured he was in town, had been to a lodge meeting and was then driving to a hotel where he expected to write some letters. In going to the hotel he had to cross the ditch, which he claimed to have never seen before. The country wagons — bringing in wood, com and hay — had crossed this ditch at the center and had, thereby, cut down the edges of the ditch. Lee was seen to pass the residence of Dr. Schovelhoffer about ten o'clock, and was then driving in a moderate "jog trot." Soon afterward Dr. Schovelhoffer heard a moaning down near the ditch, and, upon going there had found Lee lying upon the ground some fifteen feet from the ditch and his horse and buggy were standing not very far away. In thinking of the matter it occurred to me that, if, in going at a "jog trot" the sudden stopping of plaintiff's buggy by the front wheels alternately dropping into this foot wide and foot deep ditch, caused him to be thrown fifteen feet from the ditch, as was testified to by Dr. Schovelhoffer, then if two freight trains should be approaching each other on the same track, each train being made up of ten cars; loaded with ten tons to each car and each drawn by an engine weighing one hundred and sixty-five tons, and both trains running at thirty miles an hour, and these trains should meet and collide, how far would a brakeman, standing on top of one of the cars, be thrown when these two trains come together?

Of course, it is a problem which could not be even approximately solved, but assuming that plaintiff weighed one hundred and fifty pounds and the buggy three hundred and fifty pounds, and if with this insignificant momentum as compared with the momentum of the two trains, he should be thrown fifteen feet, it is certainly fair to assume that the brakeman would be thrown, perhaps, one quarter to one-half mile, and probably further. The truth is that, with his slight momentum, plaintiff should have fallen in the ditch.

Dr. Schovelhoffer procured assistance and had plaintiff carried to his residence, and then sent for Dr. Blaney. Plaintiff would not permit them to touch him and complained of some pain in his right hip and leg. They had to chloroform him, in order to examine him, as he would not permit examination without it, and they found not a mark of any kind upon his body. Plaintiff stated that, instead of driving to the center of the street and crossing the ditch where the country wagons had cut it down, he swung abruptly around and crossed near the end; that, as he was turning to the left the left front wheel of the buggy struck the ditch first, which threw him over on that side, and then the right front wheel struck the ditch and threw him up on that side, and that, after that, he knew nothing until he "came to himself" lying on the ground.

The next morning the citizens of the little town were treated to the spectacle of the plaintiff being driven through the streets, lying on a cot in a spring wagon. In a few days Drs. Schovelhoffer and Blaney placed his body in a plaster cast, which he did not wear very long.

For better treatment he was then sent to a hospital in St. Louis, which was conducted under the auspices of a Protestant religious denomination. He did not get along very well there; and, on complaint of some of the nurses, he left the hospital and went to a boarding house; but still returned to the hospital to be treated by the physician in charge. A trained nurse was then employed, who remained with him all the time— even occupying the same room with plaintiff.

It was to be proven — and it was — that he and the nurse got to bantering each other at the table one morning and the nurse ran up to their room ahead of plaintiff and locked the door, and that plaintiff, on finding the door locked, went into an adjoining room and asked permission of the young lady occupant to go over her transom, which request she granted. He then got upon a small table and jumped up into the transom, resting on his chest, slid through and went down, head foremost, alighting on his hands on the nurse's trunk, summersaulting into the room, and arose and said, "Ah I ha! you thought you had me locked out, did you?" That it would also be proven (and it was) that a young doctor was in the habit of coming to this boarding house and playing cards with plaintiff and others; and that, one day, the doctor came in in an intoxicated condition. In a wordy altercation with the plaintiff the doctor made some slighting allusion to the nurse. Plaintiff arose and assaulted the doctor. They fought their way to the head of the stairway, where they got down upon the floor, and then rolled to the foot of the stairs — the plaintiff, luckily for a paralytic who was going on crutches, alighting on top, and then proceeded to maul the doctor in true pugilistic fashion. They were separated, and the doctor made his way, on a run, through the boarding house office, and the plaintiff, in his wrath, broke away from those who were holding him, and followed the doctor up, but was restrained with some difficulty by two or three men.

After this recital and much more, I was asked: "What do you think of it?"

I answered, "Gentlemen, this young man was not thrown from his buggy as he claims at all, but drove to that point, got out of the buggy and laid down on the ground and groaned, so as to attract attention."

"Oh, I guess he was hurt some," said the Mayor, "for Dr. Schovelhoffer and Dr, Blaney put a plaster cast on him."

"I don't care what Dr. Schovelhoffer or anyone else did," I replied, "I tell you he was not hurt and that he laid down there, as I have stated, in order to lay the foundation for a suit for damages, and I will convince you of this fact before this trial is over."

The case went to trial that afternoon before a jury of fairly intelligent farmers — Judge Farmer, an able, intelligent and fair man, presiding.

In view of my last experience I asked the attorney to tell the jury in his opening statement that we admitted that plaintiff was having "fits" or "spells" and that we expected him to have one in the court room for the edification of the jury before the trial was over. We thought that, by this statement, we might keep him from having a "fit," with what success the sequel will tell.

I was mortally afraid of "fits" in court, and their influence on the jury, after my experience at Marysville, Kansas. The attorney did this and dwelt on it for a short time. The case was fought strenuously and almost bitterly from the beginning. The people, and even the ladies of the little town, turned out and filled the court room to repletion all the time. They were much concerned, for a verdict for the amount plaintiff had sued for meant an assessment of ten dollars each on every man, woman and child in the little town. The case of the plaintiff was made by the testimony of himself, his mother, the nurse and a number of his and his mother's intimate friends — including Dr. Schovelhoffer, who showed himself to be quite a partisan in the case. They swore to the facts as I have stated them. They also had the doctor from the religious denominational hospital at St. Louis, who testified that it was an injury to the spinal cord, but was not very clear as to what the nature of the injury was. The plaintiff himself was very adroit, while on the stand. He admitted climbing the transom in the St Louis boarding house, but stated that it was done under excitement and that he paid for it by feeling a great deal worse for several days. The nurse testified as to his having the "fits," and both she and Dr. Schovelhoffer testified that, when he had those "spells" his pulse always became very slow — as low as forty to the minute — in the beginning of the "fit," but that they grew gradually faster until they came to be very rapid and correspondingly weak. Taking it altogether if one were to believe the testimony of all of his witnesses, they made a very strong case.

Just as their last witness — plaintiff's mother — was closing, or had closed, her testimony and the plaintiff's attorney had said "that is all; we rest," the plaintiff arose from his seat in front of the clerk's desk and in full view of the jury, grasped his cane, horizontally in both hands (he used a cane and one crutch), and fell sprawling on the floor, the cane making a loud whang as it struck the floor. The plaintiff turned on his side and began to kick and jerk his arms quite vigorously, and his body underwent all the contortions that an accomplished athlete is capable of making. There were a number of exclamations, "There! Lee's got one of them spells," and a number of stalwart men rushed to his assistance. They raised him up and the judge ordered them to convey him into one of the jury rooms.

I whispered to the attorney for the defense and told him to ask permission for me to examine the plaintiff during the fit, and he did so, making the request in a loud voice, so as to be heard by the jury. The judge said, "It rests with plaintiff's counsel; the court has no objection." Of course plaintiff's counsel could not well refuse this request without hurting their case in the estimation of the jury, and so consented.

I went into the jury room at once. I found plaintiff lying on his back on the floor while quite a crowd stood around, and the nurse, under the supervision of Dr. Schovelhoffer, was preparing a hypodermic injection of some kind. I at first took hold of the patient's wrist, in an attempt to count his pulse, but he flexed his hand at a right angle to the forearm and kept up such a jerking that I could not count the pulse. I then laid down with my head on his chest, and tried to count the heart beats, but he sucked himself full of wind and inflated his lungs, so as to cover up and obscure the heart. I sat up and put my hand over the region of the heart, knowing that he would have to expire and let the air out of his lungs before a great while.

He had his eyes closely shut; but, when he found that I was about to gain my point, in spite of his gymnastics, he opened them very wide, looked at and located me, and then drew both feet up and placed them against my right side and gave a most vigorous kick. I was ready for him and so rolled over twice and avoided the kick. I then went and sat down above his head. I thought of Josh Billing's funeral of the mule: Josh said, "If I ever attend the funeral of a mule, I will be amongst the mourners at the head." I again placed my hand over plaintiff's heart and found the heart beat to be eighty-two per minute. This was about four minutes after his fall in the court room.

In a few minutes more it arose above ninety, and in ten minutes had arisen to above one hundred. Considering his gyrations and violent contortions, this was about what was to be expected. I then attempted to separate his eyelids with the thumb and index finger of my left hand, but he held them together so tight that I could not. I then took my two thumbs and, after quite an effort, succeeded in separating the lids. The pupils promptly responded to the influence of the light. I then separated and shut the lids a number of times, the pupils responding to the influence of the light and dilating in the dark in a very healthy manner. I then left the plaintiff to his physician, nurse and friends, as I had ascertained all that I desired to. Plaintiff was soon removed to his home, where he remained that afternoon.

Illinois has a very peculiar way in appointing examining physicians in such cases. The defendant cannot name the physician that he wishes to examine the plaintiff; but he can name as many as ten physicians and then plaintiff or his counsel may name the two that they are willing shall examine him. The attorney's for the defense were very desirous that I should examine the plaintiff, but plaintiff's counsel selected Drs. Blaney, of the town, and Chas. H. Hughes, of St Louis, an eminent neurologist, whom the defense had summoned in the case.

Dr. Schovelhoffer went upon the stand the next morning after plaintiff had the "fit" and testified that in the fall plaintiff had received a contusion at the hair line on the right side of his forehead, the size of a hen's egg, and that there seemed to be a fracture, depression or crack in the skull just beside this large contusion. As Drs. Hughes and Blaney had not yet completed their examination, they went down and finished their assigned task, and came back and both went on the witness stand and testified that there was not a mark on plaintiff's forehead, and that they could find no fracture or depression in the skull. I was then called.

I testified almost wholly in answer to hypothetical questions, and stated that, in my opinion, plaintiff was not and had not been injured; and that there was not, and could not be, any injury to the spinal cord, and told of the splendid protection that nature had provided for this important organ. I stated that the symptoms complained of were not such symptoms as would arise from an injured cord, and Drs. Hughes and Blaney gave the same testimony. I gave a detailed statement of my examination of plaintiff during the "fit" and stated that, if plaintiff was having genuine "fits" they would be in the nature of epileptic seizures and that, in such genuine seizures, the pupils were always temporarily paralyzed and immovable; that in such "fits," when genuine, the eyelids were not pressed tightly together, but were partially paralyzed and half open; that, in a genuine "fit," the invalid's face would become suffused and almost purple, and that the pulse did not behave as in plaintiff's case; and, in fact, that the plaintiff's "spells" were assumed and voluntary, as was evidenced in many ways; but, especially by his opening his eyes and locating me and then attempting to kick me; and that nothing in plaintiff's case indicated that his spinal cord had been injured, and that, had the "fit" been genuine, he could not have raised the assumed partially paralyzed leg with the other in his effort to kick me; and, in fact, the plaintiff was a malingerer — one of the very worst I had ever seen.

Plaintiff's counsel tried very hard to confuse and break me down, but he failed in his efforts to do so.

When the testimony was all in, the speaking began. The Centralia attorney made a powerful plea in behalf of the city. For the plaintiff Col. Merritt — brother of General Merritt of our regular army — spoke one hour, during which he devoted twelve minutes to the case and forty-eight minutes to me personally. He was quite witty and an inveterate stammerer, and he held me up before that audience and ridiculed me to his heart's content. He did me no harm, however, and only succeeded in raising a laugh at my expense, in which I heartily joined. I enjoyed nothing more than the high compliment he paid me by his ridicule, for it was evident that he felt that he must break down my testimony in order to win his case; and, to be singled out of all the witnesses and eminent specialists as a mark for his wit and satire was no mean compliment.

He held me up as being very egotistical and vain, and I presume that my satisfaction at the compliment he paid me went far toward verifying his statement.

The jury retired and the next morning brought in a verdict in the plaintiff's favor for three thousand dollars. We felt that we had not done so badly — having reduced the per capita assessment of a twenty-thousand-dollar suit to one dollar and a half per capita, or a saving of eighteen dollars and a half per capita. After the trial was over the Mayor came to me and, as spokesman for himself and others, said: "Doctor, when you advanced the idea that this plaintiff had climbed out of his buggy and laid down at the crossing, we thought it was monstrous, but, since hearing all the evidence and witnessing the 'fit' we have come to the conclusion that you are right. We believe that he deliberately got out of his buggy and laid down at the crossing, in order to complete his scheme to swindle our little city."

Later: — While writing the foregoing chapter, I wrote the former Mayor of the Illinois town and asked what the Supreme Court of that state did with the Webber case. I am just in receipt of a reply, in which he informs me that the Supreme Court had affirmed the case, and, as soon as the decision was made public, Lee Webber threw aside every semblance of being injured and walked the streets of the little town without halt or limp, and that he was also attending dances and taking part in the terpsichorean enjoyments of the town.

It is a wonder— considering the frailties of human nature — that somebody in the little town does not commit a violent and dangerous assault upon him, for it is most aggravating to have such a rogue to impudently and brazenly walk the streets, in perfect health and strength, after his two or three years of pretense on crutches.

No one but a born criminal would have the cheek and fortitude to face the people amongst whom he had been reared, under such circumstances.

That this young man is a moral imbecile I have not the least doubt. I feel quite sure that he has no correct conceptions of right and wrong. Such persons will not earn an honest living. They always prey upon the public. As a rule they are naturally very smart, but will not study and, therefore, rarely ever become highly educated.

They start out in life with the motto, "The world owes me a living, and I am going to have it." There was never a bigger lie uttered. The world owes no man anything until he has earned it. We are all indebted to the world for our very existence.

This is the motto of all degenerate criminals— criminals who are moral imbeciles. To this class belong the criminals who brutally murder old men and women in their beds and then rob their houses. They do not seem to ever suffer any compunctions of conscience. They are intensely egotistical and, also, intensely selfish.

To this class belonged Brooks, who murdered his friend Preller in the Southern hotel in St. Louis some years ago. Preller had befriended Brooks even to loaning him money; and Brooks returned this kindness by chloroforming Preller, under the pretense that he could ascertain whether the victim had certain troubles; and, after he had chloroformed his victim, he either continued the anaesthetic until the victim was dead or he added choking to the chloroform and then killed him.

Now, cunning as such criminals are, this man showed signs of great weakness in his manner of getting away. If he had written on strips of paper, "I killed my friend, Preller, and put his body in a trunk, in room so-and-so, in the Southern hotel, in St Louis, and I am now making my escape over the Southern Pacific Railroad, via California, and there expect to take a steamer to Auckland, New Zealand," and had scattered the strips along the route, he could not have advertised himself more effectually.

When his steamer arrived at Auckland two officers went out to the vessel and placed Brooks under arrest He even had on some of Preller's clothes — the cuffs bearing the dead man's initials.

Brooks made up an ingenious story as to how Preller happened to die — all by accident, of course — but the jury found him guilty of murder in the first degree, and he was hanged according to the laws of Missouri.

His good and respectable parents came all the way from England and tried to save their bad and undutiful son from the gallows. But the Governor of Missouri was obdurate and unmovable. The poor old mother pleaded pitifully for the life of her beloved, but all to no purpose.

She did not believe her son guilty. Few mothers who ever held a baby boy to their breasts ever believed that boy capable of committing a willful murder. They cannot see how he could do such a thing.

May God pity the dear, good mothers who must suffer on account of the bad conduct of such sons I It is, no doubt, a wise provision of nature that they cannot believe their loved ones capable of murder. It is a compensation of nature that they cannot believe it.

May God pity them, I say! May the good and loving God pity them always!

Case VII. I have the facts and details of a rare case of assumed injury to the spinal cord (which I never saw), in which the brazen assumption of the supposed injured party is rarely equalled, surely not excelled, for the courage he exhibited and the endurance which he showed.

The case was that of a brakeman on the Iron Mountain & Southern, who was injured, if my memory serves me right, by falling from the top of a box car, though it may have been a fall in some other way, and it is very probable that he was temporarily paralyzed by the bruising of the spinal nerves in the lumbar and sacral regions of the spinal column which caused a paralysis of both lower extremities, but which soon recovered.

He was taken to the company's hospital in St Louis and was under the immediate care of the chief surgeon, Dr. Warren B. Outten, and his assistants — all of whom are surgeons of experience and ability.

As said before, he claimed a paralysis of the lower extremities and, perhaps, for a time not without good ground. He also claimed to have paralysis or partial paralysis of the organs of speech or of the muscles of the larynx.

He was examined and treated in accordance with the best modem methods by Dr. Outten and his staff. for some time; when, suspicion being aroused, specialists on Dr. Outten's staff and even outside specialists were called in, who examined him repeatedly and made suggestions as to treatment and as to methods of detection of malingering, in case he were malingering.

The fellow ate and slept about as healthy individuals eat and sleep and did all of his talking in whispers.

Tests were made by sticking him with pins and needles and by the use of a powerful electric current, but all to no avail.

These tests proved nothing, for he never moved a muscle or even said "ouch!"

There was much division of opinion amongst the laryngologists and neurologists, but the strength of opinion seemed to be with those who believed that he was malingering.

This controversy and these examinations were kept up for months and still the fellow laid there and ate and slept and was serene in all respects. Watch was set upon him at night, and in daytime, when he slept, but no one ever saw him move a leg or foot, or heard him speak a word, asleep or awake. It seems incredible that any human being could have endured what he did without an outcry, or that he could have slept and never have moved a foot or leg; but he did it, and these were the strongest points in favor of his assumptions.

The claim department was anxious for a decision by the experts, for it made a great difference in the department's handling of the case. It was a clear case of liability — and it is my recollection, now, that the hand-hold of a defective brake gave way and caused his fall — and, if it could be clearly shown that he was totally paralyzed in his lower extremities, the department was prepared to give him a very reasonable compensation; and, if it could be shown that he was malingering, they were still prepared to reasonably compensate him for his temporary hurt and for the time lost, but they did not want to pay a man for a total paralysis who was really not injured to amount to much. It seems that the specialists could not settle it; but Dr. Outten, who had had much valuable experience and who knew how to utilize such experience, was of the opinion that the man was not paralyzed at all, and he stubbornly held to that opinion to the last.

Powerful lenses were used in the examination of the patient's larynx and many tests, best known to specialists in that field, were made, all to no avail. It was found, however, that the muscles of the larynx which take part in the formation of words were not atrophied, nor did his legs undergo atrophy.

The claim department finally decided to settle with him any way, and did so by paying him, I believe, fifteen hundred dollars.

He then announced his desire to go to his home, at some place in the State of Tennessee. Transportation over some of the Southern roads was procured for him and he was lifted into an ambulance, bade everybody an affectionate good-bye, and thanked them for their great kindness to him. He was then driven to the union station and carefully carried into the waiting coach, which was to bear him Southward, and there placed in a comfortable position and left.

Nothing was heard of him for about three months, when a stranger came into the hospital and asked to see Dr. Outten and members of his staff. When they had assembled he asked them if they had had a man under their care for something like a year who claimed to have been paralyzed in his legs and in his speech, and he gave the man's name, so as to surely identify him. He then said that at a certain date (this date being the same as the date of the departure of the malingerer) he was riding on a train going Southward, when he met up with and sat beside a young man — and he gave a very accurate description of the malingerer — and they got into conversation. As such conversations usually run, each inquired as to the destination of the other.

The malingerer told this man that his home was at a certain place in Tennessee — giving the name of the home of the malingerer — that he had been away from home and had not seen his relatives for a period of three years. He said he had made a sort of vow that he would not go home until he made a stake, but that he found it slow work to accumulate money on the salary he received and at the same time associate with railroad men and keep up his end of things, as is a proud young man's desire to do.

But, he said, he had fallen from a car on the Iron Mountain road and had been hurt some and that he was taken to the hospital; that there it had occurred to him to assume paralysis of his legs and larynx, and he told of the repeated examinations by the specialists and what a hard time he had had in fooling them. He put his feet upon the seat in front of him and lit a ten cent cigar and continued by saying that the claim agent had paid him fifteen hundred dollars, which he considered a pretty good sum for a poor boy who had been away from home only three years, and was going home to enjoy it in the midst of his loved ones. He said he had always been poor and had had little chance or enjoyment in life, but now he had the first opportunity to enjoy himself and to give enjoyment to his mother and sisters; "and, you bet, I'm going to have a good time, and don't you forget it!" said he.

It is my impression that Dr. Outten heard from him through other channels, and that the story was the same as to his not being paralyzed. In my opinion it parallels the most remarkable cases of malingering on record; and, in some respects, excels them all. Many surgeons — believing as Dr. Outten did, that the man was a malingerer — would have abused him like a dog and would have incontinently thrown him out. But not so with Dr. Outten. He is no more capable of doing such a thing to a man who has been hurt just a little bit, than he is of child murder.

Case VIII. I shall now narrate a case, not on account of its great importance, nor from the fact that it differs materially from other cases of assumed injuries to the spinal cord, for it was simply an ordinary, average case of assumed injury to the cord, but that I desire to speak, before I finish this manuscript, of the ability, shrewdness and peculiar methods in practice of one man, the Hon. Bailey P. Waggener, of Atchison, Kansas, and who is and for many years has been the general attorney for the Missouri Pacific Railroad Company of Nebraska and a large district in Northern Kansas, which large and important division is covered by himself and his able assistants. Of all the attorneys whom I have assisted in arranging and bringing out the medical facts in a given case, I feel sure that no other attorney will feel injured, jealous or hurt when I say that, in many respects, Mr. Waggener is the superior of any lawyer I have ever seen or expect to see.

Mr. Waggener is, I am proud to say, a native Missourian, who, soon after being admitted to the bar, removed to Atchison, Kansas, where he has resided and practiced law ever since, and where he has made for himself a reputation as an attorney and as an amiable and courteous gentleman which no lawyer need hope to equal much less to excel for many and many a day.

I think I have been with Mr. Waggener, personally, in about eight cases in my twenty-five years' experience, for he does not attend the trial of cases except those of peculiar importance, but leaves the case to one or more of his able assistants, but I can remember only one case which was tried to a conclusion — all the others finding themselves out of court early after the issues were joined; or, at least, as soon as the plaintiff's testimony was all in.

The Missouri Pacific attorneys seem to have a rule of practice which is not followed, so far as my experience goes, by the attorneys of any other corporation, and that is that of offering a demurrer to the evidence as soon as plaintiff closes his side of the case. Now, with some, this seems to be a mere formality, as the demurrer is often not even argued, but not so with Mr. Waggener. I make the assertion, which is based on my experience with him, that, in at least three out of five cases, he never permits the case to go beyond the closing of plaintiff's side of it, and, in my experience, his success is even much greater than this.

The demurrer, which the Missouri Pacific attorney generally brings with him already typewritten, is about as follows:

"Black vs. White. |

In the Circuit Court |ss.

Of Kansas City, Kansas. |

October term, 1890." |

Now comes defendant in the above entitled cause, who demures and says that plaintiff has not produced sufficient evidence to establish his case, and defendant, therefore, prays the court to dismiss this cause. I give this merely from memory.

Now, as I said before, this does not constitute a mere formality with Mr. Waggener, but this demurrer means something. He always comes into court with his aids and assistants and himself carrying stacks of books which are greater in number and importance than the library of many a young lawyer. All of those books are marked by the insertion of a card, or a book-mark, in one or more places, and he rarely uses any law books which are to be found in the libraries of the courts, but uses his own books always. He never comes unprepared. I never saw him caught or upset on a single point. When he comes to argue the point one of his assistants sits and hands him the books in turn and in the order in which they are needed.

Mr. Waggener, for a man of his ability and reputation, is not pompous or self-conceited. He has not a bit of either of these elements in his smooth and well-rounded character. He is an amiable, kind and courteous as a sweet-tempered girl; but, to use a slang phrase, "he always gets there." Mr. Waggener is not what might be called a finished orator. He never rants or makes attempts at elocutionary flights; but, simply talks, talks in a plain, not loud, smooth voice that is well modulated and which may be distinctly heard all over the court room, but his talk, together with the law he presents, amounts to something.

In the case I am about to relate I shall call the plaintiff Mr. Laystrom, as he was born in America, of Swedish parents, and had a name quite out of the ordinary.

He was a car inspector, and had been placed at a division point far out in Western Kansas. The place was not an inviting one. It was in the "Short Grass Country," where the wind blows the alkali dust into one's face and hair, and where what is called "society" has not yet reached.

Unfortunately for Mr. Laystrom (who would, no doubt, have been perfectly content otherwise) he had married an American girl who desired to enter and be a member of the society which her intelligence, beauty and position entitled her to enter, in some good respectable town.

Railroad men related that she ding-donged at him incessantly to get his position changed, to get an exchange with some other inspector, and therefore to get himself placed at a better division point. To this end he had petitioned his superiors over and often; but, in the estimation of his superiors

45

Mr. Laystrom fitted into the place where he was like a jug handle to a jug, and there they permitted him to languish.

He finally grew desperate. He loved his pretty young wife, and her smiling and loving appeals to him to "get another place," get a place somewhere where we can go to the theater and to church and see things. Oh, I'm so tired and disgusted with this hot and dusty old place," worried him no little, but Mr. Laystrom could only hang his head and utter regrets.

He could not move the "powers that be," hence he could not move his wife to another place.

He finally came to the hospital. He had been badly hurt, in cleaning up a freight wreck he said — had received a serious injury to his spine. He did not say "spinal cord," for he had not got that far along in anatomy, so it was just his "spine" that had been hurt. We stripped Mr. Laystrom and gave his "spine" a careful examination. There was not a mark on him, though it was only a few days after the infliction of the assumed injury when he came to the hospital. Mr. Laystrom said he had a "tingling all the time" and, furthermore, "the feeling seemed to be gone." He said he could not feel it when anything touched him. So we examined him with the aesthesiometer. As usual in such cases, he lied about it — said there were two points touching him, when there was only one, and vice versa, he said he felt only one when there were two.

The railroad men from his division had told me about his wife and her ambition to shine in a better town; for a car inspector is above and gets a better salary than a mere section laborer.

I felt sorry for the poor fellow, for I knew what he had to put up with; and, if I could have helped him in any way, without detriment to the interests of the railroad company, I would have done so, for Laystrom was fairly honest; in fact, he desired to be an honest man, and he had attained to his present position of car inspector by being perfectly fair and honest in his work and with the corporation for which he worked. His assumed injury of the spinal cord and the lying necessary to back it up did not sit lightly upon him.

He "herded by himself" a good deal; not because he was too proud to associate with other railroad men, but, I believe, because he was ashamed of his lying assumptions.

He used to go away to the furthermost part of the hospital gallery and then stand and look toward the Western Kansas plains with a "faraway Moses" look in his eye, and he would feel of and examine his right buttock with his right hand and a grieved expression would come over his countenance which was painful to look at.

Well, the case finally came to trial in the Circuit Court in Kansas City, Kansas.

Mr. Waggener came down, not because the case was of much importance; but, it did not happen to be a busy time with him, the place of trial was not far from his home and he could reach it in an hour, and he needed diversion away from his office.

When the issues were joined, Mr. Laystrom went on the stand in his own behalf. He looked fearful and apprehensive. The trial meant much to him and the pretty wife sat in her poor little cottage out on the hot and dusty alkili plains and waited to hear of the victory, and then hoped to be able to leave that hateful place, exchange or no exchange.

He gave the details of the wreck, which was a pretty bad one, and things had been smashed to pieces and separated from their connections with other things and all was in confusion. The division car inspector in a far out place like that is generally the boss at a wreck. That was one thing that made his wife so proud and ambitious — her husband sometimes bossing a whole lot of other men.

Mr. Laystrom, as was his habit, had been a very busy man at this wreck. They had an engine and used a big cable in pulling things off the track. Mr. Laystrom was engaged in hitching this cable on to things and then giving signals to the engineer to "slack ahead." At the time when he claimed to have been hurt he was hitching on to a pair of trucks which had been detached from their connection with the car. He stepped in front of the trucks and placed the cable around the axle. When the cable left the axle it did so to the right and at an acute angle.

Mr. Laystrom, when he went to place the cable in position, had stepped into the place where the angle was — between the cable and the right wheel of the trucks. When he had made the cable secure the engineer started up without a signal and before he had time to get out and so caught him between the cable and the wheel and he was squeezed.

Just at this point in the trial a stalwart railroad man came in bearing on his shoulder a pair of wooden car trucks. They were an exact pattern as to shape, size and everything of the ordinary freight car trucks. He laid them down in front of the judge's desk and stepped back and sat down.

"Why didn't you go on the other side of the cable and make the hitch where the cable would not catch you when the pull was made?" asked Mr. Waggener.

"Why, I couldn't," answered the plaintiff.

"Why couldn't you?"

"Well, you see, I'm right-handed, and I couldn't make the hitch from that side unless I was left-handed."

"Here," said Mr. Waggener, "take this little rope" (producing one from a bundle near him) "and go down there and show the jury how you made that hitch."

Mr. Lay Strom went down and took the rope and attached it and it was carried off at an angle as he directed. He was standing just where he said he was when caught. Mr. Waggener went down and stood on the other side of the cable.

"Now," said he, "I will make the hitch. Don't you see that this is where a right-handed man should stand when making the hitch? You are standing where a left-handed man ought to stand, although I can't see much difference. Either a right or a lefthanded man ought to make the hitch from either side, without any difficulty."

Laystrom's face was a study. He put on a weak and sickly grin; he looked down at the cable; then he fumbled it with his hands, and scratched his head and grinned some more. He shook his head, as much as to say, "I give it up."

"You may go back to the witness box," said Mr. Waggener.

Mr. Waggener then said to the court: "Your Honor will please pardon me for a moment."

He then sat down and wrote a demurrer, which was not in the stereotyped form, but which stated that plaintiff had defeated his case by his own testimony. The court read the demurrer and looked up. "Demurrer sustained," said the court. "Case dismissed. Call the jury for the next case, Mr. Sheriff," and Mr. Waggener grabbed a bundle of books and hurried out, for he always goes as if he were being chased by something, or somebody.

Now here was a good man, a man who had learned his trade of car repairer and car inspector well — but whose life was disturbed by the constant importunities of his pretty, sweet and proud young wife. She wanted to be where she could be in society.

There was nothing where they lived but the bare monotony of the plain which stretched away toward the Western horizon. It was intolerably hot there in the summer and unbearably cold in winter. She had a chance to see but few people and they were of the very commonest sort of humanity.

Laystrom was cast in a mold that gave him endurance and equanimity and he would have been satisfied almost anywhere with that pretty, sweet wife with him. But not so the wife. Her proud soul yearned for better things, and so, when the mere accident of his being squeezed, through his own dullness and lunkheadedness occurred, she, no doubt, persuaded him to assume that his spinal cord was injured.

Laystrom made a poor malingerer, for he was not naturally dishonest. What became of the poor fellow I do not know. Of course, the Missouri Pacific could not employ him again, and he would have to work at car repairing a good while on another road before he would be promoted to the position of car inspector.

Case IX. Several years ago a man was knocked down and rolled over by a Metropolitan street car at the incline at Ninth and Walnut streets, in this city. He was picked up and taken, I believe, to the University hospital.

Examination revealed the fact that the man was, apparently, not much hurt, there being only a few contusions about the legs, but no bones broken, no severe lacerations; and, in fact, the man's injuries seemed to be insignificant.

But, strange to say, the man seemed to be totally paralyzed in both lower extremities. After repeated examinations and tests by the street car company's surgeons, specialists were called in, and they applied all of the tests known to their specialty, and then decided that the man was not paralyzed in any degree whatever.

He was, I believe, an ordinary house and sign painter, or something of the kind; and it soon got abroad that he held accident insurance policies for fifteen or sixteen thousand dollars.

In due time he made a demand, on the insurance companies for the full amount named in those policies for total disability.

They refused payment and he brought suit against several of them.

There was also an attempt at settlement by the Metropolitan Street Railway Company, but his demands were so exorbitant that they could not agree.

To save expenses and prepare himself for the conflict, he sent his small, young family back to Indiana, there to remain with his wife's relations. He soon left the hospital and then he had some braces made. Those braces went around the hips and connecting, malleable, flat steel bars went down each side of both legs and was, in some way, attached to his shoes. This rendered his legs perfectly stiff. He also procured a pair of strong crutches. He then left his room and came upon the street. In walking he hopped or jumped forward with both feet at once and got around at a pretty good gait. In due time some of his suits against the accident insurance companies came up for trial. He won — receiving verdicts for the full amounts sued for.

Appeals were taken, but the insurance companies soon concluded to settle the verdicts, and did so. Others, becoming alarmed, also paid up; so he soon found himself in possession of six or eight thousand dollars — less his attorneys' fees. He now had plenty of money with which to fight the other insurance companies, and the Metropolitan Street Railway.

When he left the hospital a trained nurse, who was a good-looking widow, went with him to nurse and care for him. They took a modest cottage and lived in apparent comfort. I have never learned how he was able to live until he obtained his first settlement with the insurance companies, but presume that his attorneys must have carried him or that the nurse had some money. The latter is the most probable conclusion.

After he obtained a sufficiency of war material, he brought suit against the Metropolitan for a large sum — fifty thousand dollars, I believe.

There was a hung jury at the first trial. It was afterward ascertained that some of the jurymen were in favor of giving him a very large sum, others were more moderate and the Metropolitan had succeeded in convincing some that the man was a fraud and they stubbornly held out against giving plaintiff anything at all.

I was not present at this trial; in fact, I was not concerned in the case at all, but I learned, through medical circles, that the medical testimony was most conflicting. About all of our ablest neurologists were very positive that there was nothing the matter with the plaintiff at all, and that he was a fraud and a malingerer, but plaintiff's attorneys had succeeded in enlisting in plaintiff's cause quite a number of physicians — some of them pretty fair men, but none of them who were entitled to be called experts or specialists in neurology.

A change of venue was then taken to Carrollton, where the final trial was held. Carrollton is about seventy-five miles from Kansas City, is a county seat; and, it is said that, when the second trial came off, the hotel capacity of the town was strained to its utmost to accommodate the lawyers, witnesses and other interested parties from Kansas City — these being added to the petit jurymen and local litigants who usually remain in town during the sitting of the Circuit Court.

The trial of the case was a most exciting one, every inch of ground being contested. Attorneys and everybody seemed to take a partisan interest in the case. Those who believed in the plaintiff thought that the Metropolitan Company was treating a poor, unfortunate man, whom they had permanently maimed, very shabbily, and those who were against him thought that he ought to be mobbed.

The plaintiff came and went, amid it all, on his crutches with his clanking braces plainly in sight and hearing of everybody — always flanked by his faithful nurse — the widow.

I have always thought that he must be a man of unusual nerve, grit and sagacity, for one of his class.

The jury gave plaintiff a verdict for twenty thousand dollars. The case was appealed, but it was soon compromised. I do not know what the sum paid to the plaintiff was, but have understood that it was at least one-half or two-thirds of the verdict.

About this time the other insurance companies settled — paying up in full. The wife — back in Indiana — growing suspicious from some hints she had received, come on, to "spy out the land" and see what was going on.

When she found out how her husband and the widow nurse were living there were stormy scenes and dire threats of suits, indictments and so forth. But, what did this man care? Had he not just come out of a four years' war, in which he had learned the use of every weapon of offense and defense known among men? Pshaw! A little brush with his wife would be like a division of the United States army pitted against a few strikers in a country town laundry.

A compromise was soon effected, the wife's wounded feelings were soothed by the payment of a reasonable sum and she yielded the man to the widow nurse. This man was a diplomat as well as a warrior.

About this time — and in truth, this man did not seem to have anything but just the biggest kind of luck — the drawings for the Oklahoma lands came off. The plaintiff and the widow hid themselves away to this drawing, and, of course, drew a ranch or two. They couldn't help it. The wonder is that they didn't draw it all.

The last I heard of them, the erstwhile plaintiff and paralytic had discarded his braces, thrown away his crutches, and was devoting his valuable time to the improvement of his ranch and the investment of his money.

The press and the public make a great deal of noise about train robbers and train robberies, but, in my opinion, in the presence of such a case as this, train robbers and train robberies become eminently respectable.

Now, I insist again that these cases should be tried before a jury of three or five physicians. They, even if not specialists, would understand the facts as detailed by the specialists — in anatomy, pathology and neurology. They would also know in what doctor's testimony to place most confidence. They would know an able specialist, of pronounced ability, from a "Jim Crow" poser as a specialist, while the ordinary juryman knows nothing about it. All are specialists in his estimation.

Here is another case in which, it seems to me, an indictment could and should have been obtained and the plaintiff put upon trial for perjury, for obtaining money under false pretenses, or for any offense which is indictable under our law.

It does seem that such persons should and ought to be punished; and, for the life of me, I do not see why they cannot be. While it does look, sometimes, as if Justice had removed her blindfolds and had taken a walk and had not returned, yet it does seem that if many good men should give themselves to the task of trying to punish those persons it could be done.

Case X. In about the year 1898 I received a communication from Dr. Hopkins, banker and Mayor of Burlington, Kansas, saying that they had what they regarded as a very dangerous law suit for damages, on account of alleged personal injuries, pending against their city and asking if I could come and assist their counsel in defending it.

I had often been to Burlington, assisting our railroad attorneys in defending such suits, and knew Dr. Hopkins and the principal citizens of Burlington well, and I answered that I would come, and told Dr. Hopkins what my charges would be.

In due time I received a telegraphic message to come, and I went. I had been made acquainted with the facts in the case, by correspondence with Dr. Hopkins, so I did not have much to learn concerning it after arriving there. The facts were as follows:

A woman, of forty-five, who lived with husband and family on their farm, which almost joined, if it did not join, the city corporation, had been in the habit for years of driving an old yellow horse hitched to an old shack of a buggy, into Burlington and delivering garden stuff to the Burlington families and dispensing gossip to the women, also. She was extremely religious, had belonged to about all of the Protestant religious denominations, was a member of the Salvation Army; and was, at the time she claimed to have been hurt, attending a revival meeting of the Society of Friends, or Quakers.

The city of Burlington was doing some cleaning up of streets, and had shoveled the dirt off the crossings and piled it up in piles which resembled hay cocks. Mrs. Naylor (that shall be her name) was driving home after night from the meeting, in the old buggy, with the old yellow horse attached, and her sixteen-year-old daughter by her side. It was very dark and a storm was threatening, and she was driving pretty fast, when the left buggy wheels ran up on one of those piles of dirt and tilted the buggy up and Mrs. Naylor fell out. The daughter helped her into the buggy and they drove on home.

Within a short time suit was brought against the city of Burlington for twenty thousand dollars — injury to the spinal cord being alleged in the petition. When I arrived I met a number of physicians who had been out and examined Mrs. Naylor that morning. Their examination had been quite superficial, as they had not used a battery, nor had an examination of the uterus and ovaries been requested.

As I was going out, by arrangement with the city's leading counsel with the attorney for the plaintiff, most of the doctors went back with me. They informed me that Mrs. Naylor had been confined to her bed ever since the accident and that she had "spells" in which she "jerked all over" and became unconscious.

I said to the leading medical witness for the plaintiff: "Doctor, I will wager you a new hat that this woman is not wholly paralyzed in both lower extremities, as claimed, and that her principal trouble lies in a lacerated *ceroix uteri*, enlarged and retroflexed uterus and enlarged, indurated and prolapsed ovaries." He said he would not make a wager, but he did not believe that such was the case, as there was nothing that pointed to such a condition.

After arrival I was permitted to make a thorough examination, as had been agreed upon by the attorneys. The test with the battery for reaction of degeneration showed that there was no paralysis in any degree. I passed the uterine probe through a double laceration in the *ceroix uteri,* demonstrated the enlarged and retroflexed uterus, and had them all feel the enlarged, indurated and prolapsed ovaries.

Plaintiff could not attend the trial.

A few days before the case came to trial. Judge Johnson, of Gamett, the leading counsel for the city of Burlington, had gone out and taken plaintiff's deposition, or, rather, had cross-examined plaintiff when her attorney took her deposition. When she was being hard pressed on cross-examination, she took refuge in one of her "spells." One of the family, according to custom, ran down and brought up a bowl of hot water — too hot, in fact. When the plaintiff's feet were placed in the water she jerked them out and said "Ouch!"

Notwithstanding this, some of her physicians went on the stand and swore that she was totally paralyzed; and, notwithstanding the demonstrations as to the condition of her uterus and ovaries, all swore that they did not believe that to be the cause of her trouble; and yet, she had not one symptom or sign pointing to an injured spinal cord, which they all swore they thought to be her ailment, and that this injury had been received at the time when she fell from the buggy.

After the trial of such cases you can always get information with regard to matters which would have been of vast value if given on the witness stand. For instance, one lady told me that Mrs. Naylor had told her, when delivering vegetables and gossip, that her uterus often came entirely to the outside, which I was quite well prepared to believe; another told me that, a week after the plaintiff had taken her bed, a severe storm, which looked like an approaching cyclone, came up one night, and plaintiff became hysterical from fear and excitement and arose from the bed and ran up and down stairs and out into the yard, screaming at the top of her voice, and that the husband and daughter apprehended her after a lively chase, and bore her to her bed by force, and that plaintiff had never since left her bed, so far as any of her neighbors knew.

This would have been of great value, especially as bearing on the question of total paralysis.

A most ludicrous incident, which I shall relate, occurred during the trial. Amongst the medical men, summoned by plaintiff from other towns, was one whom I shall call Dr. Curley.

Dr. Curley was one of those physicians whom we often see, who practices medicine with a plug hat, chin whiskers and a three-button Prince Albert coat. He gave you the idea that "he knew so much that it made him unhappy."

When on the stand he was asked, on cross-examination, in regard to plaintiff's jerking her feet out of the hot water and crying "Ouch!" "In view of this fact, doctor, would you say that plaintiff is totally paralyzed in both of her lower extremities?"

"Yes, sir; I should say that she is," was his answer.

This question was turned over, changed and altered and put to him in different language and the answer was always the same. As he left the crowded court room, I saw young Dr. Harrington, who was from Dr. Curley's town, get up and follow Df. Curley out I whispered to Judge Johnson and said, "I will bet you a dollar that Dr. Curley will come back on the stand and ask permission to correct his testimony in regard to the total paralysis."

"What makes you think so?" asked the Judge.

I then told him of seeing young Dr. Harrington follow Doctor Curley out; "and," I added, "Dr. Harrington is just home from a course of post-graduate instruction, in Chicago, and is as bright as a dollar. Now he knows that Curley's testimony was all wrong, not to say ridiculous, and he will tell Curley so; and Curley, desiring to advertise himself all that he can on this occasion, will come back and correct his testimony and try to leave the impression that he thought of the correct answer himself."

It was not long after this when I saw Curley pressing his way through the crowd toward the place where the lawyers sat. He finally reached Judge Graves, the leading counsel for plaintiff, and stooped and whispered to him. "Well, wait a little while," I heard the Judge say.

At the opportune time Judge Graves arose and, addressing the court stated that Dr. Curley desired to go on the stand and correct a part of his testimony, as it had occurred to him that he had, perhaps, inadvertently given a wrong answer.

The Court said the doctor could do so then. Dr. Curley took the stand with a great strut and an air of profound wisdom.

"What part of your testimony is it that you wish to correct, doctor?" asked the court

"Well, let the stenographer read the last three or four questions," said Curley. The stenographer did so.

"Well, no," said Curley, "I wouldn't say that she is totally paralyzed."

Judge Johnson then went after him. "Why, doctor," said he, "I asked you that question over and over, and tried to get a correct answer from you ar.d yet you persisted in giving the same answer each time."

"Well, I didn't understand the question," persisted Curley.

"But, how could you misunderstand the question, doctor, when I made it so plain that a child could understand it?" asked Judge Johnson.

"I don't know," said Curley, "but I didn't understand the question." And such is the character of medical talent that daily goes upon the witness stand and either ignorantly, or wilfully, swears away tens and hundreds of thousands of dollars of the money of railway and other corporations.

The jury gave Mrs. Naylor eighteen hundred dollars. The case was appealed and I have not heard what the Supreme Court of Kansas did with it.

Here is a case in which a woman of a certain age, who has suffered for years from injuries due to the accidents of child bearing, at last receives a shock. She is religious, impressionable and hysterical.

Added to her physical, nervous and mental condition is the incentive to suddenly increase the size of the family exchequer by bringing suit against a corporation — the city near which she lives.

It is contended by some that under such circumstances a woman persuades herself that she is really hurt. I cannot agree to this. I believe that when a woman is really hurt she knows it, and that, when she is not hurt she knows it I believe that she knows when she is playing a part, although that part may be a wrongful one, and may have for its consummation the obtaining of something for nothing. But, I believe that such people — both women and men — believe that their conduct is justified by the fact that they are poor, that there are many persons in this corporation, who will have to bear the burden of the verdict, who are very rich and who will not be materially injured by the payment of the verdict, and that the very lightly increased taxation which the poor will have to pay will amount to but little, when divided up among so many.

I have no doubt that such people console their consciences with such sophistry as this and believe in the end that there is little harm in which so much good may be done to a few and so little hurt to the many.

They do not think of the lasting injury they do themselves by perjuring themselves and to their children, whom they often cause to go upon the witness stand and swear falsely, and thus lay the foundation for a life of falsehood, and, maybe, for a life of crime.

People who do wrong invariably try to sustain themselves by arguments that will not bear inspection.

Chapter Four - Fractures, Dislocations and Joints

THERE are perhaps, more personal injury lawsuits based upon fractures, dislocations and injuries to joints, or upon assumed fractures, dislocations and injuries to joints, than upon any other grounds, except that of assumed injuries to the spinal cord.

It is not difficult, except in rare instances, to make out a fracture of a bone, so in these cases, as a rule, there is no question as to the existence of a fracture, or to the fact that there has been a fracture; so, the question often hinges upon the question as to whether a fracture has united or as to whether it continues to give trouble, after it has united.

In private practice, if a patient sustains a fracture and it is properly adjusted and unites, that is the last of it, but not so always where the fracture has been caused by a railroad accident, or upon a railroad. It has always been a puzzling question with the writer as to why it is that fractures, dislocations and injuries to joints in private practice, when properly set, reduced or treated get well and give no further trouble; and in cases where the injury was sustained in a railroad accident, or caused by a railroad, they should be treated in exactly the same way; and yet, continue to give trouble by pain and disability, which the doctor cannot see, nor explain upon any reasonable hypothesis.

It must lie with the patient It must be that, in cases where the injured party has received his injuries in a railroad accident or by a railroad he does not desire his injury to get well, or to appear to get well until its pains have been soothed by a "greenback poultice."

There are some cases in which an injured party claims to have sustained a dislocation, where such is not the case and the doctor who pretended to have reduced the dislocated joint seems to become *particeps criminis,* in order to get the fee for having reduced the dislocation.

I have paid doctors a good round fee a number of times for having reduced dislocations when I knew that they had done no such thing; and this is true, especially, as to the hip joint. I have had bills sent in for reducing a dislocation at the hip joint, where the doctor claimed to have made the reduction without an anaesthetic, when I knew that he could not have made the reduction with an anaesthetic. All I could do was to protest It was either pay or stand a law suit and then pay and have the costs to pay besides.

With regard to fractures there is scarcely ever any controversy except, sometimes, in cases of supposed or real fracture of the thigh bone at or near the hip joint, or fracture of this bone within the capsular ligament — what is known as intra-capsular fracture. An able man can, as a rule settle this matter; but, sometimes it is hard to do, especially where there is what is called an "impacted fracture." This is where the bone is fractured and then driven into itself, so that it becomes immovable at the point of fracture. This is a rare injury, however. A capable surgeon can usually settle the question as to what the trouble is; or, at any rate, as to whether there is any trouble at all.

There are cases in which it is claimed that ribs have been fractured when they have not I have known doctors to get on the witness stand and swear that there had been a fracture of one or more ribs when there was no sign whatever that a rib had been broken.

One peculiarity about fractured ribs is that they always unite with a large callous. This is a lump, or an enlargement at the site of fracture and these large callouses are shown on the rib at the site of the fracture, if there has been one. This is due to the fact that the two fragments of the fracture are always in motion, caused by the breathing, while the process of union is going on. Nothing can be done by the surgeon to prevent the constant movement of the two ends of the broken rib. It leaves a large callous or lump at the site of fracture which any surgeon ought to be able to make out by touch; and yet, doctors will swear that there has been a fracture when there is no callous to be felt at all.

There is and has been much controversy as to whether there has been an injury to a joint, and as to whether that injury still exists. Yet, there should be no controversy and no ground for disagreement and cross swearing in a case of this kind. It should be plain to a competent surgeon as to whether an injury still exists in a joint and as to whether a diseased process is still in existence in that joint

There are just a few conditions which may follow a serious blow, a twist wrench or any severe injury to a joint These are synovitis, or inflammation of the lining membrane of the joint; peri-arthritis, or inflammation of the tissues around the joint; osteomyelitis, or a rapidly destructive inflammatory process in marrow and the soft or spongy ends of the bones composing the joint, and tubercular ostitis — that is, an inflammatory condition with tubercular disease, running in the soft ends of the bones composing the joint. Some of these processes are more or less rapid — viz: osteo-myelitis, peri-arthritis and synovitis, and some or one at least, is rather slow — that is tubercular disease of the soft ends of the bones which make the joint, or the same disease — (tubercular)— of the synovial membrane.

But, no matter what the disease may be, there are some things which ensue, some conditions which occur, in time, which make one fact quite apparent and that is, that there exists in or around this joint a serious condition of disease.

Any diseased condition, following an injury, and which may or does run in a joint for some time, will cause the joint, or the structures about the joint, to become infiltrated and, hence, the joint will be larger and changed in appearance, so that its symmetry, when compared with its fellow, is lost. If you do not find these changes — if they are not apparent to the eye, then you may conclude, without argument, or further examination, that there exists no diseased condition in this joint; and, in addition to the gross appearances to the naked eye, measurements with the tape line will demonstrate the fact; for, if it be the knee joint — which is the joint most commonly complained of in those cases — or the elbow, then, it will not only be apparent to the naked eye, but measurements will demonstrate that the limb is smaller, above and below the joint, than its fellow.

As I have stated the knee joint is the one most frequently hurt, and the one we see most in private practice, and the one complained of most frequently in these personal injury suits for damages. So I will take that joint as an example and shall have more to say regarding it than any other joint.

In the diseased conditions which may follow an injury to the knee I have stated that osteo-myelitis is the one which runs its course most rapidly. It cannot be said to be a strictly knee joint injury, as a rule, for the injury is usually below and near the joint in the epiphysis of the tibia — (the upper and spongy end of the shin bone) and the diseased process is in this upper end; but, as it is so near the joint, it often affects the structures around the knee and, hence, makes it appear, to the uninitiated that this joint is also affected.

The disease runs its course rapidly. It is exceedingly painful and especially so at night. The leg is more or less flexed upon the thigh, so as to take the strain off the muscles, the tendons of which are attached to the tibia in the region of the diseased end.

The patient will have a high fever — which is not true of some of the other diseased conditions of this joint; and, if it be not attacked and relieved by the surgeon's knife, the pus will soon bore its way through the soft parts and make its exit without surgical interference. This condition should be attacked early by the surgeon and not only the pus let out, but a sufficiently large opening should be made and drainage put in to permit the use of the curette (the gouging and scraping instrument) and the chisel and all of the diseased bone removed. This is easily done, and it is surprising how quickly it will recover and what an excellent limb the injured person will have afterwards. If done well the injured party need not feel, and his friends need not know that he ever sustained such an injury.

In a periarteritis — inflammation of the tissues and structures outside the joint, the process is, also, more or less rapid and should be treated by pressure with bandages and by elevation and it almost invariably gets well in a very short time.

In the tubercular ostitis, or synovitis, the process is slower and not so painful. The theory of the pathologists; or, at least, of some of them with regard to tubercular disease of the bone or a joint, following an injury is as follows: They hold that in persons in whose cases tubercular disease of a joint follows an injury, such persons already had tubercle bacilli floating in the blood or lymph channels, that these bacilli are attenuated or weak and are kept in this attenuated condition by the good health of the person in whose system they reside; that, where such person receives an injury to a joint — to a knee joint, we will say — there ensues at once, a congested condition of the arterial capillaries in the joint and the ends of the bones composing the joint — this congestion being caused by the temporary paralysis of the walls of the capillaries — this making it difficult for them to empty themselves; that, under such circumstances the leucocytes or white blood corpuscles which are the scavengers of the system — seize upon these attenuated bacilli and carry and dump them into the injured joint, where they can have a plenty of nutriment, on account of the increased and altered secretion of the part, due to the injury and that, then, the leucocytes go to work and pen these bacilli up in the joint, by throwing up and organizing a strong fibrous wall around them, and then proceed to starve them, by cutting off the fine arterial capillary circulation of the part, thereby not only lessening, but almost entirely checking the secretion of the part The bacilli then go to work and use up what pabulum there is in the joint; and when they have done so, like the cannibals they are, they proceed to destroy each other, and that they do destroy each other, leaving only a comparatively few of attenuated bacilli. This is a magnificently conservative process of nature, and all the facts in the case bear out the theory. After all of the pabulum has been used up, and the bacilli have destroyed almost their entire colony, there is nothing left, except a mass of caseous, or cheesy, material, which we find there in subsequent operations upon the joint; and we also find the destructive work of the bacilli in the spongy ends of the bones, leading up to the protective wall, but not beyond it. The leucocytes by this, their splendid and intelligent work, localize the tubercular process to this one spot; and this is true of nearly all the tuberculous processes of the body — tubercular disease of the lungs being always a purely local disease, though the process of walling off the local affection is much more difficult there than in a joint, owing to the difference in the nature of the structures — the lungs being very soft, and hence it is hard for the leucocytes to do their work as satisfactorily as in a joint.

Now, as before stated, this process takes place slowly and with nothing like the pain and constitutional excitement which attends the more rapid process in osteo-myelitis. While this is going on there is an attendant infiltration in all of the structures around the joint, so that it becomes very large, as compared with its fellow, and it loses its symmetry entirely. After six months or a year the measurements will show that this knee is from one and a half to two and one-half inches larger than its fellow, and that the calf, and the thigh, at a point four or five inches above and below the joint, are from one to two and one-half inches smaller than the opposite leg and thigh. There is no possibility of any one making a mistake in the diagnosis of such a condition; and, in the absence of the enlargement and loss of symmetry every intelligent and fair-minded physician must know that there is no disease of the joint; and yet, it will be seen that doctors, and even those supposed to be competent surgeons, differ very greatly in even as plain a case as this.

Chapter Four - Fractures, Dislocations, Injuries to Joints

Case I. I WILL now proceed to give some cases illustrative of what has been said in the introduction on this particular subject.

In the latter part of the year 1886, I received directions from the chief surgeon, Dr. Warren B. Outten, to go to a town which I shall call Mapleton, on the Missouri, Kansas and Texas road — one of the Missouri Pacific's leased lines — and there examine and report upon the condition of an old gentleman, whom I shall call, Col. Ames.

The history I had received of the case, at the time of the accident, and by correspondence with the chief surgeon since that time, was as follows: On the afternoon of the 29th of June of that year. Col. Ames, who was the proprietor of the principal hotel in Mapleton, had gone to the depot with some departing guests to meet the incoming southbound train. He was carrying the hand baggage of some of his departing guests. The train was late and came in at the rate of twenty miles an hour — thus violating a city ordinance, which limited the speed of trains passing through the town to six miles an hour.

As the train slowed down at the depot, a United States mail agent threw a leather pouch, containing mail, onto the platform. It struck Col. Ames on his right knee. He stepped backward and the heel of the shoe of the right foot caught in a hole in the platform — the hole being the ordinary auger hole found in the grub lumber of which such platforms are made, and which hole had been much enlarged by the passing over it of the wheels of the truck used in handling trunks and freight. The heel of the shoe became fast and he swung around in a spiral twist and fell — tearing the heel and a part of the sole off the shoe. He was taken charge of by friends and conveyed to his hotel and his family physician. Dr. Sheldon, sent for. The doctor came and attended him. He afterward stated and testified that the Col. complained bitterly and seemed to be in great pain. The doctor stated that the right knee began to swell at once and that he treated it by putting on a warm flaxseed meal poultice.

This was very bad surgery, for the warm poultice tended to further paralyze and dilate the arterial capillaries of the part. It did little, if any, harm in this case, however, as the doctor testified that the swelling subsided before many days.

Col. Ames made a demand upon the claim department and I believe, an assistant claim agent went to see him with a view to settlement; but the Col. wanted fifteen hundred dollars with which to soothe his injured knee, which the claim department refused to pay. The matter remained in abeyance until the 29th of October — just four months to a day from the date of the accident Some correspondence had taken place between the Col. and the claim department in the meantime, but nothing came of it.

I arrived in Mapleton late in the afternoon and went at once to the hotel kept by Col. Ames. I roistered and then looked about to see if I could locate the Col. I had a slight acquaintance with him, though he did not remember me. I found him sitting in the hotel office, near a front window. He was leaning back in an office chair and had both feet extended upon a table in front of him with the left leg on top of the right one, and was reading a St Louis paper. I walked about for some time — hoping to see the Col. get up and make his way to his crutches, which I espied upon a counter some ten feet behind him. He was so engrossed with his reading, however, that he did not seem disposed to leave his position; and, growing tired of waiting, I introduced myself, told him who I was, my official position with the railroad company and the object of my visit to Mapleton.

I watched his countenance very critically, and was much interested in noting the change in the expression of his features. He slowly and, apparently, with great pain and difficulty, unfolded his legs, arose and hopped to the place where the crutches lay, holding to chairs and the counter on the way. He placed his crutches in position and asked me what I wished him to do. I asked that his physician be sent for. Dr. Sheldon, whom I found to be a fairly intelligent physician; and, evidently a very good man, came. We three then went upstairs. The Col. had great apparent difficulty in mounting the steps. When we had reached his room he took a seat in a chair and I asked that he take off his pants and drawers.

This, with the help of Dr. Sheldon he did, though with much apparent suffering. Inspection showed the knees to be symmetrical, so far as the naked eye could judge. Measurement showed the right, or assumed injured knee, to be a little less than one-eighth of an inch larger than the left, which is about the usual difference, as the right knee, ankle and foot are always a little larger than the left, on account of the fact of their having been used more.

The calf and thigh showed no difference in size. I then made examination by touch and manipulation, and found no thickening or alteration of structure; but, when I came to flex the leg upon the thigh; and, when it had reached the position of an angle of about thirty-five degrees, he stopped me. "Oh" (staccato) "Now, there's where she catches me! hold on doc, my God, you can't imagine how that hurts."

Then I would try it over again; but it was always the same.

When I had reached about the same angle in flexing the leg upon the thigh he would stop me and "Oh" and grunt and moan as if in much pain.

Having satisfied myself I closed the examination. I then asked him regarding the pain when the part was not in motion.

"Well," said he, "she always hurts me some, and especially at night and in changes in the weather. 'My God,' nobody knows what I've suffered with that knee. If I could have it back as it was before I was hurt, I wouldn't have it hurt again, as it is now, for all the money old Jay Gould has got!"

The same old story I the same old song that I had heard so often before.

I returned home and made my report in accordance with the above facts. The Col. brought suit and set his damages at twenty thousand dollars. The case did not come to trial until two and a half years from the time of the accident. The suit was brought and the case tried at Nevada, the County Seat of Vernon County. There was quite an array of legal talent on the Colonel's side; and, for the railroad company, there was the assistant attorney for that district, Mr. Harrison of Carthage, and the local attorney, who was a young man. In the testimony the facts sworn to for the plaintiff were about as I have related them — the Col. proving by overwhelming and indubitable evidence that the train was running at about twenty or twenty-five miles an hour when it entered the town of Mapleton.

The Court appointed six physicians to examine the plaintiff — three local physicians for the plaintiff and the two local surgeons of the railroad company and myself for the defense.

We repaired to a room in the principal hotel, where the Col. was then living, to make the examination. We had the plaintiff take off his pants and drawers, and made the examination, first, by inspection. The knee seemed, to the naked eye, to be symmetrical with its fellow, and the leg and thigh were also in appearance, the same. Measurement showed the right knee to be a little less than one-eighth of an inch larger than the left and the calf, and thigh, four inches above and below the knee, measured almost the same as the opposite limb. Examination by touch showed no induration, or alteration of the structures about the joint; and, in manipulation the joint was perfectly movable, but, when we flexed the leg upon the thigh the plaintiff checked us when it reached an angle of about thirty-five degrees. "Oh!" ouch! hold on there, doc, my! don't move it any further that way. Now there's where she catches me, oh! My! doc, you've almost killed me. I tell you, boys, I can't stand to have her bent that way beyond a certain point."

Almost all of the physicians took part in the manipulation and the Col. complained afterward that, as a consequence of so much rough handling his knee joint was quite sore.

The doctors for the plaintiff testified that they thought there was some disease running in that knee joint, but would not name the disease, further than to say, "it might be some nervous condition." The two local surgeons for the company and I all testified in about the same way. I was put on the stand first and detailed the facts of my former examination of the plaintiff, on October 29, 1886.

I stated that there was no disease known to surgery that could possibly exist in that joint for two and a half years, without showing a great alteration of structure and a loss of symmetry of the joint I gave the differential diagnostic points between the different diseased conditions that might exist in a joint, and stated that there was no disease in that knee when I saw it first and there was none at that time. The company's attorney asked me, if it was not true that, in disease of the joint or when no disease existed in the joint, if the leg and thigh of the leg that was held up so long should not become smaller than the other, from what is known as "atrophy of disuse" or "perishing away" from its not being exercised. I answered that such should be the case.

"Then," asked the attorney, "how do you account for the fact that the Colonel's leg, which has been held up and out of use for two and a half years, is not smaller than the other leg?"

"He walks on it and exercises it in his room at night," I answered.

This created a howl amongst the Colonel's Counsel. "Hold on! hold on, stop right there. Now, how do you know that he walks on that leg and exercises it at night?"

"Because, if he did not, it would be smaller than the other one now."

"Now, Dr. King, do you swear that he walks on that leg at night?"

"I do, to the best of my knowledge and belief."

"Then, you will not swear that you know he walks on it at night?"

"Yes, I do, to the best of my knowledge and belief."

"And, upon your oath, you swear that you know that plaintiff walks on that leg at night."

"Yes, I swear that I know it, as well as do any other fact or circumstance in this life that I did not see." And so we had it.

"Then you swear that when the Colonel says that that leg hurts him, he tells a lie!"

"I do not care, Judge Burton, to call the Colonel a liar, thus publicly, on the witness stand. He is an older man than I am; the jury has heard his testimony and mine, and it is for them to say whether one or the other of us lies; and, if so, which one of us is lying."

"Well, but I want you to say, in so many words, whether or not you believe the plaintiff is lying." I protested; called attention to the disparity in our ages, and again said that the jury must be the judges of our testimony.

The attorney then appealed to the Court to make me answer the question; and, for the first time in my experience, the Court said, "You must answer the question, Dr. King."

I answered the question upon the order of the Court and under protest I said, "Yes, I think he is lying; I know that he is lying, as well as I know any fact or circumstance in this life, which I did not see with my own eyes."

I described to the jury what the process of infiltration about an inflamed, or diseased joint was, and likened it to the enlarged hock of an old horse, whose joint had been inflamed for a long time. "Everybody knows Smith's old, big legged horse," I said, "and there is no material difference in the two cases — the process in both being the same."

The medical and surgical facts were clearly against the plaintiff; but he and his friends stuck to their story, and good Doctor Sheldon went on the stand and swore to the linseed meal poultice, and said that, so far, as he could see, it was a case of periarteritis (inflammation around the joint) and that there had ensued some "nervous trouble" the nature of which he could not name.

There was an occurrence during this trial which I cannot refrain from mentioning especially as it indicates how railroad companies bribe juries.

During recess one day, an old acquaintance came to me and taking me aside, said, "Doctor, do you people want to hang this jury?"

"Why, yes," I answered, "We would prefer to have a straight verdict in our favor; but, as I fear this cannot be had, I presume the next best thing is to hang the jury."

"Well, I can hang the jury for you, if that is all you think you can get; but I tell you that unless somebody can be induced to hang the jury, you are going to have a big verdict against you."

"How would you go about hanging the jury?" I asked.

"Why," said he, "There are two men on that jury that I can buy for twenty-five dollars each, and make them hang that jury until doom's day. I know, because I have bought both of them when they were on the jury before. All I want is for you to guarantee that I shall have my fifty dollars again. I wouldn't trust the railroad company, unless I had arrangement with some official connected with the management, but your word is good to me; and, if you say that I shall have my fifty dollars back again, I will see them and fix them, after the adjournment this afternoon."

"This is an entirely new kind of business to me, Mr. Blank," I said, "and, under no circumstances, would I do anything that might, in the most remote way, connect me with the commission of a felony. As long as I have been with the Missouri Pacific railroad company, and as many of these cases as I have helped to try, I have never heard the bribing of a juryman or witness so much as referred to once. You can go to the assistant attorney and make your proposition to him; but, I don't believe that he knows any more about such things than I do. However, if you should make arrangements with him let me beg of you to not let me know anything about it, for I would have a guilty feeling were I to know that such a thing was being done."

After the afternoon adjournment, the company's attorney came to me and asked, "Did Mr. Blank have a talk with you?" I answered that he did. "What did he say?" the attorney asked. I told him what Mr. Blank had said. "He came to me," continued the attorney, "and made the same proposition. I told him that I was not authorized by the management to engage in any such business; and, even if I should be, I would have nothing to do with such work. I would resign my position before I would be compelled to commit a felony. I am not going to violate the laws of my state and lay myself liable to go to prison for a term of years; and, from what I know of the management of the Missouri Pacific road, I am sure that they would not only not require you or me to engage in such work; but, they would not furnish the money for anybody to do it."

And, that is the whole of my experience in railroad's bribing jurors and witnesses during an experience of twenty-five years.

The jury gave Col. Ames a verdict for eight thousand five hundred dollars! The case was appealed to the Supreme Court; and, afterwards reversed and remanded.

When the United States Court broke the Gould lease of the Missouri, Kansas and Texas, in 1888, and ordered the corporation into the hands of receivers, the claim department at once got busy in settling claims and suits against the Missouri, Kansas and Texas road. When the general claim agent reached Col. Ames he found that the Col. had discarded one crutch and had substituted a cane on that side; and had also had a brace put on his right ankle. Why he had it put on the ankle — since he never complained of the ankle, I never could divine, unless it was that the brace on the ankle could be seen by the public, and a brace on the knee could not

The general claim agent found the Col. still staunch in his demand for fifteen hundred dollars. This the claim agent paid.

I was curious to know what the Col. did with his crutch and cane, after he had received his money; and, upon inquiry, learned that he discarded both within ten days after settlement.

A few days afterward an old and esteemed friend said to one of my sons:

"I desire to send an apology to your father by you."

"What do you want to apologize to my father for?" asked my son.

"Why," said he, "I have done your father a real injury in my mind. I was present at the trial of the Col. Ames suit and heard your father' give his testimony, and I thought that I had never heard anything like it in my life, and hoped to never hear the like again. It really almost made me sick. I went home and told my wife about it, and said to her, 'Why, just to think that our old family physician whom we esteemed so highly and thought so good and honest, could be so prejudiced by drawing a salary from a railroad company as to go on the witness stand and testify as he did is shocking. And the way he abused that good old man, Col. Ames, was simply outrageous. We sorrowed over the matter together, for it hurt us infinitely to have to believe such a thing of our old and esteemed family physician."

"Well," he continued, "about ten days after the settlement of the Col's, case I was walking down the street and saw the Col. standing on the street facing the sidewalk and talking to some gentlemen who were standing on the sidewalk; and I was not only astonished to note that the Col. had not only discarded the crutch and cane; and, what I supposed to be the very necessary ankle brace, but, I was almost horrified to find that he was standing on his left foot and was digging the toe of his right shoe into the dirt under the sidewalk; he was kicking, I tell you, and *kicking hard!* hard enough almost to have hurt a well leg.

"I felt so indignant that, had he not been an old man, I believe I would have assaulted him. I went home and told my wife, and your good father resumed his old place in our estimation and affections."

The trouble with the public is that its indignation usually comes too late to do the cause of justice any good.

This was one of the most remarkable cases that I ever took part in the trial of. Of course, it is impossible to make the average juryman understand what we mean by hypertrophy, atrophy, etc., although I always used the plainest and commonest words and speech in our language, and then explained every word if there was not an equivalent in common use.

But, with all this care and trouble, and absolutely true as it was, I presume that I failed to make the jury understand that, in a case where a diseased condition had existed for two and a half years, the knee should be large, boggy, shapeless, and the calf and thigh smaller than its fellow, they either could not or did not understand, or they thought that I was swearing falsely because I was employed by the railroad company.

It was true, and is yet true, that it was impossible that this man could have suffered in any degree whatever, on account of the slight blow that he received on his knee from the thrown mail sack. I mean that he did not and could not suffer from this cause two and one-half years afterward.

I have submitted this matter to the very ablest surgeons, east and west and have had their opinions in regard to it, for, I did not wish to do injustice, even in my thoughts, to any man that lived, and their opinions have invariably been the same as mine — that it was impossible for this man to have suffered, as he claimed to have suffered for two and one-half years, and even longer — in fact until the settlement was made in September or October, 1888, and for there to have been no alteration in appearance, for there to have been no change in the structures around the knee joint, but that it should still be symmetrical with the other knee.

It should have been enlarged, infiltrated and boggy to the touch. This they all say and agree with me in every word of my testimony on the witness stand.

I have no compunctions of conscience, therefore, in regard to my testimony. If I could be made to believe that I had inadvertently injured any human being, under such circumstances, I would even yet try to repair that injury, for I do not look at such things lightly. I believe that the conduct of every man should be measured with an eye to the very highest conceptions of justice. That he should wrong no man, under any circumstances.

I may be foolishly sensitive about such things, but I believe that the conduct of all men toward others — toward the highest and even the humblest, should be such, not only so as to meet the approval of his own conscience, but that it should meet the approval of the very best men everywhere.

If such men as Col. Ames would square their lives by such rules I am sure that there would be less sueing of corporations and that less money would be collected unjustly.

How such men can reconcile their conduct, and be satisfied with their ill-gotten gains is to me a problem that I cannot solve.

But the hardest problem to me to solve is as to how such people can see their way clear in coaching and drilling their own children — little boys and girls — and then putting them on the witness stand to swear falsely.

Of course there were no children in Col. Ames' case, but I have often been in cases where there were children, and have witnessed the mental contortions of those innocents while they were being cross-examined. They often acquit themselves in their dishonest role as well as, if not better than, their elders.

But, think of the moral blunting of this child's conscience! Think of the effect it will have on this boy or girl in after life.

I do not believe that a little girl can be coached in this way and then put on the witness stand and made to swear falsely without a blunting and benumbing influence that robs her, not only of all honest and moral feeling, but of all ideas of virtue and true womanhood. I wonder if such people could foresee what such training may do for their little ones, if they would not hesitate and then change their course.

I fear not. "The love of money is the root of all evil." There was never a truer saying.

In this training the foundation is laid for the moral ruin of the boy or girl, and hence the foundation for the bringing into the world of more moral degenerates. May God pity the little children that are thus trained by their dishonest parents. May God pity them always.

Cases II, III, IV, V. On March 6th, 1886, a local train, running between Independence and Kansas City, was derailed while *en route* to the latter place, and about forty persons were injured. The passenger list was made up almost entirely of citizens of Independence, and most of them were going to Kansas City to attend a theatrical matinee — the versatile and famous Lottie being the attraction.

An account of the wreck, with a list of the injured, was sent to the general claim agent and to the chief surgeon and his chief assistants. I had a full list of the injured and a short statement of what their injuries were, late in the afternoon. It was too late to get to Independence that afternoon so it was arranged by wire that I should join the assistant general claim agent at the depot in Sedalia in the early morning of the seventh, and proceed with him to Independence, to see and examine the injured and to do what I could in assisting him to make settlement with the injured persons, or their guardians and legal representatives.

I found the assistant general claim agent to be quite crestfallen, and he informed me that the general claim agent was feeling the same way — both of them feeling quite sure it would cost the company tens of thousands of dollars to settle with all of those people, and it would increase the average for settlements for that year, on the general claim agent s books, to alarming proportions.

"Do you know anything about the people of Independence?" I asked the assistant general claim agent, Mr. Henry B. Kane. No, he did not.

"Well," I said, "if you don't know them then you are not capable of judging of them; but, let me tell you something about them. The population of Independence is made up principally of native Missourians, of Kentucky, Virginia and Tennessee ancestry, and of Virginians, Kentuckians and Tennesseans — principally from the two former states, that is Virginia and Kentucky. They are the most high spirited and the proudest people on earth. They hate a mean action and they despise the actor as much as they hate the act."

"They are not speculative and they are not going to speculate on you. Of course, if any of them have sustained very serious, permanent injuries they will, no doubt, desire to receive a fair compensation; but the slightly injured, though they know they could now make exorbitant demands and they know that you will be willing to pay a goodly sum to get out of this miserable wreck, but they will not do it Mind what I tell you, those people are going to be reasonable and they are not going to rob you." "Ah," said Mr. Kane, "You will find when it comes to a show down, that your Missourians, Kentuckians and Virginians will be just as greedy and speculative as any other people, and they will rob us, if they can do so."

We arrived at Independence in the early morning and went to a hotel and got our breakfast. We then took our lists and began to make inquiry as to where this or that injured person lived. We got started and began the rounds — the hardest part of our work being in going from place to place. When evening came we found that we had settled with thirty-four injured persons, and had paid out the enormous (?) sum of six hundred and eighty-two dollars!

Mr. Kane, to use a slang phrase was simply "bug-eyed." He couldn't believe the evidence of his own senses. In all his experience he had never encountered anything like it before.

"You are right, doctor," he said, "but, it beats anything I ever ran across. I would just like to have a good home here and sit down and spend the balance of my days right here. What a delight it would be to live amongst such a people." And, I was correspondingly proud — being a Missourian of Kentucky parentage myself.

It is a fact that we found one case where they didn't want to take anything at all. They were Virginians, and, I think the old gentleman was a retired merchant. I know that he was said to be quite well fixed, financially. He had had two daughters in the wreck. The oldest — a most beautiful, amiable and gracious young lady (now the wife of one of our Kansas City Judges) had not been hurt at all; but the youngest — her little sister of ten years of age, had received quite a cut on the right side of her forehead, near the hair line.

"No, suh," said the old gentleman, "No, suh, I don't want youah money. I am happy and thankful that we got our little gurls back, and that they were not killed. If you have any papahs to be signed, releasing you, I will gladly sign them, but I will not take youah money."

Mr. Kane insisted and the old gentleman persisted in his refusal to take money. A release without a money consideration is not valid, so Mr. Kane at last induced the old gentleman to accept ten dollars on account of the fact that the little girl's clothing had been torn, and as a present.

"It will buy her something that she can keep as a souvenir of the occasion when two kind gentlemen visited us and treated her so kindly," said the old gentleman.

In fact, they treated our presence as a social visit and seemed to be proud of the fact that two gentlemen had come all the way from St. Louis and Sedalia to pay them a kindly visit of sympathy, after so many of their loved ones had been put in jeopardy of their lives. God bless them! I wish there were more of them.

The general claim agent arrived on the scene the next morning; and when his assistant showed him the result of our work the day before, he could hardly believe it. He said to me, "Doctor, it is simply almost incredible," and he always spoke of them and their kind to me afterwards; "Oh, he is one of your Missourians," or Kentuckians or Virginians.

On that day we settled with two more — but not so cheap; at least not with one of them — an Eastern drummer to whom we paid thirty-five dollars for the loss of a three dollar hat!

There was a Mrs. F. on the train, who was the worst hurt of any of them. Her husband was a prosperous business man at Independence. They were people of the very highest character, and Mrs. F. is one of the six, whose cases I have seen tried, who never exaggerated her injuries in the least. After the wreck she was taken to a hotel in Kansas City. She had sustained a rare injury — the separation of the hip bone from its attachment to the spinal column on the right side. She was so disabled and helpless that she could not be gotten home, until I went up and her physician and I put the hips in a plaster cast.

After that I went to Independence and her family physician and I put her in plaster again. There was a failure to settle and the suit was brought by herself, in her own right, and by her husband for the loss of her services. I do not think their proposition to compromise an extravagant one but the general claim agent was limited as to what he might pay in such cases.

The cases were tried at Harrisonville, in Cass County. She received a verdict for fifteen thousand dollars; but the Supreme Court made her attorney remit five thousand before they would affirm it, and her husband received a verdict for five thousand dollars. This, with interest, was all paid, and all of which amounted in the aggregate, to a stun in the neighborhood of seventeen thousand dollars. The case could have been settled for considerably less than half of that sum. They asked in compromise just half of what the verdict gave them.

Mrs. F. got onto crutches after a long time, but it was two years before she discarded her crutches and walked with no other aid than a cane.

There was a lady who was injured in this wreck — a young married woman — who lived in the East Bottoms inside the corporate limits of Kansas City. The husband worked in a brick yard. I went to see her on the second day of our visit to Independence and Kansas City. I found that she had an abrasion — the size of a silver dollar, over the ribs on the right side of the chest, but no ribs were broken.

The blow that produced this abrasion and the general shake up she received had revived an old, slumbering asthma.

Efforts at settlement were made and a very liberal offer was made to her, but they would listen to nothing within the bounds of reason.

Suit was brought in her behalf and the husband also sued for the loss of her services. My recollection is that she was entirely well in less than two weeks. I made a discovery at the trial of the case, which gave it a most ludicrous aspect. In drawing the petition the attorney had complained amongst other things, that plaintiff, by reason of her injuries could never have children, that she and her husband were very fond of children and had looked forward to the time when she would bear a child and they could enjoy the innocent prattle of the little one as it played about their knees. In fact it was pathetic.

As the trial progressed, I had noticed a peculiar arrangement of plaintiff's dress waist in front which, I thought, was quite suggestive. In wandering about the corridors of the court house for a little air and exercise I heard the cry of a child in one of the ante rooms. I went in, for I am very fond of children. There I found two ladies — one of them holding a nine months' old baby in her lap. I went over to it and chucked it under the chin and made it laugh. I asked the lady its age, sex, etc., and then asked if it was hers. She answered that it was not, that the mother was in the Court room.

"Oh, it is Mrs. Block's baby, is it not?" I asked. She said that it was. The plaintiff's name was not Block, but that will do.

"Yes," said the nurse, "it is her baby."

The jury gave her one thousand dollars, which we promptly paid, and we then compromised with Mr. Block for one hundred and fifty dollars and he dismissed his suit.

Amongst others who were injured in this wreck was a gentlemanly bachelor from Platte County. He received a very severe blow on the head which seriously disabled him and from which he suffered for years. There was also failure to settle with him and he brought suit; but, before the time for trial came our general claim agent settled with him — giving him three thousand dollars, and he didn't give him any too much, for he was one who might truthfully say, "If I could be put back where I was before that wreck I wouldn't be injured m the way that I am for all that old Jay Gould is worth."

The last of the cases was a maiden lady, who lived with relatives in Independence. She was from Kentucky and belonged to one of the most distinguished families of that Commonwealth. Unfortunately, she had been afflicted with hip joint disease from her early childhood. She had been operated on for temporary relief quite a number of times, as I understood; on the sixth day of the previous October — just five months previous to the wreck to a day — two of Kansas City's most distinguished surgeons had operated on her for the removal of *carious* and *necrosed* bone from the upper part of the femur. The operation had been quite formidable, in some respects, as she was confined to her bed and room for a long time.

She had a sweet and most lovely face and manner and, in all respects, she exhibited those higher qualities of heart and mind so characteristic of the better class of the women of the South.

On the day of the wreck she was on her way to Kansas City for the purpose of having her hip examined again. She was quite badly shaken up in the wreck and received a quite severe scalp wound from which a very serious erysipelas developed. This soon got well, however. She thought that the shake up aggravated her hip trouble, and it may have done so. There was also failure to settle in her case and suit was brought.

The case was tried at Lexington, on a change of venue, and the jury gave her a verdict for five thousand dollars. This was appealed and reversed; but, before the time for the second trial came on, settlement was made for one-half the verdict

A rather funny thing occurred at the trial of this case, which only two of us knew anything about. The company's attorney, Capt. Robert Adams, who tried this case, had a morbid fear of offending women litigants or witnesses. He handled them, on cross-examination, as if they had been wax dolls.

I took down with me to the trial a pelvis with the femur attached on one side. In my room, the night before the trial, I showed it to the attorney and told him that, when on the stand, I would use it to demonstrate to the jury the extent of the operation which had been performed by the Kansas City surgeons.

"Oh, no, no," said he, "never, never in the world do that, doctor."

"Why not?" I asked, with some surprise.

"Why," said he, "if you do that she will get to looking at it, and then she will think about her own pelvis and thigh bones, then she will imagine these are her bones, and she will get to crying, and that will make the jury indignant and they will soak us like sixty. No, don't use it, for heaven's sake, it will ruin us."

It was Capt Adams' natural refinement and his high regard for the sex which caused him to feel this way.

I thought this a little far fetched, but he was the attorney and I yielded without an argument. I went on the stand the next day and gave my testimony without any bones to demonstrate.

Just after I had finished, one of her Kansas City surgeons was put on the stand, in rebuttal. When he got under way, he reached down and picked up an old valise, opened it and took out the pelvis, with a femur attached and he turned this around and overpointed out to the jury the site at which the operation had been performed, the extent of it, etc., etc.

I looked at the plaintiff and she was looking up at the bones and watching the doctor's demonstrations, with that sweet Kentucky smile on her face and she didn't cry even a little bit.

You may rest assured it was some time before I ceased drawing that weeping picture to the attorney and laughing at him about his vivid imagination; for it was he who had the imagination and not the plaintiff.

We thus settled all the cases, either in or out of Court, and when the amount of the cost of the personal injury liabilities, with interest was figured up, it amounted to between twenty and twenty-five thousand dollars. No one could have persuaded the general claim agent the next day after the wreck, that the company would get out of it without paying out from one hundred and fifty to two hundred thousand dollars.

It was a lucky thing for the Missouri Pacific Railroad Company that Independence was settled by the brave, honest, proud and peculiar people that she has.

Case VI. A number of years ago a lawyer of Warrensburg, Missouri, brought me a case with a view of having me examine it, and of also testifying in it, in case I thought the man could recover damages for malpractice against a doctor at Holden in Johnson County.

The doctor in the case was a physio-medicalist, a man whom I knew, and a man of average ability.

The case was one of ununited fracture of both the radius and ulna. They had both been fractured in the middle third of the right forearm.

I questioned the man and ascertained that the doctor had put it up in a properly padded Levis perforated tin splint, that had fitted the dorsal surface of the forearm neatly. There had been no swelling, no oedema and no pain.

After thoroughly examining the arm and questioning the would-be plaintiff, I told the lawyer that, so far as I could see, the case had been properly treated and that, should I be put on the stand in the case, my testimony would surely be for the defendant.

I then made a proposition to the attorney and his client, and that was, if he would come to Kansas City and go into a hospital, and would give me a suitable guarantee that he would not sue me for malpractice, I would operate on the forearm, and, if possible, make it unite and would charge nothing for my services, provided he would agree to not bring suit against the doctor.

But, no. That was not what he wanted. He was looking for testimony, not for successful surgery.

I heard nothing more of the case until the sitting of the next Circuit Court at Warrensburg, when I received a telegram from the same attorney, who was also the local attorney for the Missouri Pacific Railway at Warrensburg — calling me to Warrensburg in a Missouri Pacific case.

When I arrived at the depot in Warrensburg I was met by five doctors and two attorneys — amongst the doctors being the Physio-medicalist, who had treated this man's arm.

They informed me that the case was then on trial and that "old B," a noted Kansas City quack, "had got on the stand and just torn Doctor D. to pieces."

"How had he torn him to pieces?" I asked.

"Well, he said that the arm had not been put in the sling right; as the thumb and not the palm should have been toward the face."

I said to them, "The palm toward the face is the proper position in the sling, as it then leaves the radius and ulna parallel, and, as for old B., he is one of the biggest quacks in Kansas City and can't give any reputable physician in Kansas City an orange on the end of a forty foot pole, as they will not let him get near enough to them to do it."

"Well, old B. being a quack is one thing, and you saying so on the witness stand is another. Will you get on the witness stand and say about him what you have said here?"

"Will I?" I asked, "well you just put me on the stand and put the proper questions to me and see if I will. I will say anything on the witness stand that I believe to be true if the whole Mexican army had their bayonets at my abdomen.

We then retired to a hotel and prepared for war — the Kansas City quack being set down as the common enemy.

After lunch I was put on the witness stand. I took the same bones — the *radius* and *ulna*, and showed the jury how, when the palm is toward the face, these bones are parallel.

After I had finished my demonstrations and had stated that, according to plaintiff's own statement to me. Dr. D. had treated the case according to the very latest and best methods, these questions were asked me:

"Dr. King, do you know Dr. B. of Kansas City?"

"I have a slight acquaintance with him." I answered

"What is his reputation as a physician and surgeon in Kansas City?"

"Amongst the people, or in the profession?" I asked.

"Well, amongst the people?"

"I do not know, as I have never heard his name mentioned or his abilities or character discussed." I answered again.

"What is it in the medical profession?" was asked. "We object," came promptly from plaintiff's counsel.

The point was argued and the Court decided that I should answer the question.

"It is that of a quack of the very worst kind." I answered again.

Here came more protests from plaintiff's counsel and then I was turned over to the tender mercies of said plaintiff's counsel for cross-examination.

"Dr. King, whom did you ever hear say that Dr. B. was a quack?"

"Well, the first time I ever heard the expression in regard to him was soon after I went to Kansas City, in the latter part of 1888. I was called in consultation with a young man, in the case of an old friend, named Hatch. When I arrived at the house I found that Dr. B. had been in consultation before me and he was there to take part in the consultation on that day.

After I had thoroughly examined my old friend we retired. There was no disagreement regarding the case, as it was apparent that my friend was a dying man. As we prepared to leave Dr. B. went back and fixed the cover about the patient's body and quietly gave some extra instructions to the wife.

I had noticed that he was busy making his own importance known in the case — in fact, giving more attention to his own importance and position in the case than to the welfare of the patient.

When I returned to my office, I stepped into the office of Dr. S. on the same floor. Dr. S. was an old resident of Kansas City and knew all the doctors, good and bad.

"Do you know Dr. B., Dr. S.?" I asked.

"Yes," he answered, "why?"

"Well, I met him and a young man in consultation this morning, and, as I never met him before, I thought I would ask you?"

"What!" exclaimed Dr. S. "You don't tell me that you have been consulting with old B.? Why he is the d---dest quack in Kansas City!"

"Well, what other doctor did you ever hear say that Dr. B. is a quack?"

"I heard Dr. G., a prominent surgeon in Kansas City, say so once."

"Tell the jury the circumstances and what was said."

"Very well, I will, sir. I was standing on Main street in Kansas City once. It was between tenth and eleventh. Several doctors had accidentally met and we were talking. While we were there Dr. B. passed in his buggy. After he had passed Dr. G. said, 'there goes old B., the biggest quack in Kansas City.' "

"Well, who else?" asked the lawyer.

I gave the names of others.

"Well, who else," came the parrot like question.

"Oh, I do not know," I answered, "that I can give the names of others, specifically, but I will say this, I never heard Dr. B.'s name mentioned where there were a number of doctors together, when someone did not speak of him as a quack, and if the speaker was disposed to be profane he always called him a 'd—d old quack.'"

Dr. B. was sitting by plaintiff's counsel, and his face grew red, purple and spotted by turns.

As soon as I left the stand he went on again — no doubt at his own request.

He stood up in the witness stand and roared, like the "bulls of Bashan."

"Dr. King has insulted me," he exclaimed.

"Dr. if I have insulted you we will settle that on the outside," said I arising from my seat.

"Sit down I Dr. King," exclaimed Judge Sloan.

"I don't want to settle it on the outside," said Dr. B. and as he was then excused, and as the train whistle on the passenger train from St. Louis to Kansas City blew just then he made a bee line for the depot and left for Kansas City. The jury was out ten minutes and found for the defendant.

A day or two afterwards I received a letter from Dr. B. through the mails, in which he complained bitterly of the great injustice and injury I had done him. Said he had consulted with one of my intimate personal friends, and had told him of what I had testified to in Warrensburg.

"I had contemplated bringing suit against you for damages," he said, "but, this friend says you are a good man, but disposed to act on the impulse of the' moment and to do and say things, which you regret afterwards. He also said that you were a poor man and that, even should I bring suit I could not collect anything."

I answered him: "My friend, in his fears, has deceived you Doctor B., while it is true that I am not a rich man, yet I have several thousand dollars lying idle in the National Bank of Commerce at this time. "Now, I make you this proposition, doctor: You and I will join in the expenditure of a few dollars. We will have a few hundred letters printed in which we will detail the facts of my testimony at Warrensburg and we will mail one of those letters to each of the respectable physicians in Kansas City and we will put up in bank any sum, from one thousand to five thousand dollars each. If a majority of the doctors do not answer that my testimony was true you can take down the whole sum in bank. If they say it was true then I take it. "Furthermore, you say that; if I (you) had injured you, as you did me, I would go back to Warrensburg and on my knees I would retract it before the Court and the community."

"Now, doctor, if you win in this case, I will go back to Warrensburg and into that Court room. I will not get down on my knees, for I get on my knees to no one but God, and I fear I do not get on my knees often enough to Him, but I will stand uncovered before that Court and that community, and I will make a statement that will set the people of Warrensburg and of Johnson County twenty years ahead of their generation."

Dr. B. did not accept my proposition, but he continued to write letters and to *mouthe* about the injury I had done him.

As I was disposed to be very lenient in our correspondence this encouraged him to be a little more and more impudent, until, at last, he became actually insulting. I then wrote him, "Doctor, I have made you a fair proposition as to how we may settle this matter, but you do not even refer to it in your reply, but you are disposed to grow more and more insulting in each letter. Now, let me say this, once for all; if you wish to settle this matter in any way as gentlemen should settle such matters, while I do not recognize you as a gentleman, yet I will not deny you that satisfaction which any man feels that he has a right to expect, when aggrieved. Now, name the way in which you wish to settle this matter and the time when you wish to settle it. I will be with you. Otherwise stop writing me, or I shall handle you on the street. Now, in the language of the sports 'either put up or shut up.'"

I never heard from Dr. B. again.

He has now been "gathered to his fathers" and I hope may learn better methods and better manners in the "Sweet bye and bye" than he ever knew or practiced here.

Case VII. In about the year 1888 there was brought to the hospital on a November day, an old man; at least he appeared to be fifty-six to fifty-eight though he gave his age at forty-six. He had a young wife, however, and was to be excused for forgetting his age. He had been in a wreck the night before and was injured to some extent.

He had been a conductor on other roads; but had, for some cause, lost his position and was then breaking on our Lexington and Southern branch for a train. This branch extended from Pleasant Hill to Joplin at that time and Pleasant Hill was made the end of the division — in fact the L. & S. constituted a division.

On the evening before the accident, Williamson, with the others of his train crew had left Pleasant Hill on a freight train for Joplin, Williamson — the old man, being the middle brakeman.

At six o'clock p. m. it was snowing hard; and, somewhere between Harrisonville and Butler the train broke in two. It is the rule, when an accident of this kind occurs for the engineer to let his engine out and run at top speed, until he passes a low section or depression in the track and then ascends the opposite hill and to then stop. This is to prevent the, perhaps, unrestrained rear section from running into the front section of the severed train. This was done in this instance. When they had reached the summit of the next hill a half mile or more away, they stopped and could discern the caboose lights of the rear section standing still — showing dimly through the blinding snow. The conductor and rear brakeman had discovered the accident and had used the caboose brakes to bring the rear section to a standstill. The engineer proceeded to back up, so as to pick up the rear section. It was the duty of Williamson as rear brakeman to stand on the last car of the front section; and, by his lantern, signal and guide the engineer in backing up.

At the bottom of the low piece of track between the two sections the car upon which Williamson stood left the track and went into the ditch and five more cars were piled on top of them. Williamson was in the midst of this terrible smash up. When the accident occurred Williamson testified that they were backing up at about twenty miles an hour, the front brakeman and fireman testified that the speed was about six miles an hour. The engineer could not testify as he died before the case came to trial.

Well, as before narrated, Williamson was injured. He had a transverse cut just under his nose, extending entirely across his upper lip, another cut under his left eye; and, he complained of an injury to his left shoulder and several of the ribs on that side.

Williamson's wounds were neatly stitched up, a body bandage was put on and the old man tenderly put to bed. He proved to be a very restless patient. During the nine days that he was in the hospital my senior house surgeon — Dr. Ned. Yancey, now chief surgeon of the M. K. & T., came to me and said, "Doctor, that old man complains of his left side and insists that his ribs are broken. I can't find any broken ribs; and, as you are an older man than I am, I am satisfied that he would feel better if you should examine him." In both instances I went to Williamson's bed — although he swore at the trial that he never saw me and didn't know me, that he was "treated by a boy," and I carefully traced all the ribs in the region complained of, and found — nothing. I could not keep him beyond nine days — he just must see that young wife and the baby.

There was an attempt at settlement, but Williamson's figures were so high that the general claim agent could not reach them. Then Williamson brought suit and the case was tried at Kansas City, in 1889.

In his petition he placed the cause of his injury to the negligence of the engineer; who, it was proven by the testimony of the hotel keeper at Pleasant Hill and others, was in the habit of getting gloriously drunk just as soon as he came in from Joplin, and of remaining drunk until the next day; he would then sober up a little until time to go out, when he would take just enough to brace him up for his run. The chronic inebriety of the engineer was established beyond a per adventure or a doubt, and that, too, by the testimony of the very best people.

The testimony at the trial was about as related above, except that a physician, who saw Williamson just before he brought suit, testified that three of Williamson's ribs were torn from their attachment to the breast bone and the ends shoved out and elevated above the surrounding surface about an inch, or an inch and a half. I could never account for this testimony, except upon the theory that the doctor was drinking to excess about that time, for he was a most honorable and capable man.

To rebut this and sustain my own statements, I made this proposition: "The plaintiff is an old man, and his bones have the hardness of the bones of an old man; if those three ribs were thus displaced three months after the accident then they are displaced yet; and the best proof of what the condition is that can be made would be for the plaintiff to make profert of his person, bare his chest and let the jury see what the condition is." He didn't do it.

The jury gave him a verdict for eighteen hundred dollars. This was appealed and reversed and remanded by the Supreme Court; and, at a second trial. the jury gave plaintiff three thousand dollars, which verdict was affirmed by the Supreme Court, and paid, with the accrued interest.

At the time of the trial plaintiff was running as conductor on the "dummy line" between Kansas City and Independence.

He swore that his greatest disability was in the stiffness of his left shoulder; that in his then position he had to ring the bell a great deal in stopping and starting his train; and that, the left shoulder being stiff, and as he carried his punch in his right hand, he had always to transfer the punch to his left hand and ring the bell with his right, which gave him a great deal of trouble and annoyance.

Three weeks after the trial I was going down to Independence on an afternoon and just happened to strike Williamson's train. There were two very particular friends of mine on the train and I told them of Williamson's testimony as to his disability in his left shoulder and asked them to watch him and see if he rung the bell with his left hand. At every station between the two cities Williamson stopped and started his train by ringing the bell with his left hand! And yet that was only mild perjury. He just established the permanency of his injury by this adroit falsehood.

There was an amusing episode at the conclusion of the first trial which I must relate. After both sides had rested, the late John W. Beebe, who was plaintiff's chief counsel, arose and addressed the Court and asked for a delay of twenty or thirty minutes, until he could recall some of his medical witnesses, as he had forgotten, when they were on the stand to ask them what the effect was on an engineer's capacity to do his work — an engineer who drank as it had been shown the deceased engineer had drunk.

The Court refused the request. Mr. Beebe insisted. "Mr. Beebe," said the Court, "you promised me when this case came to trial, that it should not last but one day. Now, two days have been consumed and now you come in here, after having had six months in which to prepare your case and ask to delay this court by recalling witnesses whom you have already had on the stand. I will not allow it."

Mr. Beebe and his co-counsel were in consternation. Beebe stooped and whispered to his assistant; the assistant shook his head; Mr. Beebe insisted and the assistant still shook his head. Finally the assistant nodded — indicating that he yielded the point, whatever it was.

Mr. Beebe said, "Dr. King, take the witness stand." I did so. "Doctor, you heard the testimony given in this case with regard to the excessive drinking of the engineer?" I answered that I had. "Now, doctor, I will ask you, what is the effect of such excessive drinking on a man's capacity as an engineer?" I answered that it might be very different in two individuals. It might destroy the capacity of one man, altogether; and yet, another and stronger man might go on and automatically do his work, and do it very well. "Well, doctor, what is the effect generally of such drinking on a man in his position where he must rapidly co-ordinate his mind and his hand, especially in emergencies?"

I answered that it was to diminish his capacity.

"Very much?" persisted Mr. Beebe.

"Yes, very much as a rule."

"That will do, doctor." Mr. Beebe went back and punched his assistant in the ribs, as much as to say, "I knew this man better than you did." Mr. Beebe never caught me in a crowd in the later years of his life, that he did not tell this story; and, always, as a "good joke on Doctor King," but Mr. Beebe really meant it as a compliment to me.

I could not testify otherwise than as I did and tell the truth, and the only way for our own attorney to keep out of such a dilemma would have been to get me out of the way as soon as he was through with me.

This was done a number of times, where the company's attorney was afraid that the plaintiff's counsel would get an inkling of my opinion of the case and would have me summoned.

In many cases I did not go to the trial at all — notably in the case of Mrs. F., who was injured in the wreck between Kansas City and Independence, on March 6, 1886.

Her counsel knew what my opinion of her case was and, of course, would have put me on the witness stand had I been there.

A great many people have an idea that a railroad surgeon is pulled around and made to testify as suits the company's attorney, without regard to what his opinion may be.

I can only speak for one road, and I must say that, in my twenty-five years' experience I was never called upon to yield my individuality in any degree, nor was I ever called upon or expected to do a wrong thing.

If I had been there would have been a severance of my connection with the railroad company at once.

It is strange that people cannot understand that railroad officers are taken from our citizenship and that they are moved by and act from the same motives that move people in the ordinary walks of life.

There are mean railroad officials, of course, so there are mean men in all of the relations and walks of life; but, I believe that they are the exception and not the rule.

There is only one particular in which I have been compelled to give up my ideals as to men and women, and that is in regard to their false swearing in order to cheat corporations.

This has been to me a most painful experience, and one that I am sorry I ever had. I would have much preferred never to have had it. I would much rather have gone on in my innocent belief in the honesty and incorruptibility of the people generally. But, a little money is, unfortunately, a great temptation.

This, I presume, has always been so, and it will be to the end.

I find that women are just as bad as men. There was a time when I could not have been made to believe that any virtuous woman would go upon the witness stand and perjure herself for money, but I was sadly mistaken.

Unfortunately for the women, those who usually advise and control them are personally interested in seeing them win their cases and hence they are willing that wife, mother, sister or daughter shall go upon the witness stand and perjure herself.

Case VIII. In 1893, if my memory serves me right, I was directed by the chief surgeon to assist Judge Elijah Robinson in the trial of a case at Independence, Missouri.

Judge Robinson is an attorney, who, it is a delight to help in bringing out the medical testimony. He is not only a bright and strong lawyer — a lawyer who knows the law — but he is as belligerent as the "Tasmanian Devil." He is a fighter "from the old house," to use a sporting phrase.

I have assisted attorneys who always went into the trial of a case with their "tails between their hind legs," so to speak; who went into the case whipped; who were "afraid to say 'boo!' to a goose."

I have assisted lawyers who were afraid to make a decent, vigorous cross-examination — fearing that they might offend the witness and thereby offend the jury, and prejudice the case. But, not so with Elijah Robinson. He is a manly and a courteous attorney at the bar, but people do not come over and step on his favorite corn without hearing from him.

If he knows that a witness is lying, and he can get him into a comer he pounds him unmercifully — jury or no jury, and it pays.

This case was one I had never seen until the day set for the trial. I shall, for convenience, call him Mr. Monroe, for he really did have the name of one of our earlier Presidents. Mr. Monroe was a farmer and a renter as well; he lived about one mile east of Independence.

He was a little wizened, dried up sort of fellow. He looked as if he didn't have enough substance in him to furnish the material for a tallow candle. A half dozen mosquitoes would absolutely have destroyed him!

Well, as I have said, he lived on a rented farm one mile east of Independence. It was in the haying season when Mr. Monroe was hurt.

He was hauling a load of hay and was sitting on top of the load. He had to cross the railroad track, unfortunately for the railroad company.

The section men were repairing the crossing at the point. They had removed the planks from alongside the rails and had dumped in a lot of fine cinders at the places from which the planks had been removed.

Mr. Monroe had to cross the tract diagonally. When his front wheels struck the rails they slid. This caused the wagon to careen, the load of hay to tilt and Mr. Monroe fell off and struck his right ankle against a fence post and bruised and sprained it. Now, if Mr. Monroe had been a heavy weight he would, no doubt, have been hurt enough to make a fuss about it; but, being so light, it didn't amount to much. Really the case should have been settled for about twenty-five dollars, and in a season that was not a busy time such a sum would have been a big thing for Mr. Monroe, under the circumstances.

A very competent physician went out and bound up his ankle and it soon got well; and while Mr. Monroe lay in bed he began to grow speculative. Some old codger who, perhaps, had more brains than money said a long, long time ago, "An idle brain is the devil's workshop." Mr. Monroe lay there and, not being inclined to literature, he just thought about that injured ankle and what it would bring him. He, no doubt, started out with the idea of getting twenty-five dollars; and, honestly, fifty dollars would have been ruinously high for that ankle. But, Mr. Monroe began to think of things he needed and got up to a hundred. Then the contemplated trip of his wife back to "Ellenoy" occurred to him and ankle stock jumped at once to two hundred. It is surprising how rapidly such stock will advance at times. When he thought of renting a large farm and of hiring a hand or two, that ankle jumped up to four hundred dollars. Ankle stock firm and still going up.

Then he thought of buying a thresher and running it in the beautiful autumn days and making "dead oodles" of money, while his less thrifty neighbors, who have no ankles that are worth as much as a pig's ankle in a barrel of brine, go to town, stand on the comers and chew "dog leg" tobacco and fight flies and tell how the government ought to manage its finances. Mr. Mcwiroe, he of the speculative ankle, continued to quote stock on that ankle on a rising market until it got up to a farm of his own — just a small farm, and that small farm grew larger and larger and, at last, it must be stocked with cattle; not your ordinary cattle, but thoroughbred cattle with a long pedigree, and he saw himself taking his pedigreed bull to the fair and leading him around the county fair with a ring in his nose and of leading him around before the admiring gaze of people whose ankles are not worth five cents on the dollar, and stock, ankle stock jumped to ten thousand dollars; and then Mr. Monroe got scared for fear that he might lose all of that money and so he went to town and took a lawyer into his confidence and full partnership with him, to help him take care of that ankle money.

Well, after a feeble effort to settle which failed, Mr. Monroe's lawyer brought suit for ten thousand dollars damages and putting that speculative and valuable ankle forth as the cause.

Well, as I said before, I had never set eyes on Mr. Monroe nor on that ankle until the day the case was called for trial. It had been alleged that Mr. Monroe's ankle was stiff — permanently stiff. I watched plaintiff walk on the street and noted the fact that he "walked over his foot." We all "walk over our feet" when the ankle above that foot is in a healthy and normal condition. In "walking over a foot" we do this: We put the right foot forward, we will say; we set the foot firmly and flat on the ground in front of us. In this position note that the leg joins the foot at the ankle at an acute angle. Now, we bring forward the left foot. When the body is straight over the right foot the leg joins the foot at a right angle — straight up and down. As we place the left foot forward and plant it flat on the ground this leg also joins the foot at the ankle at an acute angle; the right leg joins it at an angle — the leg pointing backward.

Now, this goes on all the time we are walking, and we walk first over the right foot and then over the left foot.

But, when the ankle is stiff, when it is ankylosed, as we say, we do not walk over our feet. We cannot.

Now, note the difference: We put the right foot, the one with the stiff ankle, forward, we cannot place it flat on the ground, we can only put the heel on the ground. Then, as we bring the left, or good foot, forward, we let the right foot down on the flat; and, as we advance the left foot to the front and, especially if we advance it very far, we must raise the heel of the right foot and put our weight on the ball of the foot.

So, plaintiff plainly "walked over his foot," and he did it constantly. In fact, as much as he had thought about that ankle, I am quite sure that he did not yet know what "walking over the foot" meant.

He did another very foolish thing, and one that would have been ruinous to his case, and to the prospective value of that ankle, if it had not been true that the men on the jury knew as little about ankylosis as he did. He put a wooden brace on that ankle! He, no doubt, made the brace himself, for it was made of something like old wooden barrel hoops. He fitted this into his shoe, between the "upper" and the lining, and then had it extended up his leg and bound it to his leg by some straps which extended around the leg and buckled. But, here is a very pertinent inquiry: Why brace a thing that is already braced? Why brace a joint to render it immovable — for that is the object of joint braces — when it is already immovable? There can be but one explanation: That brace was put on there to be "seen of men." It constantly called the attention of the neighbors to that speculative and valuable ankle. People who don't know will say: "What a pity about Monroe! He's got a stiff ankle and he has to wear a brace on it all the time."

I wonder if it ever occurs to one of those sympathetic noodles to ask himself, "What in thunder is the use of bracing an ankle that is already stiff?"

Well, the case came to trial, before what seemed to be an average jury. In due time a commission of physicians was appointed to examine plaintiff's ankle, and I was one of said commission. When plaintiff took off his right shoe it was discovered that he turned up his toes on his right foot — that is, he pointed the toes on that foot upward as near to a right angle to the foot as he could make them point.

I wondered at this, but soon discovered why he did it. I looked at his shoe and saw that he did not do this when he had his shoe on; for, had he done so there would have been a ridge across the shoe at the place where the toes came in contact with it There was no ridge on the shoe. The ankle was symmetrical with the other and the measurements at every point were the same. When I came to make attempts to move the ankle I found that I could not move it at all. I did everything in my power to move that stubborn ankle, but I couldn't budge it. Others tried it with a like result. When adjournment was taken for lunch I took a friend to my room; and taking off my shoe and sock, I turned my toes up like Monroe did his. I asked my friend to move my ankle. He made the effort, but failed utterly.

When I was put on the stand I told the jury how that ankle should look, after one year of inflammation. I described hypertrophy of joints to them and told them that, were this ankle completely ankylosed, as the plaintiff made it appear, it would measure from one to two and one-half inches in circumference larger than its fellow, and I told them that he could not put his toes down and keep that ankle stiff for a moment.

Mr. Monroe came before the jury with his foot bare and several of the jurymen took a hand in trying to move that ankle, but they failed. I stated that he could not keep it unmovable for a moment if he would put his toes down. I then tried to get him to put them down, but he would not. I then grasped them and started to force them down, but he howled.

I then stated that anybody could stiffen his ankle by turning his toes up.

"Can you do it?" asked plaintiff's counsel.

I answered that I could.

"Let's see you do it," said he.

I removed my shoe and sock, turned my toes up and said, "There is Mr. Monroe's ankle. Now, you gentlemen of the jury may try to move my ankle." Two stalwart farmers came forward, with much confidence and determination expressed on their faces; and, in turn took hold of my foot and tried to move it. They sweat and panted and grew red in the face and yet that ankle of mine was obdurate. It would not move and these stalwart jurymen could not move it.

I then let my toes down and said, "Now, you can move it." They took hold in turn and the ankle proved to be perfectly flexible.

I stated: "If Mr. Monroe would let his toes down as I do, and as he can do, if he will, his ankle can be moved just as easily as mine."

"Are you testifying or arguing the case, doctor?" asked plaintiff's counsel, who was much chagrined at my demonstration.

"I am testifying and arguing my testimony," I answered.

"Yes," said he, "I thought so. Doctor, how long have you been practicing law?" he asked, still bent on "showing me up" before the jury.

"I have never practiced law," I answered.

"Why, have you not been practicing law to-day?" he asked.

I answered that I thought not — not intentionally, at least.

"Didn't you sit beside Judge Robinson to-day and write and suggest questions when the other doctors were on the stand?"

I answered that I did.

"Well, what do you call that?"

"I call that assisting the counsel to bring out the facts from the medical aspect of the case."

"Well, now, doctor, don't you think you ought to have been a lawyer?"

"Yes, my friends of the legal profession have flattered me by telling me that I should have studied law, and they tell me that, had I done so, I would have made a good lawyer, and that I might to-day be earning large fees by assisting consciousless, but impecunious clients to rob corporations of large sums of money. The truth is, though, that I rarely ever saw a lawyer who didn't think that he would have made a good doctor, nor a doctor who didn't think he would have made a good lawyer and, to be frank with you, I think I might yet be admitted to the bar, considering the character of some of the talent that gets there."

"That's all," said he.

The jury gave Mr. Monroe one thousand dollars, which we paid and which will go far toward stocking a larger rented farm.

Should Mr. Monroe grow speculative with regard to some other joint, a knee or a hip joint, for instance, and should run the stock up, as he did in the case of his ankle, he may yet be able to buy that farm and to own the fine, pedigreed cattle, and to lead the big red bull, with a ring in his nose at the county fair at the head of the herd, with several cows, yearlings and calves following behind.

Mr. Monroe's perjury did not differ from the ordinary article, as I had met with it time and again. The playing of a part by Mr. Monroe, and learning how to walk without "walking over his foot," was too much for his histrionic abilities, for Mr. Monroe was not a talented actor.

He just kept right on "walking over his foot" as if nothing had ever happened to him; and he had no idea that a lynx-eyed expert would ever watch him walk on the street and detect the fact that there was nothing the matter with him.

In fact, if Mr. Monroe had not luckily had a lot of jurymen as blunt headed as himself to help him out he would have made a dismal failure of the whole thing.

I often wonder how a man, even a small farmer, a renter, feels after having gone into court and "made a stake" by perjuring himself.

How such a man — a man born and reared under the aegis of our free institutions, can go home and face his good wife and take off his brace and quit limping, when he knows that she knows that he is an arrant fraud, I cannot understand.

How does a man feel to have the one person in all the world, to whom he would appear great, and before whom he would like to exhibit such qualities as will make him appear to be a man amongst men, when he knows that she knows he is a little cowardly, perjured fraud?

How does he feel when he knows that she knows he is a fraud and a cowardly, lying puppy, and that he has exhibited those lying and puppy qualities before her in such a way that she cannot help but know that he is a weak and lying rascal in every atom, in every fixed cell of his weak and lying body!

Bah! What can you expect from the offspring of such people? And yet people marvel at crime.

Why, criminals are made and bred in the fixed cells of the bodies of such men, long before their mothers conceive or give birth to them.

Such a man breeds criminals every hour that he is awake. A decent and respectable monkey is a proud and honorable citizen beside such a nit.

I do not understand how men who hold themselves to be honest and honorable men can tolerate such a creature, or have anything to do with him. I know that I cannot and that I will not do so, so long as I live.

I may and will lend countenance to those who have made mistakes and who have paid the penalty of the law. So long as I find such persons, who show a desire and a willingness to live upright lives, I shall not only countenance them, but I shall aid them, when they need aid. But, for the malingering, perjured and cowardly fraud, who goes brazenly about in a community where he has acted the part of the malingerer and fraud, I have nothing but denunciation and hard words.

I would be as good to him as the others, if he should admit his fraud and try to make restitution of his ill-gotten gains, but so long as he pretends that he has been injured, when I know he was not, and that he was entitled to what he got as a compensation, when I know he is lying, I can give him no countenance, and it is hard for me to see how a good, virtuous and honest woman can live with him.

Case IX. Not long since I was called upon to assist the assistant city counselor of the corporation of Kansas City, Mo., in the trial of an extraordinary case; at least, I so consider it to be.

The plaintiff was an unmarried woman of, perhaps, thirty-two years of age. She was rather large and came into court on crutches — her right thigh having been amputated at about the junction of the middle and upper thirds of the femur.

The history of the case, as the testimony developed it, was that, on a certain day — about one year ago — plaintiff, whom I shall call Belle LaHarpe, fell upon the sidewalk at or near Tenth and Wyandotte streets, in Kansas

City, Mo. Quite a crowd gathered around, when a man and his wife (who shall be, for the purposes of this narrative, Seth Venner and wife) pressed their way in to where the prostrate woman lay and, with the assistance of others (for she is a large woman), placed her in a surrey and took her to their electric bath and massage parlors, where Mrs. Seth Venner, then not a doctor, but a simple masseuse, treated her.

When the issues were joined Mr. Latshaw, of Kansas City, a noted criminal lawyer, and also a noted anti-corporation lawyer, appeared as counsel for plaintiff; and Mr. Joe Williams, an able attorney, appeared for the city. The case was tried at Platte City, Mo. The testimony developed the facts that plaintiff was a native of Cairo, Ill.; that she had been an orphan for many years and had worked in North-eastern Arkansas and, afterward, in South-eastern Missouri; that about twelve years ago she fell upon the sidewalk, in a small South-eastern Missouri town and injured her right knee quite severely; that she afterward came to Kansas City and, between 1892 and 1902, she had been in two hospitals in Kansas City, Kansas, once each, and in the city hospital of Kansas City, Missouri, three or four times— once in the maternity ward, where she gave birth to a child, out of wedlock. This latter fact she swore to herself, as no doctor, who knew of the fact, was allowed to refer to it.

There was a strong effort made to get the fact before the jury that the disease of the knee joint, which, at last, necessitated the amputation, was tuberculosis, but the effort failed, and the fact got to the jury through hypothetical questions to a surgeon who had never seen the case, as not one of the eight or ten doctors who had seen it was allowed to testify as to his diagnosis. Some of them had been shown the case merely while plaintiff was in bed in the hospital, one had remarked, "Why, that looks like a tuberculous knee;" another had said, "that is undoubtedly a tuberculous knee," all had said something about the knee or done something for it, and all were supposed, or declared to have "made a prescription" by the remark he made. It seemed quite ludicrous that eight or ten doctors were debarred from telling what their diagnosis was, while the plaintiff, herself, was allowed to tell that she had been in the maternity ward of the City hospital and had there borne the child, out of wedlock.

If any man can reconcile this matter to ordinary common sense he certainly has a more critical and a better analytical mind than I have.

No country can make much progress, in matters of legal justice, so long as such nonsensical rules are permitted to stand. It remains for some bold, big brained judge to decide that this is not a proper rule of practice, and then for a Supreme Court, with brains and courage to back him up by sustaining his ruling.

Unfortunately, after the leg was amputated — which was done at the City hospital — the joint was examined and then thrown away.

Mr. and Mrs. Seth Venner appeared in the role of chaperons for the plaintiff, and swore that they had not known plaintiff until the day she fell, yet it seemed quite significant that they should have appeared on the scene so soon after her fall, and should have taken her to their place without any prospects of remuneration; and that, now, they acted as if they had a personal interest in the verdict.

Mrs. Seth Venner testified that she was not a graduate in medicine at the time plaintiff was injured, but had graduated at a Homeopathic school since that time.

She showed the effect of a profound knowledge of anatomy and physiology by advancing the opinion that the reason why plaintiff's knee swelled so rapidly, after the injury was inflicted, was that the joint was opened and the joint water escaped into the tissues I If the swelling was as great as she testified that it was, there was at least a quart of synovial fluid in the joint before the injury!

Strange to say, Mr. Williams did not put any of the four Platte City physicians whom he had summoned nor myself on the stand. I was prepared to say that, in a tubercular joint — which this undoubtedly was — (I could say this, for I had never "prescribed" for plaintiff by making a remark about her knee) it is a very difficult matter to inflict an injury, unless you should use a spike maul or a sledgehammer; that the arterial capillary circulation being cut off, the structures entering into the formation of the joint were practically dead; and, hence, could not be easily excited; that, therefore, Mrs. Dr. Seth Venner must be mistaken about the rapid and large swelling that ensued immediately following the fall.

The plaintiff made her case almost upon the point that the injury inflicted by the fall on the sidewalk necessitated the amputation of the limb. All of the Platte City doctors — and there were some able and experienced men amongst them — and I were prepared to swear that this was not the case; that the Kansas City injury did not necessitate the amputation of the limb; and, in the very nature of things, could not have necessitated it.

The jury gave her a verdict for five thousand dollars. The case was appealed.

Here was as great a piece of injustice as I ever saw perpetrated against a city. This young woman had fallen on a sidewalk in a small country town twelve years previous to the amputation of her thigh. She had had trouble in the knee ever since. It had been operated upon — opened and curetted — twice, I believe, and the doctors who performed these operations were there ready to testify; but, no. They were not allowed to do so. One of them has since told me that, when he curetted the joint, it was full of caseous material and swarming with attenuated tubercle bacilli. But that fact could not be gotten to the jury and the only information the jury had on this point came to them through hypothetical questions, answered by a surgeon who had never seen the case.

The truth is that, when we consider the case, from the standpoint of common sense, she could not have hurt that knee by falling on the sidewalk, as she claimed. Why not? For the reason that that knee joint was in a condition of fibrous ankylosis. The knee had only a very limited motion — the foot moving over the arc of a circle of only a few degrees.

Now, anyone knows that she could not fall on the sidewalk and strike on the knee. You must bend the knee in order to fall on it. Otherwise you must fall flat on your face in order that the knee shall come in contact with the sidewalk at all. Such a person in falling will, naturally, extend that leg outward, or forward and then come down in a squatting position, and, in such case, which was the way witnesses testified that she fell, the injured and ankylosed knee does not come in contact with the sidewalk at all. And her's did not. I know this as well as I know any fact in this life to which I was not an eye-witness.

I do not know that I and the Platte City doctors could have made the jury see the case in this light, but it is my impression that we could have done so.

It is strongly probable that our Supreme Court will reverse and remand this case. If they do I have no doubt that I shall be called upon to testify in the case, if I live.

I wish this unfortunate woman nothing but good, and would be glad to join in any public or private effort to help her, and thereby add to her happiness, but I am not willing to see her rob the city in which I live.

I believe such a thing to be a great public wrong; and, while a great public wrong may help a few, it is bound to hurt the many; and, in the end, no good can come of it.

No good can come of any wrong doing, and hence, should this young woman collect this verdict, it will bum her fingers.

Some adventurer, who would not look at her now, will come along and marry her, just to get hold of this money and then proceed to squander it.

I have known of such things heretofore.

Heigh, ho! I would that all men and women were honest, good and true. Then we should have little use for courts and lawyers.

May God help and pity the weak, and stay the hand of him who covets his neighbor's ass.

Case X. About the year 1887 I was directed by the chief surgeon to go to Leroy, Kansas, to see Link Miffin, who, while working as a section laborer, was supposed to have sustained and claimed to have sustained a very serious injury of his right hip joint.

When I arrived in the little town I called upon our local surgeon, who had been appointed before I had charge of the division, on account of services rendered the company at a wreck near the town. He informed me that Link Miffin had sustained a dislocation of the femur and that he had reduced it without chloroform. I would have wagered almost any sum that he could not reduce a dislocated femur with patient under the most powerful anaesthetics. I asked him what method he employed, but he could not tell me. I had him send for Miffin, who came. He was on crutches. Placing him on a table; and, after stripping him, I made a careful examination of the joint, of which he complained bitterly. There was nothing whatever wrong with the joint, and I told him so.

The principal object of my visit was to induce him to go to St. Louis and see the general claim agent After much talk he finally consented to go within a few days. He wanted three thousand dollars, as a salve to soothe his assumed injured hip; but, when he went to St. Louis, he finally accepted seventy-five dollars.

Upon a part of this he got gloriously drunk before he left the city, and was very boisterous on the train. In his blowing he threw his crutches out of the window of the train; and, arriving at his home at midday, he walked up town in the middle of the main street with his hands thrust deep down into his pockets and a big cigar in his mouth.

We ascertained afterwards that there was evidence, could we have procured it, which would have obviated the necessity of settling with this scoundrel.

He was a big, powerful man and the section foreman and all of his men were mortally afraid of him. The section men were not Irishmen, else otherwise. The evidence was this:

The section men were with a snow train, engaged in "bucking snow." The day being bitter cold, they were allowed to have whiskey. Link got drunk, as usual, and was swaggering and threatening and wanted to fight.

The foreman and his men tried to induce him to sit down, but he would not do it. The engine was just about to make a rapid run against the snow bank, and they did everything they could to induce him to sit down in the caboose, but he would not. The engine made the run; and, when it struck the snow bank and stopped suddenly, Link fell to the floor of the caboose. He howled and swore and complained and was soon conveyed to town.

The section foreman told me that the doctor laid Link on a lounge and "pushed around his hip a little," and then said, "There; she's in."

He bulldozed the section foreman into re-employing him. It was not long before he claimed to have been hurt again. This time the claim department refused to settle on any terms. Link brought suit for ten thousand dollars. I forget what the nature of his assumed injury was, as I was not at the trial, but I remember two things, which the attorney told me afterwards; that Link admitted, when on the stand, that when he came to Leroy he came in the custody of the sheriff serving a sentence for petit larceny; and that the jury gave him thirty-seven dollars and fifty cents.

This, of course, to saddle the costs on the railroad company.

Now, you could not expect anything better of such a man, for Link (his first name was Lincoln I save the mark!) was naturally and admittedly a degenerate and a thief. The jury knew this, and hence the small verdict Juries do not like thieves — that is men who admit that they have stolen, and who would steal from them. He may steal from a railroad corporation and they will still respect him and even assist him in his nefarious designs, but they don't like a man who is liable to steal from them.

He is the wrong kind of a thief and one to be watched and when caught handled without gloves.

The action of juries is a puzzle to me. It seems that the average man of moderate means is naturally prejudiced against large corporations. He cannot believe that any good can come out of them. He believes that all officials connected with such corporations are overbearing, dishonest and mean; and, while they do not like a small thief — a thief who would steal from the jury if given a chance — yet, they will give him a verdict against a railroad corporation, when they know he is attempting to rob it.

But not a large verdict — just enough to show their preference for the small thief over what they believe to be the large thief.

If Link Miffin had been an honest man, and had not been compelled to admit that he was a small thief while on the witness stand, the jury would have, no doubt, given him anywhere from two to four thousand dollars.

But they could not see their way clear to give such a large verdict to a common thief, and so Link got only thirty odd dollars and the despised railroad company paid the costs.

Case XI. I shall now relate a case in which there was none of the false swearing recorded in preceding chapters; indeed, there was no need for false swearing, but, if there had been, I am quite sure that the family would have stuck to the truth, as they were a highly educated and most honorable family.

In the year of 1888 I was ordered by the chief surgeon to go to the town of Spring Hill, Kansas, and there see and examine an old lady, whose name shall be Mrs. Holman in this narrative, not that there is any reason for changing the name, but they may not care to have their name paraded before the public. I went and found that she had a son just home from an Eastern Medical College, where he had graduated. He proved to be a capable and bright young man, and he gave me valuable assistance in making the examination.

The history of her injury was that, some three months previous to this time, she had started to visit friends at her former home at Louisburg, Kansas. In order to reach there she had to go to Osawatomie on one line of road and then take the Missouri Pacific to her destination. At Somerset, between Osawatomie and Louisburg, the train men did some switching.

I omitted to say that she was riding in an improvised caboose attached to a freight train. The regular caboose of the train being in the shops for repairs, a caboose had been constructed by taking an ordinary box car and putting in side seats, whi.ch they unfortunately made too high.

In setting in a car the two sections of the train came together with quite a jar — throwing the old lady out upon an iron spittoon and producing an intra-capsular fracture of the hip joint. She was taken on to Louisburg and there taken to the residence of an old friend, and Dr. J. D. Bryant, our local surgeon, was called to see her. Dr. Bryant gave her all needed attention; and, on the eighth day, her son took her from Louisburg to Spring Hill, a distance of sixteen miles, in an ordinary buggy, she being afraid to ride on a train.

Examination revealed an unmistakable intra-capsular fracture. She was fifty-five years old; and, as the fracture had not united in three months, it was strongly probable that it never would unite, and I so reported. Failing in settlement suit was brought for ten thousand dollars personal damages. The case came to trial at Paola, Kansas, within the year. Judge W. A. Johnson, of Gamett, a most capable attorney, was for the company, and a very brilliant young man, named John C. Sheridan, was counsel for plaintiff. A verdict for about three thousand dollars was obtained and appeal taken, the case reversed and remanded and tried again, when a verdict for five thousand dollars was given plaintiff, which the Supreme Court affirmed, this, with interest, making a total of sixty-three hundred dollars, was finally paid the plaintiff and her attorney, which, I was informed, they divided by the figure two.

It is some of the amusing episodes and incidents of these two trials that I propose to relate; so as, if possible, to relieve this narrative of the awful record of fraud, malingering and perjury.

In the first trial the contest between counsel was quite spirited. On the question of contributory negligence we had nothing, and the only thing that could possibly help us in the least was the ride of plaintiff, on the eighth day after her injury, from Louisburg to Spring Hill, and we worked that for all it was worth. When I was on the stand Judge Johnson asked me what effect it would have on a woman of her age to take such a ride. I answered: "In a woman of fifty-five nature begins to throw out bone. material in fractures near the upper end of the femur m about six to eight days. Now, in taking such a ride, with the thigh bone flexed to a right angle with the body, and being subjected to the grinding that it necessarily would be subjected to, the material thrown out would necessarily be destroyed. It is like the building and burning of a frame house; the builder gets the frame up and the roof and siding on, when it burns."

"Now, he has not only got to bring new material there with which to rebuild, but he must cart away all of the ashes and cinders, and the scorched and twisted scantling. So it was in the case of plaintiff's fractured thigh bone."

On cross-examining me John Sheridan asked: "Doctor, suppose the patient should be worrying; suppose she felt she was imposing on her friends and wanted to go home, wouldn't that interfere with the union of the bone?"

"No," I answered; "it would not."

"Then suppose that she did not have confidence in the attending physician, would not that retard union?"

I answered that it would not.

"Now, doctor," said he, "is it not a well-established fact in medicine that, if the patient has not faith In the physician, the medicines do not act so well?"

"No," I answered. "It is not a well-established fact, on the contrary, every competent physician knows that such is not the case. I admit that there is such an idea amongst the laity; it is a part of their 'chimney corner' medicine, but if you were to sustain a fracture of your leg and I should be the only doctor you could secure, though you might have no confidence in me whatever, if I should set the fracture properly it would heal, and, if I should give you three compound cathartic pills, you could not keep them from moving your bowels to save your life."

The effect was electrical. The audience, the jurors, witnesses, attorneys, and even the grave and dignified judge, broke into uproarious laughter and even the judge did not come to order for some time.

In both trials the plaintiff had for witnesses her son, the doctor, and her two daughters, both school teachers, and both very bright, intelligent and very good young ladies.

In the prosecution of the case it, of course, behooved their attorney to make out the plaintiff as a very strong and capable person before she was injured. To this end the son and daughters all testified to their mother's great ability as a worker. At Louisburg, where the son was preparing for a course in medicine and both daughters attending high school, with a view of becoming teachers, they all testified that they took some boarders, and plaintiff then did the cooking, the family washing and housekeeping, except the girls' rooms, which they attended to themselves.

"Now, Miss Alice," said Judge Johnson, "do I understand that your mother did all of this work and that you and your sister did none of it?"

"Yes, sir."

"What were you sisters doing while your mother was working so hard?"

"We were studying; we were preparing to teach, and we had our lessons mornings and evenings, and we had no time to do anything else."

"Then, if I understand you. Miss Alice, your mother did the cooking, the washing, did up the rooms of the boarders; and, while she was in the cellar splitting stove wood, you two girls sat back and sang, 'Oh, What is Home Without a Mother?'"

I don't think that I ever heard such boisterous laughter in a court room before or since. All joined in, and even the plaintiff, the son and the two girls laughed. Miss Alice laughed until she broke down and became hysterical and laughed and wept together.

Case XII. In all my twenty-five years of service in the hospital department of the Missouri Pacific Railroad I never changed my diagnosis with regard to an injury but once; and, in that case, I was "taken down" in a way that was amusing and which furnished a good deal of enjoyment to the plaintiff's attorneys.

In the year 1886 there was brought to the hospital a young section hand who had been injured in a hand car accident. He was a young, green country boy, about twenty-two years old. He was tall and gawky and showed by his manner that he had never been far away from the parental domicile — poor and uninviting as that domicile must have been.

He had been working as a section laborer for only a very short time when one day a handle of the hand car that he was working gave way or some other accident caused him to fall in front of the car. They were running pretty fast and it whirled him over a number of times. As I have before stated, hand-car accidents are, as a general rule, the very worst that the railroad surgeon has to deal with; for the spine of the injured person is almost invariably injured, and, generally, there is a fracture of one or two vertebrae and a consequent resulting paralysis of the parts below.

The young man seemed to suffer greatly — more, in fact, than the nature of the injury seemed to warrant. I thought that, perhaps, his apparent suffering was due to the fact that he had never been hurt before and that he was scared. He was not smart enough nor versed in the ways of the world sufficiently to assume that he was suffering nor to malinger.

Examination revealed nothing more than a slight puffiness or swelling of the back at the junction of the last dorsal and the first lumbar vertebrae, or in the upper part of the "small of the back."

Neither I nor my house surgeons could find anything more.

He complained and wept a good deal and wanted to go home almost as soon as he arrived.

I don't think that he remained as long as one week. He begged to go home so constantly and so pitifully that I finally gave him a pass and permitted him to go.

When he came into my office to get his transportation, I had him back up to me, as I sat at my desk, and I stripped up his shirt and examined his back again. There was nothing more to be seen there than what had been seen before. The region complained of showed a slight discoloration, as in a bruise, and that was all.

There was an attempt at settlement, but his claims, in view of my report, seemed to be exorbitant and the claim agent refused to pay him or his attorney the amount.

Suit was brought and, in due time, was called for trial at Butler, in Bates County.

Plaintiff had for his attorneys a firm of young lawyers— Jarratt & Whitsett, of Pleasant Hill. After plaintiff's side had been heard, I was put on the witness stand for the defense.

I stated the case as I had seen it, stated that it was insignificant, amounted to nothing, and should not keep a man from work more than ten days, or two weeks at the outside.

Judge Jarrett asked me: "Doctor, have you seen this plaintiff's back since he left the hospital?"

I answered that I had not.

"Will you look at it and examine it now?"

"I will be glad to do so," I answered.

Plaintiff was ordered to stand up near me and to put himself in a position for examination. I unbuttoned his suspenders behind and stripped up his clothing, and then glued my eye to the upper part of "the small of the back," and then you could have pushed me over with a straw. In all my professional life I had never been so deceived.

There, in the region first complained of, was a lump, or what seemed to be an enlargement about the size of my thumb; and, what was more, when I put my fingers on it I found it to be bone!

I examined it very carefully, Judge Jarrett and his partner enjoying my discomfiture. Nobody else in the court room could guess why I grew red in the face and looked as if I would like to jump out of the window, or go through the floor — anywhere, anything, just so as to get away.

I turned to the court and said, "If your Honor please, I would like to correct my testimony."

I then explained to the jury the condition of plaintiff's spine then and the difference between it's then condition and when I last saw it and the reasons for it.

When the young man was injured he sustained a fracture of the spine of one of the vertebrae.

These spines project out backward; and, if the lay reader of this will think of the backbone of a hog which he has eaten he will remember how each vertabra has a projecting spine on it, about an inch and a half in length. In the accident one of these spines in plaintiff's spinal column had been broken off at its attachment to the body of the vertabra.

When he was at the hospital it was still in its old position. Though broken it had not been moved from its place. But, when he went out and exercised, the erector muscle of the spine, attached to this particular spinous process, in its contractions, had simply pulled the detached bone out and made it prominent. You could not only feel it, but you could see it the length of the court room. It was all very plain now, and I made the explanation to the court and the jury, as I have made it here. Adjournment for lunch was taken at about this time, and, you may rest assured, Jarratt and his partner laughed at me, and it wasn't a snicker, either.

At the noon hour the attorneys on both sides and our general claim agent, who happened to be present, got together and settled the case — the railroad company paying plaintiff fifteen hundred dollars, as I now remember it.

The then Mr. Jarratt is now Judge Jarratt of the Warrensburg Circuit.

The last time I saw him, which was only a few weeks ago, he came down from the bench at the noon hour, and, calling together a group of mutual friends, he told them of the young section man's case and of my discomfiture while on the witness stand, and then had me explain to our mutual friends the reasons for my mistake.

A railroad surgeon may and can be dishonest if he is disposed. He may cheat a plaintiff litigant, especially if he is an employee, by lying to him about his condition and inducing him to settle his case, when, had he brought suit, he could have realized a great deal more, and, it may be, that he was entitled to all that he could have realized at the end of a suit.

I am glad and proud to say that in my long connection with the Missouri Pacific corporation I have never heard of an accusation against the chief surgeon, nor against any assistant chief surgeon, in any of the hospitals, of doing anything that looked like misleading or cheating an employee in behalf of the railroad company. I am quite sure that there was never any grounds for any such accusation.

When I first took charge of the hospital at Sedalia, Missouri, it was the rule, when an injured employee was ready to resume work, for the general claim agent, or one of his assistants, to come to the hospital and go into the ward or call the convalescent employee into my office and settle, or attempt to settle, with him.

I found this to be a very bad policy. It was often the case where a man had been quite severely hurt, and when he had been guilty of contributory negligence, and where there was, therefore, no liability on the part of the company and in such a case, of course, the claim agent could not afford to pay the employee as much as he would have paid him had the company been liable. While the settlement was in progress the other sick, injured and especially convalescent employees would gather in groups and wait news of the progress of the settlement; and, after settlement had been made and the claim agent had departed, these same groups would gather and discuss the settlement. If, as I have said, the amount paid looked meager for such an injury — for they did not consider the question of liability — there would be much anger expressed and the claim agent would receive a general denunciation; and, I fear, the doctors often came in for a share, however little we may have deserved it.

Dr. Outten and I discussed this phase of settlements by the claim agent and we agreed that such settlements should not be made in the hospitals; for it had a bad effect on the patients and it made it more difficult to enforce discipline; for it is hard to maintain discipline with angry men, even if their anger is not directed against you.

It was agreed, therefore, that I should write the chief surgeon on the subject and give our arguments against the practice, and our reasons for desiring that settlements should be made elsewhere than in the hospitals, and Dr. Outten was to then personally endorse my letter to Mr. Hoxie, the then general manager, and also verbally argue the matter with him.

Mr. Hoxie was a brainy, reasonable and sensible man and he was not hard to convince that we were right.

If a settlement was ever made in or about the hospitals after that, it was done to accommodate the employee, whose condition was such that he could not go to see the claim agent. I believe that there were a very few such settlements made in the hospital, but I cannot remember to-day the name of any employee who was settled with under such circumstances.

I do not believe that there is a railroad hospital system in the country, or in the world, where the men have received and where they yet receive better treatment, in every respect — medical, surgical and personal —than the employees of the Missouri Pacific system.

This is all due to a liberal policy inaugurated by the present chief surgeon, and by his selection of subordinates who were and are in accord with him on all matters pertaining to the maintaining of this liberal policy.

Dr. Outten has always selected men of ability (I will here except myself, and will let Dr. Outten speak for me), who knew how to do their work and who were and are progressive and kept abreast of the times in all material advances in modem medicine and surgery.

Chapter Five - Assumed Local Paralysis

Case I. ONE of the most remarkable cases of fraud, malingering and readiness to commit perjury, if necessary to accomplish his purpose, was brought to my notice not long before I severed my connection with the Missouri Pacific road.

The case had, no doubt, been reported to my office by the local surgeon who attended the man at the time of his insignificant injury, but it was so trivial and so small an affair that I had not remembered it.

One afternoon our general claim agent, Mr. William E. Jones, of St. Louis, and who, I may say *en passant*, is in my estimation the superior of any other claim agent in this country, and that is equivalent to saying in any country, appeared at my office in the hospital, accompanied by two men. I did not know that Mr. Jones was in the city until he stepped in.

I had a slight acquaintance with one of the gentlemen — a Kansas City lawyer, who had at one time held a very important position in the legal department of the government of Kansas City — but the other man I did not know, never having met him before. The latter, for the purposes of this narrative, I shall call Mr. Malin; for I think that, in some respects, he was the *Chief Malingerer* of all the distinguished malingerers whom I have met, though his malingering was in a small way, but it went to show what Mr. Malin could do if given the opportunity.

It seemed that some two or three months previous to that time, Mr. Malin had ridden on a Missouri Pacific train into Rich Hill. At Rich Hill two passenger trains meet — one from Joplin and one from Fort Scott, Kansas.

At Rich Hill some switching is done, a coach being set in and out and the train that comes on to Kansas City is made up of a part of each train, and, if I mistake not, another train is made up which goes to St Louis via Pleasant

Hill; or, at least a Pullman coach is set in behind the Kansas City train and dropped at Pleasant Hill, to be picked up by the regular St. Louis night train.

While this switching was being done Mr. Malin was standing in the rear coach of one train, watching the approach of a Pullman coach which was to be attached to the rear of the train upon which he stood.

The coach struck the car in which Mr. Malin stood with considerable force and he plunged his right hand through the glass in the door in front of him. He received a cut on the outer knuckling or knob of bone just above the wrist. This knuckle is the lower end of the bone of the forearm, which is called the ulna. The cut was through the skin and about three-fourths of an inch in length. Our local surgeon was hurriedly sent for and came down and attended him. He really did not think enough of it to take a stitch in it. but simply closed it with a strip of adhesive plaster and put on a light bandage.

In due time Mr. Malin made a demand upon the claim department, through the attorney who accompanied him and the claim agent this afternoon, and who, by the way, was his brother-in-law, for a settlement—claiming paralysis of the right hand. The general claim agent did not know of the location and insignificance of the wound, and, not being a physician, did not know but that the hand might have been paralyzed through the severance of some nerve which supplied it.

The general claim agent informed me that he had come to Kansas City to meet those parties and, if possible, to settle the case; and that he desired that I examine the hand and frankly say to him and Malin's attorney what my opinion of the case was.

At my suggestion we repaired to our operating room, and there, at my request, Malin extended his hand to be examined.

"Umph humph!" I said, "a cut, isn't it. Where did you get that?"

He informed me.

"Well, but it is healed up; what do you complain of now?"

"Hand paralyzed," said Malin, assuming a sheepish air, which well befitted him.

"Paralyzed!" I exclaimed. "Oh, get out! That hand is not paralyzed?"

Honestly I thought for a moment that some job had been put up on me, with a view to making me set up the cigars.

"Yes, it is," said Malin; "it's totally paralyzed."

"But I tell you it is not paralyzed," I insisted; "it can't be. You might as well tell me that the hairs of your head are paralyzed."

"Yes, it is paralyzed, doctor; at least he tells me that it is," said the brother-in-law attorney.

I honestly believe that this attorney was deceived in the matter, and I am the better prepared to believe it when I consider that he was not a physician and is known in Kansas City as a most honorable gentleman.

The fingers of the hand were extended and held in one position. There was not the least swelling, bogginess or change of color in the hand or fingers.

"Shut your hand," I commanded.

"I can't," said Malin, looking still more sheepish.

I don't think that I ever desired to knock a man down, who had done me no harm, so much in my life.

"Yes, but you can," I insisted, seizing the fingers and starting to bend them.

"Oh, doc! don't do that; that hurts, oh my I how you have hurt me. Now, just that little attempt to shut that hand makes it pain me so it nearly kills me," insisted the malingering rascal.

"I tell you it don't hurt and that it is not paralyzed; shut your hand!" I again commanded, but it did no good. He would not shut the hand, nor would he permit me to do it.

I gave it up.

At my suggestion we then went to my private office. On the way to my office I frankly told the general claim agent what I thought of the case. "You go into the sitting room," I said to Malin.

He half arose, stood in a semi-squatting position, and gave his brother-in-law an appealing look, as if for directions.

'That's right," said the lawyer.

Malin went to the door and opened it and then, turning his face toward us, stood there.

"Go out and shut the door," I commanded. I was so indignant and had such a profound contempt for this malingering scoundrel that I could not treat him with decent courtesy — not even in my own house.

"Well," began the claim agent, "tell us what you find in this case, doctor."

"Do I understand that this man is your brother-in-law?" I asked the lawyer.

"Yes," said he. "He married my sister, and she died and now he is married again."

"I am sorry," I said, "for I respect you, and I am sorry to say to any man what I am now going to say to you about this sweet-scented brother-in-law of yours. I have been in this business about twenty-five years, and during that time I have examined, counting employees and others, hundreds, yes thousands, of persons who had been injured or who assumed to have been injured. In that great number I have of course run across a great many frauds, liars, malingerers and have heard many of them swear themselves into purgatory, just for the chance of getting a little money, but this fellow, this brother-in-law of yours, is the biggest liar, the worst pretender and malingerer I have ever met. If there is a belt or a chromo anywhere which is held by the champion liar and malingerer, I am going to insist that he have it. He is getting ready to go on the witness stand and perjure himself; and. if you respect the memory of your dead sister, or care anything for her children, if she left any, let me beg of you to not permit him to do it. Bind him, gag him, kill him, do anything rather than permit him to go on the witness stand and swear in this case."

Mr. Jones looked astounded. In all of our work together he had never heard me talk to any one or about any one as I did about this fellow to his brother-in-law; for it was the policy of the claim and hospital departments to show the greatest courtesy to the people whom we hurt. Mr. Jones could himself turn a rascal over "to the Queen's taste," when it became necessary, but he had never heard me do it before, and I think he would have been willing to acknowledge me as his superior on this occasion.

"Well, now, doctor," began the surprised lawyer, "isn't it possible for you to be mistaken about this case?"

"It is not possible," I answered.

"Well," he continued, "not long ago there was a case in which two doctors gave an adverse opinion; and yet, in the end, it turned out that they were wrong," and he gave the details of the case.

"The cases are not parallel," I said.

"There is nothing in common between them. In the case you relate it is possible for even a fairly good man to be mistaken, but the merest tyro could not make a mistake in this case.

"Now, as I said before, he is prepared to go on the witness stand and perjure himself until he is black in the face; and, if he does, we will put every surgeon, of any note, and every neurologist in Kansas City on the stand to contradict him, and if I can, I will have him indicted for perjury and will send him to prison. And, I will make you any kind of a wager that I can prove that he works on his farm, down in Kansas, every day and uses that hand, without let or hindrance, in chopping, pitching hay and in all kinds of farm work. He is too shrewd a rascal to lose the valuable time he would have to lose in malingering all the time, when at home. He just put that paralysis on for this occasion and for a purpose. I will tell you what I will do: You and I will go down to this neighborhood and investigate this case. If it is shown that he has not been using his hand right along, I will pay him one thousand dollars out of my own pocket, 'and I will give him another thousand,' said Mr. Jones, for he had great respect for my opinion in those cases, "and if it is shown that he has been using it, you to pay me one hundred dollars just to pay my expenses."

Mr. Malin was sent for. He came in and sat down, holding his right hand in his left, as real paralytics do.

"Malin, the doctor don't think there is much the matter with you," said the lawyer, putting it as light as he could by the use of the word "much."

"Oh, he don't know — he don't know how I have suffered with that hand." (Paralytics do not suffer, as a rule, with paralyzed hands — Author)

"If I could be back where I was before my hand was paralyzed I wouldn't be where I am now for all that old Jay Gould —" I got up and went out I just could not stand that old stereotyped rigmarole from this villain. The general claim agent settled with him for one hundred and fifty dollars and I heard a few weeks afterward that Malin was using his hand and had been using it all the time since the skin had healed.

Now, here was a man who was prepared to bring suit for, perhaps, ten thousand dollars damages and to allege a permanent injury to his hand and to claim that it was totally paralyzed, and he was prepared to go on the witness stand and solemnly swear that his hand was paralyzed and that he had not used it since the day the slight cut was made. And, unfortunately this was not all. He was the kind of man who would not hesitate for one moment to drill his little boys and girls— children of tender years — and put them on the stand and have them perjure themselves; and his wife unless she should be a woman of unusually strong mind and determined will — would have been drilled and put on the stand to play her part in the fraud.

This man, after bringing suit, would have worked only at such times and under such circumstances as he could and not be seen by his neighbors, for such rascals get to be exceedingly wise and cautious after they have once brought suit, for they know that, after they have brought suit, they are, in many respects, the subjects of comment, of criticism and inquiry, by their neighbors and sometimes, if a neighbor is not very friendly, or if there is an enmity existing between them, he may give a "pointer" to the railroad company's attorney, and thus defeat the malingerer.

Hence, it behooves such a person to be careful before every one, except the members of his own immediate household and relatives, whom he can control, or who expect to be benefitted by the success of the fraud.

But, think of such a man putting his own children, his little boys and girls on the stand, and of his teaching them beforehand as to what they shall say and as to how they shall answer certain questions if put to them on cross-examination!

Does any one undertake to tell me that this child, this tender little boy or girl, may not be injured and may not be ruined morally, for life?

I do not see how it can result otherwise than in the moral blunting and corrupting of the child's mind for the period of its natural life.

Such persons will, no doubt, read, or have read the story of old Pagan teaching Oliver Twist and the Artful Dodger, how to steal handkerchiefs, and other things, and manifest — and perhaps, feel horrified at the idea of a young and tender child being so corrupted and ruined and, at the same time, drill and train their own tender little ones to go on the witness stand and commit perjury! Human nature has some queer kinks in it. Now, I certainly cannot see but that such a person does his child as much or more harm by what he teaches it to do than old Pagan did to poor little Oliver and the Artful Dodger. And, it must be remembered that they were not Fagan's children, nor were they of kin to him. But, such men as Malin will drill their own tender offspring to swear falsely and yet feel horrified at the story of Oliver Twist.

It is hard to reconcile such contradictions in human character. In fact we cannot reconcile them. We can only accept the facts as we see them and know them to exist and wonder as to why they are so. But they cannot be explained in any other way than upon the fact of the great part *Self* plays in all human actions.

Case II. I was directed, at some time during the year 1892, as well as I can remember, to go to Mound City, Kansas, and assist Judge W. A. Johnson, of Garnett, and Judge Kelso, of Atchison, in the defense of a very peculiar and unusual case. The plaintiff was a rather pretty girl of eighteen or nineteen years of age, a school teacher by occupation at that time, and she had brought suit against the company for ten thousand dollars damages on account of paralysis of the left side of her face, or, what is called "Bell's paralysis," and, sometimes, simply "facial paralysis," which she claimed to have been caused by fright.

The facts, as developed by the evidence were these: Something over two years previous to that time, and when Miss Nellie (Miss Nellie Abbott shall be her name in this narrative) then about sixteen years of age, was attending school in Pleasanton. Her family were farmers and she, of course, lived in the country when she was at home. She was ambitious and desirous of becoming a teacher; and so, she boarded with a family in Pleasanton and assisted the lady of the house in doing her housework of mornings and evenings for her board.

Some one or more of her family came for her on late Friday afternoons and she was brought back to Pleasanton again on Sunday afternoons.

On this occasion, when she claimed to have received the fright, which she claimed caused the paralysis of her face, she was returning to Pleasanton in a two-horse wagon, accompanied by her mother and fourteen-years-old brother. They were all sitting on the ordinary spring seat which is commonly seen on farm wagons — Miss Nellie sitting in the middle and driving.

It was a cold, blustering November day. However, there was a controversy on that point — the family with which Miss Nellie was boarding testifying that it was cold and blustering, while Miss Nellie and her mother and brother testified that it was warm and pleasant and the sun shining brightly, but the records of meteorological observations, in the nearby towns, showed that it was cold and blustering, a quite sharp wind from the Northwest prevailing.

They were driving East on a good country road, and, at the point where the fright occurred, were gradually approaching the railroad track, a branch line which ran from Butler, Mo., to the town of Madison, in Kansas.

Between the country road and the railroad track there was a hedge fence which ran parallel with the country road and which also gradually approached the railroad track. At the point where the country road crossed the railroad track, this hedge fence crossed the track at a quite acute angle, and, at this point, the hedge had been cut down for about fifty feet on either side, either way.

The country road crossed the railroad track by a square turn to the right, so that it crossed at a right angle.

The railroad track at that point was elevated about four feet above the surrounding ground. The country road, therefore, approached the railroad track by a gradual rise — this rise gradually ascending to the track by about twenty feet after the turn to the right was made. Just as the front feet of the horses were about on the first rail of the track Miss Nellie looked to the right and saw a passenger train, only one or two hundred feet away — the train running at about twenty-five miles an hour.

Miss Nellie jerked upon the lines quite violently and the team reared and backed down the twenty foot incline.

Neither the horses or wagon was struck, but they were all frightened a good deal. After the train had passed they proceeded on their way without further trouble, although Miss Nellie was quite nervous. When they arrived at Miss Nellie's boarding place the family testified that they remembered they all sat around the stove in the sitting room for about a half hour's time and warmed up before they took off their wraps. This was given by the family as the reason why they remembered that it was a cold and windy day, but the Abbotts all flatly contradicted this statement. This point was important only that the railroad company desired to show that they had their heads so closely wrapped and bundled that they could not hear the approaching train. The mother and brother returned to their home, after getting warm, and Miss Nellie went to bed to sleep off her nervousness.

When she arose the next morning, and while washing her face, she discovered that the left side of her face — the side next the Northwest wind the day before — was paralyzed. She continued to go to school, however, until, I believe, she finished in the Pleasanton high school.

It was stated, but not in evidence, that Miss Nellie tried to induce her mother to bring suit at once, but that the mother refused to do so.

As soon as Miss Nellie passed her eighteenth birthday she brought suit in her own name. At the time the case came up for trial she was teaching in the State of Arkansas, and dismissed her school and came all the way to Mound City to prosecute her suit.

The testimony was about as I have detailed it. The attorney for plaintiff — Hon. Jas. Snoddy — tried to put the physician who attended Miss Nellie on the stand, but the doctor refused to testify unless he was first paid his fee.

Upon motion of the company's attorney, the Court appointed a commission of physicians consisting of the family physician and myself to examine the plaintiff.

I had noticed all day that plaintiff's face had a *hanging* appearance, but I could note no difference between the two sides.

However, I supposed that plaintiff's face had practically recovered, as occurs quite often.

When we had retired to one of the jury rooms to make the examination, I pinched up the two sides of the face, which I found to be quite flabby and soft

"Why, Miss Abbott," I said, "both sides of your face are paralyzed."

"Y-e-e-e-s," interposed the mother, "but the right side wasn't paralyzed until about a year after the left was."

"And she has a discharge from both the ears?" I asked.

"Yes, I believe you have, haven't you, Nellie?"

Miss Nellie answered that she had.

"And it has a bad odor?" I again suggested interrogatively.

"Yes," said the mother, "I believe it does smell bad sometimes, don't it, Nellie?" Nellie answered that it did.

I happened to have some absorbent cotton with me; so I took out a piece and wrapped it on the end of a toothpick and quietly inserted it in each ear, in turn. From both ears I obtained quite a quantity of characteristic tubercular *pus*, which had the characteristic odor of *tubercular pus.*

We returned to the Court room, I to testify, if called, and the other doctor to demand his fee, in case he should be called.

The company's attorney had demurred to the evidence, alleging that plaintiff had not produced sufficient testimony to make a case. This is the almost invariable practice of the Missouri Pacific Railroad attorneys.

In the argument of the demurrer no case like it could be found in the reports of the Supreme Courts of any of the states, but the company's attorney had a case which had recently been published in a law journal which the Court permitted them to use.

It was the case of Mrs. Kelley vs. the Pennsylvania Railroad Company. Mrs. Kelley lived in a house of several rooms down near the railroad track. One night a freight train was derailed at that point and about ten cars were piled on to Mrs. Kelley's house — smashing in all the rooms, except the one in which Mrs. Kelley and her babe slept, but missing that room entirely, so that neither of them was hurt.

Mrs. Kelley brought suit for quite a large sum, alleging fright as the foundation for her claims. She got quite a substantial verdict in the lower Court, but the case was appealed and the Supreme Court reversed and dismissed it. The Court stated in its argument that it would not do to permit fright to be alleged as an element in a claim for damages, for, if such should be the case then all a person who desired to raise some money would have to do would be to go to some point on the railroad and get frightened — alleging that the train made a loud and unusual noise.

Our Judge sustained the demurrer, and so Miss Nellie did not collect anything on her tuberculous ears and the doctor did not get his expert fee. I presented Miss Nellie with a pretty fair picture of both herself and her attorney, however, which I had drawn while the case was in progress and which she took back to Arkansas with her. She said, "It is not much, but it is something."

I omitted to say that Miss Abbott had tuberculous degeneration of the ossicles — the three small bones, the *stapes,* the *malleous* and the *incus* (the stirrup, the mallet and the anvil) which take part in the making up of the hearing apparatus.

The ear was, therefore affected by a low grade of inflammation and a process of gradual infiltration into the soft parts was taking place. On the day that Miss Nellie was frightened, the cold northwest wind blew on that side of her face and head and, of course, excited the parts, and a more rapid process of infiltration was set up. This resulted in the rapid deposit of inflammatory material upon and around the nerve — the portio-dura of the seventh, and which is the motor nerve of the face. This rapid deposit of inflammatory material had bound the nerve down at the point where it emerges from the foramen — thus cutting off the transmission of the nerve current beyond that point, and, hence, paralysis of the face followed. A year afterward the same thing occurred to the other side, and so, Miss Nellie found herself with both sides of her face paralyzed, something — the paralysis of both sides — which does not often occur.

It is strange that so capable a lawyer as the attorney for the plaintiff in this case should bring suit based on so frail and flimsy a foundation as was the basis of the suit in this case. Yet, it was an untried issue in the State of Kansas, and in any other State so far as plaintiff's attorney knew, for I believe he did not know of the Pennsylvania case until the attorney for the defense produced the law journal.

Lawyers seem to be always looking for "new points" in law, and to work most ingeniously to get those "new points" into their cases and before the Courts. Indeed I have known some "new points" — points that have never, so far as could be ascertained, been tried before, and, in one instance, I knew a young lawyer who established quite a reputation on account of his taking a criminal case up to our Missouri Supreme Court on an entirely new point, and winning his case on it.

All of the old attorneys were against him, but he had studied his case and his point and stuck to it tenaciously and won.

It would seem, however, that almost anyone ought to see that fright cannot be made an element of damages; and yet, "no game is out until it is played out," as the sports sometimes say, and so, no law point is decided until the Courts have passed upon it, and you cannot always tell just what the Courts are going to do, or how they will decide a given point.

However, if such a case should be decided favorably, to the plaintiff once — I mean damages given on the ground of fright, and it should become an established decision, my! oh, my! how many there would be who would rush out and get frightened and then rush in and claim damages for it! It would be simply awful.

You would find more delicate little women, more big iron jawed women and more great hulking stalwart men getting scared and claiming damages as

103

a consequence, or as compensation for their fright, than was ever heard of before.

Fortunately, for the railroad corporations, however, our Supreme Courts which, as a rule, constitute the only safeguard that such corporations have, have got some sense and some decency left. I believe that the Supreme Courts, as a general thing, have remained pure, uncorrupted and incorruptible.

I know it is charged, and it may be true of some Courts, that they do take bribes, but I doubt it. I mean that I am quite sure that it is not true as often as charged and not true even one-tenth of the times when it is charged. I know that there was a time that one of our United States Supreme Judges was charged with having taken a bribe, and I know that the case against him looked very black and very bad, but it is to be hoped that he did not.

If that great Court can be and is corrupted then it IS a very bad thing for our country; and yet, his sudden flop on the income tax law looks very ugly — almost convincing.

Of course, nothing could be nor was proven against him, but the way he summersaulted was extremely suspicious, and, strange to say, he never gave any reason for, or explanation of his grand "ground and lofty tumble," which it would seem that, if an honest man, he should have done.

Case III. About the year 1898 we received a young man into the hospital, whose name shall be Lester Bloom. This sounds so much like his name that I have adopted it. Lester was a physical degenerate. He had all the stigmata that Caesare Lambroso — the great Italian criminologist — gives as the unmistakable marks of degeneracy. His head was small and asymmetrical, his nose was deflected and crooked, his teeth were riding upon each other and his ears — great big saddle skirts, stood straight out from his head, and looked more like they had been placed there for fighting flies or fanning the individual than for the purposes of conducting sound waves to his tympanic membrane.

Lester stated that his hip joint had been dislocated the day before, and had been reduced by the local physician, and the right side of his face was paralyzed. There was no mistake about this latter lesion, as it was plain to be seen; but, as Lester was walking on his right leg, we had our doubts about the dislocation. However, I paid for the reduction.

We could not keep Lester in the hospital. I am not sure that he did not demand a return pass the same day he came, but of one thing I am sure — he kept ding-donging about going home until, in four or five days, we sent him home. It was a long time before we understood why Lester was so persistent in wanting to go home; but, we ascertained at last — he had been married only one week when he came to the hospital.

I do not know what effort was made to settle with Lester Bloom, but I know it was made, for it was against the policy of the management to fight its employees in Court and settlement was always made when it could be made on anything like a reasonable basis. Whatever effort that was made failed. Lester being newly married, perhaps, had visions of stately mansions, great fields of waving grain and pastures in which roamed lowing herds of thoroughbreds.

In due time suit was brought and I was directed to go to Eureka, Kansas, where the case was to be tried, and assist Col. Richards, General Attorney of the Ft S. W. & W. to try the case.

Lester had a large, handsome Kentuckian for his attorney, whom I shall call Col. Davison.

The case came to trial and the issues were joined. As said before. Bloom had paralysis of the right side of the face. The seventh nerve had been bruised against the bone and the transmission of the nerve current cut off.

The testimony developed the fact that Bloom had been hired to work on a section near Eureka. His foreman was an oddity. His name was Jimmy McCarty. Jimmie had been a Confederate soldier for four and a half years, of which fact he was very proud. After Bloom told his story, and a few other unimportant witnesses had testified, plaintiff's attorney rested, and Jimmie was put on for the defense.

The company's attorney asked, "What is your name?"

"It was all his own fault He hadn't a damn bit of business to be there for I hadn't called him."

It took half a dozen questions to get Jimmie to tell his name, and oven before he did this he had to be instructed by the attorney for the company and warned by the Court. Finally, however, he was made to understand, and he then went on and told his story.

He stated that, at the request of plaintiff and the urgent solicitation of interested friends, he had given him employment, and he did so because he had just married, and he felt sorry for him.

Jimmie had the big-hearted sympathy of the Irish race. He said that Lester was not built for section work, but there was nearly always light work he could put such a man at and still feel that he had not wronged the company. He said that, on the day plaintiff was hurt, he was putting in a spur track. In the prosecution of this job it became necessary to have a rail that was shorter than the ordinary rail. Under such circumstances it was the custom to cut and break a rail. This was done in this way: One man was set to the task of cutting the rail. With a cold chisel and hammer he cut a groove entirely around the rail at the point where it had been decided to cut it, deep enough, so that, when the rail was raised and dropped on an anvil, it would break at the point where the groove had been cut.

When this man announced that the rail was ready to be broken Jimmie called, "Come, men, and let's break this rail."

The anvil, which was a piece of rail about two feet long, was placed across the track. The rail was then placed so that, when it was let fall, the groove would strike on the anvil, or just beyond it.

When all was ready they raised the rail to a place above their heads as far as they could lift it with their hands and, with a "now" from Jimmie, the rail was let fall and all hands jumped back out of danger.

On this occasion, after the rail had been permitted to fall, a cry was heard from the other end. In looking in that direction they saw Lester Bloom lying under the rail only a short distance from the other end. They lifted the rail and released Lester, who was found to be hurt.

Jimmie and all of his men testified that before the rail was broken, Lester had been placed about forty feet in the rear and put to unscrewing bolts and taking off "fish-plates" from a rail whose position it was necessary to change; but, when the order came, "Come, men, and let's break the rail," which Jimmie gave, all of his other men came to that end of the rail.

They swore that the call was not intended for Lester Bloom, and that they did not suppose that he had heard it.

However, he did hear it; and not having time to reach the place where Jimmie and his other men were, he grabbed hold of the rail only eight or ten feet from the other end; and, when the rail was let fall; and, as he had not been working in unison with the others, the weight carried him down and he slipped and went under the rail. The result was a dislocated hip and a paralyzed face. His face was still paralyzed at time of trial.

One thing which plaintiff complained of, which was false, was that the paralysis of his face interfered with his swallowing.

Every anatomist knows that there is no connection between the seventh nerve and the nerve which controls the muscles of deglutition.

When a commission of physicians, of which I was not a member, examined him he gave a demonstration of the difficulty he had in swallowing.

He took a large bite of an apple and chewed it very fine and then made an effort, apparently, to swallow it. When the finely chewed apple reached a point behind the soft palate, plaintiff began to hump his shoulders and cough and snort. The result was that a part of the apple was ejected through his nose. He swore that this occurred at every meal, and, in fact, whenever he ate anything. Some of the jurymen desired that he should give a demonstration while on the stand, but he was not permitted to do so.

When I testified I exhibited drawings, showing that there was no anatomical or physiological connection between the seventh nerve and the nerves which govern the act of swallowing; and I further testified that almost anyone could eject a part of the food through the nose; that I could do it; and that when anyone threw up a meal, a part of the ejected material almost invariably came out through the nose; and that, so far as plaintiff's demonstration was concerned, it was purely voluntary. The case was bitterly fought, and the jury promptly brought in a verdict for the company. However, plaintiff's attorney came before the Court the next morning and charged one of the jurymen with "misconduct," while the jury had the case under consideration. It seemed that, when the jury was discussing the phase of plaintiff's case which related to his difficulty in swallowing, one of the jurymen chewed a piece of apple and ejected a part of it through his nose, in the presence of the other jurymen.

This was very convincing, but contrary to rule, as it amounted to the juryman giving testimony before the jury after the case had been given to them to decide.

One of the jurymen, to justify the jury in its verdict, after the jury had returned its verdict, said, "Why Bill Smith chawed an apple and coughed and spurted a lot of it through his nose; then we knowed that Bloom had lied; and, if he would lie about one thing, when under oath, he would lie about anything and everything." This, coming to plaintiff's counsel, he went into Court and asked for a new trial, and made proof of the misconduct of the jurymen. The Court could do nothing less than to grant the motion. We then soothed Lester and his attorney by giving them five hundred dollars to quit, and this ended the famous Lester Bloom suit.

Lester got two hundred and fifty dollars, I suppose, and this was, no doubt, more money than he or any member of his family had ever possessed at one time in the whole history of the family.

It would have been a study worthwhile for one to have kept an eye on Lester and his new wife for a few weeks, just to see how they spent that money. It is strongly probable that he didn't have a dollar of it at the expiration of one month, but the things, the almost useless things, that he and that young wife purchased!

Now, it was not astonishing to me to see Lester go on the stand and to hear him swear as he did, for what could one expect from a young man whose head and face seemed to have been made in order to exhibit an assemblage of all of the stigmata of degeneracy?

I was curious to see his wife. I wanted to see what kind of a woman would marry such a degenerate as Lester, but I did not have my curiosity in that regard gratified.

She did not come to the trial, and, hence, I did not get to see her.

I stated to the jury that I could if I tried, snort a portion of a chewed up apple through my nose, and Col. Davidson, Lester Bloom's attorney, demanded that I should give an exhibition of my powers in that regard, while I was on the witness stand, but I am glad to say the Court refused to compel me to give such an exhibition, nor would he have permitted me to give such an exhibition, even had I desired to do so. I was really afraid, from some decisions of law points made by the presiding judge, that he would order mc to go to chewing, coughing and snorting. But he did not, and, taking him by and large, he was a pretty fair judge. He was reared in the mountains of Kentucky, in the feud regions, I believe, but was not a feudist himself. In fact, he was quite a just judge. Such was his conduct, in fact, that his constituents in that Congressional District have sent him to Congress one term since the Lester

Bloom trial, and have defeated him once, so that now he is in private life and practicing law again.

His decision in reversing the jury's verdict, on account of the misconduct of the juryman, was all right, I was told by the company's attorney, as it should have been done by any honest and fair judge.

Judges, I am sorry to say, are too often swayed by public sentiment — fearing that they may not be elected again, if they are even reasonably fair toward a corporation, but, as a rule, I have found the judges to be men of a good deal of courage, and ready to mete out even and exact justice without regard to what the voters may do at the next election. This is as it should be.

I seriously doubt if our judges should be elected by the people; but am inclined to believe that they should be appointed by the Governor, as our United States Judges are by the President; but, not for life, for our United States judges become too autocratic as a general thing. They know that, no matter what happens, they are safe in their positions.

Well, I do not know but what it is best to have a judge entirely free from fear of any kind. Then, if he is an honest man, he can give his decisions without fear or favor.

Cases IV, V and VI. These cases might all except that of Mr. Johnson, come under the he?iding of assumed spinal injuries; but, since the attorney, who drew the petitions did not place them as such, but simply claimed paralysis of one lower extremity, I shall treat them as local paralysis; and, as the case of Mr. Johnson was one of injury to local nerves; and, as there was paralysis of the part, with atrophy of the soft parts, I shall place his under the same heading.

They were all from the same county, two of them received their injuries in or by reason of the same wreck, and all were tried in the same county within the same week.

In about the year 1891 I was directed by the chief surgeon to go to a small town in Chautauqua County, Kansas, and examine a man whom I shall call Joe Benton, a section laborer, who claimed to have been injured while helping to clear a wreck at the Wolf Creek bridge, some three months previously.

When I arrived at the little village and inquired for Benton I was told that I would find him "at the store" where he had "been helping since he was hurt."

I went to "the store," which was the only one in town and which sold everything in every line that the people usually desired to purchase.

I very soon recognized Benton, from descriptions I had had of him. He was a low, heavy set, knotty headed Englishman, whose *H's* were scattered all over the floor, where he had dropped them.

Benton had leaned his crutches against the shelving and was bouncing around behind the counter without them.

He was climbing a ladder and handing down canned goods, weighing out sugar and coffee, and, in fact, was making a general hand in the store.

It was a very hot day and I found a seat and put in a half or three quarters of an hour in watching Benton climb the ladder.

After I was thoroughly rested and had cooled off, I approached him and asked, "Are you Mr. Joseph Benton?"

"Hi ham, sir," he answered, and then I had no further doubts about his identity.

I then told him who I was and the nature of my business there.

There was the usual spectacular change in the countenance, and he had more than the ordinary difficulty in reaching the crutches.

He at once hoisted his right foot upon which he had been both standing and walking and, holding to the counter, he made his way by hopping to his props. He adjusted them and then went over and talked with the proprietor, as I had told him that I wished to see him at his home.

We then repaired to his residence and I then placed him on a lounge and made the best examination I could. I desired to induce him to come to the hospital, where he was entitled to be treated, as he paid his monthly assessment with the rest; and, in lieu of that, to induce him to go to St. Louis and see the general claim agent with the view to a settlement of his case.

"Hi'll 'ave to see Mr. Witney, me attorney," said he. I promised that if he would come to the hospital and let us care for him, I would guarantee that the claim agent would pay him five hundred dollars when he was ready to go to work. I was perfectly safe in making this proposition, as the general claim agent had authorized me to make it; but all I could get in reply was, "Hi'll 'ave to see Mr. Witney, me attorney."

Examination revealed the fact that there was nothing whatever the matter with him.

The general claim agent refused to settle by correspondence, "Mr. Witney" would not allow Benton to go to St. Louis — fearing, no doubt, that, should settlement be made and should he not be present, he would fail to get his fifty per cent "rake off."

Suit was soon brought for twenty thousand dollars damages and, in due time, the case came to trial. Sometime before this case came to trial another case came up in the same county, which was, in all respects, a *facsimile* of the Benton case.

The case was this: Mr. George Bilson, a saw mill hand, had been to Sedan on a trading expedition for himself and others at the saw mill. He was driving a team of old long sorrel mares, hitched to a long wagon tongue of a very long wagon, with a long coupling pole sticking out behind and a mule colt and a dog following. Taken altogether, it made quite a lengthy procession.

At a crossing of the railroad, five miles east of Sedan, they were struck by a passing train, the horses killed, the wagon ruined and Bilson and his half idiot son were thrown about twenty feet, and Bilson's head plowed up the soft ground — producing a few scalp and facial wounds, but nothing serious. The boy was hurt very little.

Bilson brought suit for twenty thousand dollars in a very short time, procured a pair of crutches, lifted his right foot and assumed partial paralysis of his right leg. Strange to say, the same lawyer wrote both petitions and did not allege spinal injury in either case, but alleged a partial paralysis of the right leg, with general contusions and internal injuries.

These two cases with another all came up at the same term of Court and within the same week.

Mr. Joe Benton's case was tried first. It was in evidence that a mixed train — made up of eight or ten freight cars and one passenger coach was wrecked on the Wolf Creek bridge. The wrecking train, with the section men from several sections, was engaged in clearing the wreck off the bridge. To this end they carried a large cable under the bridge and across the creek to a tree, where they fastened it, with block and tackle attached, and by this the engine was to "pull the wreck."

Benton and another man went along with the torches, so as to light the way for the men who were coming carrying the cable, as it was night.

After lighting the way until the cable carriers were across Benton and the other man stopped under the bridge, and we were prepared to prove that they were taking tobacco out of a caddie, which had fallen under the bridge and burst open.

Benton was standing on one end of the stringer, when the engine made a pull and a pair of detached car trucks fell on the other end, broke it loose from its moorings and threw Benton ten feet in the air and he came down head foremost into the creek and came up with both hands full of mud and gravel. This was his own statement.

A passenger named W. H. Johnson, a contractor and builder at Sedan, was hurt in the wreck worse than any one else — he having been thrown across the coach, his hip striking on the comer of a seat and badly contusing the superior gluteal nerves.

Mr. Johnson is one of the six or seven persons I have mentioned who never tried to exaggerate their injuries — hence I give his correct name.

All three of these cases came up for trial during the same week — Benton's case being tried first. Mr. Joe Benton was very adroit but, unfortunately for him, he had not been well coached.

The cross-examination was conducted by Mr. Geo. Gardner, who was acting in the absence of Col. Richards and his assistant, Mr. Benton.

When Mr. Gardner had got the plaintiff down under the bridge he asked:

"Now, Mr. Benton, when you were under the bridge, did you, at any time, think it a dangerous placer

"Yes, sir, hi did," answered plaintiff.

"Do you tell this jury that you at any time, when under the bridge, thought that you were in or were going into a dangerous place? Now, be careful."

"Yes, sir, hi did."

"Now take this drawing, Mr. Benton, and show the jury just where you were when you thought you were in, or were going into a dangerous place."

Benton took the drawing and pointed out the place where he first thought that he was going into a dangerous place. "Hi was a standin — right there," said Benton.

"Now, Mr. Benton, show the jury where you were when you next thought you were in a dangerous place."

Benton again pointed out the stringer he was standing on when he thought he was in a dangerous place.

"What made you think you were in a dangerous place, Mr. Benton?"

"Well, hi looked hup hand saw them trucks a 'anging hover the bride, hand hi thought they might fall w'en they got to pullin'."

Mr. Gardner made plaintiff repeat over and over what he had already sworn to, always beginning with a bantering, "Now, do you tell this jury?" and Mr. Joe Benton grew more positive and emphatic at each repetition of his answer.

All of these answers were absolutely fatal to plaintiff's case; for, in Kansas — and I presume in most of the states — the Supreme Court had decided, time and again, that if the plaintiff went into a place where he believed there was danger, he could pot recover.

The plaintiff's attorneys were in a cold sweat! They had forgotten to post Mr. Benton on this most vital and important point.

Adjournment was here taken for lunch.

When court convened for the afternoon session, plaintiff's attorneys arose and asked permission to put him on the stand again.

"Now, look here," said Judge Troup, a most honorable and just judge, "do I understand that you gentlemen desire to put plaintiff on the stand again, in order to have him contradict his testimony of this morning?"

"Well, yes," sheepishly answered the attorney. "He didn't understand the questions."

"Yes, but he did understand them, for Mr. Gardner repeated the questions over and over and made them so plain that a child might understand them, and yet he persisted and was positive in giving the same answer each time."

Plaintiff's counsel protested mildly, but it did no good.

"I wish to say, once for all," said the judge, "that I will not permit any such practice in this court."

Counsel conferred together very seriously, and then the leading counsel said: "Well, if we can't prove by him what we want to prove, I guess we will not put him on."

"Case dismissed, with prejudice," said the judge.

Now, the lay reader may not know that a case may be dismissed, "without prejudice," and the suit may be renewed, in that or in any other court, but, where a case is dismissed "with prejudice," that ends it and plaintiff cannot renew it in that or in any other court.

Mr. Joe Benton found himself out of court, unable to renew his suit and holding up one leg, minus the five hundred dollars I had offered him and which he might just as well have had in his pocket or in bank at that moment. All he had to show for his perjury and his mule-headed stubbornness was a pair of crutches, which he didn't need, and which, I learned, he discarded the next day.

Before any of the cases were called the court appointed a commission of six physicians, of whose examination and conduct I will speak later on, to examine all of the plaintiffs. By reason of our conclusions all three of the physicians, who had been appointed for the plaintiff, went to counsel for Benton and Bilson and told them that they would better not put them on, as their testimony would be against them. This left counsel without any medical expert witnesses on their side.

Just before Benton's case was called his leading counsel came to me and said: "We have just found out what Benton's trouble really is. It is locomotor ataxia," said he.

"Is that so?" I asked. I did not tell him that locomotor ataxia did not come from an injury, but thought I would let him ascertain that fact during the trial of the case.

"How did you find that out?"

"Haven't you seen a doctor around town that you other doctors call an 'advertising quack?'" he asked.

I admitted that I had seen him.

"Well, we had him examine Benton, after you scared our other doctors off, and he pronounces it *locomotor ataxia,* and he is as smart as lightning, too," said he, "and this is one of his specialties, too. Oh, he'll make you fellows sweat when he gets on the stand."

I didn't offer any objections to having a good sweat, but I thought then that I knew who would do the sweating. This fellow I shall call Kessler; that is very much like his name. When I was introduced to him, I asked: "Did I understand your name is Kessler?"

"Yes," said he; "you've heard of me. I'm commonly called 'Old Kess.'"

"Old Kess." wore a broad brimmed hat, long hair and a three-button Prince Albert coat, and was given to standing on street corners and posing.

Well, at the opportune time, in the trial of Mr. Joe Benton's case, "Old Kess." was put on the stand.

He testified that he had practiced medicine, as a specialist, in Kansas for nineteen years, and, during that time, had treated and cured a great many cases of locomotor ataxia, just like Mr. Benton's.

The plaintiff's attorney handled "Old Kess." very gingerly and disposed of him in short order, for I think he instinctively feared some kind of disaster in connection with his expert.

He did not even ask "Old Kess." how he arrived at the conclusion that plaintiff had locomotor ataxia, nor how he made the examination. When "Old

Kess." was delivered over to the slaughter I sat near Mr. Gardner and wrote questions and otherwise prompted him as well as I could.

I had picked up one of "Old Kess.' hand bills which were thrown around the streets and which bore the heading, "Permanently located in Sedan."

Mr. Gardner then began: "Doctor, how long have you been in Sedan?"

"Four days," answered "Old Kess."

"Where did you come from to Sedan?"

"From Topeka."

"How long were you in Topeka?"

"Two weeks."

"Where were you last before you went to Topeka?"

"McPherson," answered "Old Kess.," and in a very short time Mr. Gardner had chased "Old Kess." into and out of fifteen different towns in Kansas.

"Is this your advertisement, doctor?"

"Yes, sir."

"I see that you have at the head of this advertisement, 'Permanently located in Sedan;' are you as permanently located in Sedan as you were in all the other towns to which you say you have been?"

"Just about, I guess," said "Kess."

"Now, doctor, you say that Mr. Benton has locomotor ataxia, please tell the jury how you arrived at that conclusion."

'Well, sir, I ascertained it by percussion."

"Please tell the jury what percussion is and how you make it."

"Well, sir, you place one hand on the back and strike the fingers with the tips of the fingers of the other hand.

"What did you elicit when you percussed Mr. Benton's back?"

"Well, sir, I elicited resonance."

"Please tell the jury what resonance is, doctor."

"Well, sir, it is a kind of hollow sound."

"Please describe what kind of a hollow sound you elicited when you percussed Mr. Benton's back."

"Well, sir, it was like striking an empty barrel."

"What did that indicate to you?"

"Well, sir, it indicated inflammation."

"Does resonance, obtained by percussion, always indicate inflammation?"

"Yes, sir."

"Invariably?"

"Yes, sir; invariably."

"There is no exception to that rule is there, doctor?"

"None that I know of."

I was busily engaged in writing questions and handing them to Mr. Gardner. I now handed him one which gave "Old Kess." his first real hard fall.

"Doctor, what kind of a sound do you elicit when you percuss over the stomach of a man who has missed his dinner?"

"A hollow sound."

"Is it like the sound you elicited when you are percussing on an empty barrel?"

"Yes, sir."

"It is what you call resonance, is it?"

"Yes, sir."

"Now, doctor, has every man who has missed his dinner got inflammation of the stomach?"

"No, sir."

"You said a few minutes ago that a hollow sound, or resonance, was always indicative of inflammation."

"Well, but you see, Mr. Gardner, this is an exception to the rule."

"Yes, I understand; but you said that there was no exception to this rule."

"No; I don't think I said that exactly."

"Stenographer, read the doctor's answers to the last five or six questions." The stenographer did so.

"Well, if I said that, I didn't understand the question."

The same old refuge, "didn't understand the question!"

"Doctor, what is the cause of locomotor ataxia?"

"Well, sir (when you get those fellows worried they always begin every answer by saying, "Well, sir").

"Well, sir; it is caused by inflammation of the blood vessels there."

"The blood vessels 'there,' but where?"

"Why, in the back there, along the spine."

"What are the names of those blood vessels, doctor?"

"Why, it's just the blood vessels there, along the spine."

"But, doctor, they have a name, have they not?"

"Old Kess." was getting worried and was sweating on the nose and showing other signs of distress. The audience got to laughing at him, and then he began laughing at himself. He would lean back in his chair, shut his eyes and laugh the silliest laugh I ever heard.

"Now, doctor," persisted the tormentor, "you certainly must know the names of those blood vessels; give the jury the names."

"Old Kess." gaped, which showed that he was either bordering on a chill or a collapse.

"Well, now, Mr. Gardner, you understand that I have been practicing as a specialist for nineteen years, and it is not necessary for me to remember the names of blood vessels and little things like that."

"I know, but is not locomotor ataxia included in one of your specialties?"

"Yes, sir."

"Then, doctor, don't you think you ought to know and remember the names of those blood vessels?"

"Well, no; not in a case like this."

Mr. Gardner whispered to me and asked: "Can you think of anything more?"

"This is cruelty to animals, Mr. Gardner; ask him if he would like to make his escape."

"Doctor, would you like to make your escape?"

"Well, yes sir; I believe I would."

"You may make it then," said Mr. Gardner,

"Old Kess." arose and went through the isle so fast that you could have played dominoes on the tail of his Prince Albert. Even the farmers stood up and roared and clapped their hands, so that the sheriff had difficulty in restoring order.

After adjournment I found two mechanics at the door waiting to see me. They grabbed on to me and, pulling me aside, one of them said: "We was jest awaitin' to get a chance to thank you for what you did for us."

"What have I done for you?" I asked.

"Why, you saved us some money."

"Please tell me how I saved you some money."

"Well, this friend of mine and I was raisin' twenty-five dollars apiece to pay that quack for prescribing for our wives. My friend had raised all of his and I had all but five dollars and was promised that this evening; but, since you fellers made such a monkey of him, we wouldn't let him prescribe for a dog of our'n."

The late "Old Kess." took the early train the next morning and was soon "late" from Sedan.

Mr. George Bilson's case was then called. The testimony was about as heretofore detailed, with the addition that we were prepared to prove that, when the engine struck the horses and wagon, Bilson was lying back under a partial cover of the wagon eating cheese and crackers and his son was driving.

To the right of Bilson's train of horses, wagons, mule colt and dog there was a hedge fence which ran parallel to the country road and at right angles to the railroad.

Bilson swore that this hedge was so thick that he could not see the approaching train through it, at any point. We had had that hedge examined and were prepared to prove that there were openings in it every few feet that you could throw a horse blanket through and not touch the hedge.

Bilson was a typical "Branch water man" (see "Stories of a Country Doctor," by the author), had always "lived at the back of some one else's field and drunk branch water, in preference to digging a well," and was extremely ignorant.

However, for an ignorant man, he was quite adroit in evading Mr. Gardner's questions.

Mr. Gardner pressed him, however, got him into corners, made him contradict himself again and again, until it got so hard that Bilson broke down and bawled like a calf.

The controversy over the hedge fence became so hot that Mr. Gardner was prepared to take the jury out to the place on a hastily made up train and permit them to see the hedge. The court had given its consent for this to be done, so the plaintiff's counsel took a voluntary dismissal — fearing, no doubt, that this case might also be dismissed "with prejudice."

Bilson's attorney had a long conference with him; and, soon afterwards, Bilson went out into the court house grounds and cut up some peculiar antics; amongst others he tried to climb a tree.

Bilson's attorney went into the Probate Court, swore out a warrant and had his client arrested — charging him with being insane. This was done for the purpose of getting rid of Bilson's testimony — given that day — when they renewed the suit in some other court.

In case Bilson could be shown to have been insane at the time he testified that day, no court would permit the counsel for the defense to read from this testimony, and use it against him.

Mr. Gardner came to me and said: "Doctor, I want you to go into the Probate Court and try this insanity charge against Bilson. The case is going to come up right away. I have got to defend some overflow cases in the Circuit Court and cannot attend to it and I want you to go in there and try it for me."

"Will the Probate Judge permit me to appear as counsel?" I asked.

"Oh, yes," said he, "anybody can act as counsel in the Probate Court, in Kansas."

"All right." I answered, and I went out to where Bilson was sitting under the tree he had made an effort to climb. There was a crowd around him and Bilson was batting his eyes like a toad that had just hopped out from his habitat under a stump on a frosty morning. Two of the doctors who had been summoned for plaintiff came along just at this juncture and I seized onto them and said: "Here, I want you doctors to examine this man with a view to testifying in the Probate Court."

They examined Bilson, tested the reaction of his pupils, and found them normal. They asked him several questions, but Bilson stared at them and did not answer.

The case was called immediately and I went in and announced that I appeared for Bilson to defend him against the charge of insanity.

The situation was quite ludicrous. There was one of Bilson's attorneys appearing against him and I, the chief medical witness against him in the other case, defending him.

A jury was soon impaneled and the attorney put on two or three witnesses whose testimony amounted to nothing. Both of my medical witnesses testified that they had heard Bilson testify, and that, while he was not an educated man, they regarded him as having shown a great deal of shrewdness in

116

evading and parrying Mr. Gardner's questions, and they regarded him as having been perfectly sane when testifying. I called up three men from amongst the spectators, who had heard Bilson's testimony, and they corroborated the doctors.

"Do you want to argue the case?" asked the attorney.

"No," I said, "unless you do."

'Well, we will not argue it then," said he.

I was so swelled up with the importance of my position that really I would have liked to address the jury, just for the novelty of the thing, but the case was submitted without argument.

The jury retired and, in a few minutes, brought in a verdict finding that Bilson was sane.

The Johnson case was then called and heard. The testimony was brief and the case soon submitted.

The jury hung; and on a very peculiar point. In Kansas counsel may submit any number of special questions, to be answered by the jury, and the answers to these special questions must tally with their general verdict. They failed to agree on the cause of the wreck.

During that week Mr. Gardner tried cases which amounted in the aggregate to fifty-two thousand five hundred dollars.

One case was dismissed "with prejudice," one took a voluntary dismissal, and a verdict for eight hundred dollars was rendered against him in the overflow case. This was considered a fair showing for one week's work.

Bilson again brought suit in another court and the jury rendered a verdict against him. Mr. Johnson's case was tried again — the jury giving a verdict for three thousand dollars. This was appealed and the Supreme Court reversed and remanded it.

At the next trial the jury gave him a verdict for nine thousand dollars. This was also appealed, and, after several years, they affirmed the verdict.

The company paid Mr. Johnson, in interest and all, between ten and eleven thousand dollars, and he got no more than he was entitled to.

When he was on the stand his attorneys tried to get his trouble into the hip joint, but Mr. Johnson would not have it.

"No, sir," he would say. "It is not in my hip joint. It is above the joint and right where Dr. King says those nerves are, and I believe he is right about it."

I should have related something regarding the action of the commission of six physicians who were appointed to examine the several plaintiffs.

We met in the local physician's office. We first assembled in the private office and I said to them:

"Now, gentlemen, you know how a lawyer enjoys getting a doctor on the witness stand and, if he can, making him appear ridiculous before the public. The attorneys on the plaintiff's side will 'make monkeys' out of my two local surgeons and myself, if they can, and we have an attorney here who, I understand, is a perfect terror on cross-examination. Now, let me tell you what is the sensible thing for us to do. Let us examine those men and then meet in this room and hold a consultation— just as if we were going to treat them. I have with me a battery by which to make the test for reaction of degeneration."

I then went on and explained how this test was made.

"Now," I said, "after we have examined those men, I am prepared to go upon the witness stand and swear that they are paralyzed, in case our examination shows that they are; and, if we find that they are not paralyzed and that there is nothing the matter with them I am sure that you gentlemen will be just as frank and will go upon the stand and testify to the truth."

They were all bright and honorable country physicians and they readily acquiesced in my proposition. After our deliberations they went to the attorneys for the plaintiff and withdrew — telling them that, in case they put them on the stand, their testimony would be against them in the Benton and Bilson cases.

That was what so upset plaintiff's counsel and caused him to put "Old Kess." on the stand.

The arrangement that we made and our consultation and perfect agreement in all the cases was the most satisfactory arrangement that I ever saw made in the trial of an important case.

Chapter Six - Paraplegia

Case I. NOT long since I had notice that I had been appointed as one of a commission of three physicians, who were to meet at a certain office at a certain hour and on a certain day, there to examine a five-year-old child, a boy, who was paralyzed in both lower extremities, and was told that suit had been brought against the city by the father, as the next friend, for twenty thousand dollars damages.

We met and found the mother there with the child, a boy, in advance of us. We questioned the mother and got a fairly good history of the child and of the accident, which was supposed to have caused the paralysis.

We stripped the child and examined him carefully and found him to be totally paralyzed in both lower extremities, except the anterior muscles of the thighs. Otherwise the child was in perfect health.

The mother gave the history of the accident which preceded the paralysis, which was as follows:

When the child was three years old she and her husband went out walking. There was an old board sidewalk and at one point there was a part of one board that had decayed and had been torn out, leaving a hole about six by ten inches; that the child stepped into this hole with its right foot; that the leg went into the hole up to the body, when the child toppled over to one side and screamed. The father took it up and carried it home. It continued to cry and to complain of its right foot, which was limp, hanging helpless and highly sensitive.

The accident was on Wednesday, and the child continued to suffer until Saturday, when they sent for a physician. It continued to grow worse until the next Tuesday, when they discovered that both of its legs were totally paralyzed.

The child's general health grew better then; but, notwithstanding treatment, he had continued to be paralyzed.

The case was, from the standpoint of the mother's story, a puzzling one. Of course, we did not believe for a moment that the fall had had anything to do with the subsequent paralysis; for, if a child could be paralyzed from such an insignificant fall as it sustained, roystering, romping children, which fall quite often, would be paralyzed every day.

It could not well be polio-myelitis, for that usually results in paralysis on one side only. I say "usually," for I never saw a case of paralysis of both lower extremities from polio-myelitis — that is, from inflammation of one of the anterior columns of the cord.

The only conclusion that we could come to, under the circumstances, was that it must have been a case of transverse myelitis, or a haemorrhage, and, even then, we were not satisfied as to the cause.

We had two meetings and discussed the case; and, soon afterward, the case was called for trial.

The witnesses had been put under "the rule;" that is, only one witness was allowed in the court room at a time and he the one who was testifying.

The doctors assembled in an ante-room — waiting to be called. Finally I was called in. The assistant city counsellor asked me about my having examined the child and then asked me the following hypothetical question:

"Supposing a child, three years old, healthy and active, is walking on a street on a Wednesday afternoon, that it steps into a hole in a board sidewalk, that the leg goes into the hole up to the child's body, that it topples over and screams and complains of its right foot, that the right foot is limp and helpless and exceedingly sensitive to the touch, that it is taken home and that it continues to be helpless, that on Saturday the child is growing worse and a physician is called and that he finds the child has a temperature of one hundred and five degrees, that the child becomes unconscious, on Saturday, and continually draws its lower extremities up, and that this continues until Tuesday, when the fever abates, consciousness returns and the legs are extended on the bed and are found to be paralyzed, and that they have continued to be paralyzed until the present time, what would you say as to whether or not the paralysis was caused by an injury received in the fall on the sidewalk?"

"Why," said I, "this is an entirely new case. There are elements in that question which the mother did not give us at the time we examined the child

— the high temperature, the unconsciousness and the drawing up of the legs."

"Well, what would you say, since hearing the statement of the case as you have just heard it, and as it was given by the parents and attending physician?"

"I would say that the child had cerebro-spinal meningitis and that the paralysis was caused by the cerebro-spinal meningitis," I answered.

I was then permitted to give my reasons for my opinion, and to go into a differentiation between the symptoms arising from cerebro-spinal meningitis and spinal cord injuries and diseases.

When plaintiff's attorney cross-examined me he asked if the child had had an injury to the spinal cord from which an inflammation had ensued, would not the symptoms, which I attributed to cerebro-spinal meningitis, have occurred. I answered that they could not and that children did not have high temperatures and become unconscious from spinal cord injuries or inflammations. We had an unusually bright and able lot of physicians for the defense and they all testified that it was an unmistakable case of cerebro-spinal meningitis, and that the fall could not, in the very nature of things, have had anything to do with the paralysis.

The physician who had attended the child had testified that the high temperature and the unconsciousness had arisen from an inflammation of the cord and that this inflammation had been caused by an injury to the cord received in the fall, which went to show that he was not an expert neurologist.

And this kind of doctors are ignorantly swearing away the money of corporations every day.

Strange to say, the jury gave a straight-out verdict for the city.

Some persons were mean enough to say or suggest that the child had not fallen at all, but had become paralyzed and then the parents, in looking about them to secure the future of the crippled child, had bethought them of a suit against the city. Others thought that, perhaps, the child had fallen, as testified to by the parents, and that the meningitis was wholly disconnected from the matter of the fall, but that the parents had ignorantly associated the two together.

The man and his wife seemed to be fairly reputable people, of the working class, and it was hard to associate anything dishonest with their effort to recover damages from the city. So that it was easier and more reasonable to suppose that they had ignorantly associated the fall with the child's future condition than that they had attempted to do anything dishonest.

Case II. Several years ago, in a conversation with a superintendent of the Missouri, Kansas & Texas Railroad, at Denison, Texas, he told me of the following remarkable case:

"Several years ago," said he, "a suit was brought against this company by an Irishman, on the extreme southern part of the road, near Taylor. He alleged that, at some time previous to the bringing of the suit, he had gone to a small town a few miles distant from where he lived, and that, on his way home in the late afternoon, being somewhat intoxicated, he sat down on the end of a tie to rest near a country road crossing. He was afoot and was using the railroad track as a highway.

"He claimed that he went to sleep and that the passenger train came along and did not ring the bell nor blow the whistle for the crossing, and that the engine struck him and knocked him off the end of a tie, and produced a severe lacerated wound of the scalp, and so, permanently injured him.

"He placed his measure of damages at ten thousand dollars.

"We regarded the case as being an exceedingly dangerous one, for, while the Irishman was guilty, in a certain sense, of contributory negligence, by sitting down and going to sleep where he did, yet this was a question for the jury, and juries in Texas are always disposed to give the plaintiff the benefit of the doubt, and to give the railroad corporations the worst of it; and their verdicts for damages in such cases are simply outrageous.

"The Supreme Court is our only protection, and it does not always protect us as we think it should.

"We sent a special man down to that part of the country to investigate the case and this is what he learned: The Irishman did go to the small town at the time he said he did, as alleged in the petition. He also got drunk and bought a gallon jug of whiskey and took the railroad track for home. When he came to this particular spot he ran across the section foreman and his three or four men of that section.

"They were all Irishmen and this plaintiff invited them to partake of the contents of his jug, which they did quite freely.

"They all got drunk, and, after a time, got into a general all around free for all fight. In the melee one of the men grabbed the Irishman's jug and struck him on the head with it, producing the severe scalp wound which he claimed had been produced by the engine.

"Our special man found the pieces of the broken jug and brought some of them back with him, which he turned over to our law department. He also procured affidavits of the section foreman and his men, in which they all stated the facts as above narrated.

"Of course, our attorneys showed these affidavits to plaintiff's attorney and they at once withdrew the suit But, if we had not investigated the case, as we did, this man would, perhaps, have secured a large verdict against us."

Chapter Seven - Female Organs of Reproduction

Case I. IN a wreck on the Lexington and Southern near Nevada, Mo., on June 29, 1889, a lady, whom I shall call Mrs. Pryor, claimed to have been injured. She was a married woman, married the second time, in fact, she having been divorced from her first husband, but had no children. She was about forty years old. It was in evidence at the trial that when she came out of the wrecked car she stood on the bank above the wreck and exploded in the following language:

"Oh, yes! this is the way old Jay Gould treats his passengers is it? Well, I'll show him. Just look at my clothing and at this sealskin sacque! Oh, I'll make him pay for all this, and I'll make him pay me two hundred and fifty dollars for this sealskin, for that's what it cost when it was new. I'll show him! and, besides my clothing I'm hurt and all bruised up and he'll pay for it all. I'll show him whether he does, or not!"

This testimony was given at the trial, but Mrs. Pryor denied it in her deposition — which was used at the trial — she having resorted to the familiar trick of not coming to the trial, but remained at home in bed, and her husband and friends testified that she was confined to her bed on account of the injuries received at the wreck, a year or more before.

The case was hotly contested. The plaintiff's counsel got in a good deal of testimony as to her serious injuries and of her consequent disabilities. The Court appointed Dr. Geo. Halley and myself to examine her at her residence. When we got ready to make the examination Mr. Pryor informed me that I couldn't examine her. I asked, "why not?"

"Well," said he, "there is no use in so many examining her. Dr. Halley can examine her and tell you what he finds."

"But, I cannot testify to what Dr. Halley finds, Mr. Pryor, that is hearsay evidence."

"I don't care. I'm not going to have so many examine her and hurtin' her. I don't care what the Court orders."

"Very well," I said, "The Court ordered me to examine her. I have no desire whatever to examine Mrs. Pryor, 'except to obey the order of the Court. I shall have to report to the Judge that you would not permit me to carry out his order."

"I don't care what you report You are not going to examine her."

And, so, we returned to the Court. When I was put on the witness stand Judge Robinson asked me:

"Did you examine Mrs. Pryor this morning, doctor?"

I answered that I did not.

"You didn't examine her! Why, didn't I order you to examine her?" asked the trial Judge.

"You did, your Honor, but Mr. Pryor refused to permit me to examine her."

I then told the Court the whole of Mr. Pryor's conduct, and expected to see Mr. Pryor arraigned and fined, for contempt of Court; but the Court did not do it. In fact, he never referred to it again.

As stated before the fight was a hot and bitter one. Every inch of ground was fought over and contended for.

After the plaintiff closed Judge Robinson began to put on roadmasters of other roads and have them testify as to "creeping of rails" and as to the effect of intense heat on the rails. He went extensively into the question of laying track, and of the use of the "shim" between the ends of the rails in order to provide against expansion from heat and for the "creeping of the rails." It seems that the traffic between Joplin and Kansas City is much heavier towards Kansas City; and that, as a consequence, the rails are always creeping toward the latter place.

One section foreman testified that, in the time he had had charge of the section they had cut out one whole rail, piece by piece.

Then came the question of the effect of heat on the rails. It was shown that when the rails creep in one direction until all of the space between the ends is used up, then, when the rails get hot, something must give way. It is usually one of two things — the rails will spread outward or, else, "buckle," that is, bend upward, and this is apt to occur on a curve and while a heavy engine is passing over them.

Judge Robinson was almost ready to put the agent at Nevada on the stand to prove that at the very hour when this wreck occurred the temperature at his station — six miles from the place of the wreck — was one hundred and two degrees in the shade.

The plaintiff's attorney, who was sitting just in front of Judge Robinson leaned back and whispered to the latter. The Judge whispered to him; then they both nodded.

The witness, in the meantime, was waiting to be further examined.

"That will do." "We rest," said Judge Robinson, "We have settled the case Your Honor."

I don't think I ever saw more surprise and curiosity manifested over a little matter as there was over this. Nobody knew when or how it was done. It seemed that, when plaintiff's attorney, leaned back and whispered to Judge Robinson, he asked:

"How much will you give me to quit?"

"A thousand dollars," whispered the Judge.

"How much will you give me in the husband's suit?" again whispered the attorney.

"A hundred and fifty," answered the Judge.

"All right," said plaintiff's attorney. And then the case closed.

I understood that Mrs. Pryor got up as soon as the settlement was made and that she did not complain further either of her head or of her left ovary — the latter having been her chief complaint before and during the trial of the case.

I have spent a great deal of my time within the last forty years in studying the female organs of reproduction, and in operating upon them and treating them when operations and treatment were needed; and I have also taught both students and the profession what I had learned of those organs, and I feel, therefore, that I can say, without being accused of egotism or boasting, that I think I know more than the ordinary "backwoods doctor" about those organs and I confess that it is very, very hard for me to see or understand how a woman can hurt her ovaries, or how they can be injured in such a wreck as the one in which plaintiff in this case claimed to have been injured. The truth is, I do not believe it possible.

If some brother who reads this book thinks that he knows, will he kindly tell me and the profession and the world at large how it can be done?

She is seated in the ordinary coach and, when the derailment and the sudden stop come, she pitches forward.

I confess that she may bump her forehead or receive an abrasion on her knee, or on her elbow, and I can see how she may sprain her wrist or her finger or her thumb, but I cannot see how she can receive an injury to her ovaries. It is simply impossible and the woman who claims to have received such injuries is either self-deceived, or, I fear, she is trying to deceive others.

I don't like to say this of the sex; but, I have heard so much and so many of these impossible stories from women, about injuries to their wombs, ovaries and spinal cords that I have lost much of the respect I once held for many of the sex.

A good woman is today just what she has always been and always will be — the very best and loveliest of all of God's creatures. Mind you, I say "a good woman," but, a bad woman is just what she has always been and always will be — the very worst of all of God's creation.

Where a woman decides to abandon the paths of truth, honor, righteousness and to sell her immortal soul for a little money, with which to make a vain and gaudy display before the world, she sinks lower than anybody and she stops at nothing. I know that she will teach her tender little daughter and her little boy to perjure themselves to the best advantage and she will do this with, apparently, no compunctions of conscience at all.

It would be a painful task for me to write the fact if I thought that every woman would commit perjury, or if I thought that even a considerable percentage of them would do so. I do not believe such a thing to be true.

In a railroad wreck, where there are thirty or forty in an overturned coach, where the coach has been suddenly stopped or jarred, where no one is hurt at all, where no marks are shown on anyone, one or two perhaps will complain of being badly injured, while the others will rejoice publicly that they are not hurt at all. Or, there may be women and men who have been hurt and who can exhibit wounds, injuries, discolorations, swellings and so forth, but who, in time, recover.

Now, if a person claims to have been injured, although the surgeon cannot discover any signs of injury, he is bound to admit that such person has recovered. The great objection I make to some women and to men also, who claim to have been injured, is that they never get well, or at least, so long as there is a suit for damages pending, or so long as they have not been paid.

Men and women get well from hurts in other walks of life, or from hurts inflicted in other ways, and under circumstances where there is no opportunity to get money, now why do they not get well from a small cut, laceration or contusion when it has been inflicted in a railroad accident, or by a railroad corporation, in such a way, or under such circumstances as will permit them to bring suit for large sums of money?

People who can and do get over insignificant injuries which are inflicted in a way and under conditions and circumstances where there is no chance to recover damages, ought to recover from the same character of injury when inflicted by a corporation, or by some one and in some way which will permit the person to collect damages.

I cannot understand either, why such a person should remain disabled and in pain so long and then recover so soon after settlement has been made. I have known a woman to recover and leave her bed in one day — a woman who had been in bed and complaining of pain and disability for months.

One cannot help saying that such persons are dishonest and that they are guilty of falsehood and false pretenses under such circumstances.

No man can consent to live with such a woman, unless he is such a man as she is a woman — a dishonest pretender and willing to perjure himself and to have his wife and children do the same, in order to get a little money. I know that, in this commercial age, a majority of people pay little attention to such things and seem to regard the matter of a man or woman committing perjury, or teaching their little sons and daughters to do so, as a matter of course, and to be expected under the circumstances.

This kind of lax morals seems to be percolating into and permeating our whole social fabric, and, in time, it cannot do otherwise than to cause that social fabric to rot to its very foundation.

This is enough to cause any good man or woman to fear for the future of his country and his people.

As the race grows older and as so-called, civilized conditions increase those things will and do grow worse.

I feel very much like advocating a return to the primitive conditions that existed when I was a boy and when this good state of Missouri was young.

I prefer to see the day again (which, however, I shall never see) when there are no locks on the front doors, when "the latch string is always on the outside," when neighbor thought more of the welfare of others than he did of self, and when people did not need money with which to dress and to make a fine appearance before the world.

However, I presume that this has been the history of the world. Nations rise up and grow and what is termed civilization comes to them, want and desire increase, people grow selfish and begin to covet the neighbor's ox and his ass, and, in time, the whole fabric grows rotten and, by its own rottenness and its own weight, falls to the ground.

Then come confusion, fear, riot, murder, ruin, and the army steps in and, in the name of law and order, settles things and then— ABSOLUTE MONARCHY.

Case II. Several years ago a doctor of my acquaintance wrote our general claim agent and continued to write him, making claim against the company for an alleged injury to his, the doctor's wife. He stated that on a certain afternoon his wife had returned home from a visit to a nearby town. She came in one of the coaches of the regular Missouri Pacific train. The doctor had met her at the depot. He stated that when she alighted from the coach she had their ten or twelve months' old babe in her arms, and that the porter was slow in assisting her, so that when she stepped upon the platform her 'limbs gave way and she fell upon her knees, skinning and seriously and permanently injuring them.

The general claim agent replied to him and promised to call and try to adjust the matter. The doctor kept writing, as the claim agent did not find that he could go right at once.

Finally, however, he found himself in that region and so stopped off at the little town, where the doctor lived. He called upon the doctor at his office and after some conversation, they repaired to the doctor's residence.

After he was introduced to the doctor's wife and some commonplace remarks, he told the doctor's wife that he had come to talk with her about her injury and, if possible to settle it.

The woman looked at him with wide open eyes and exclaimed, "My injuries! What injuries?" "Why the injury to your knees, falling on the depot platform," said he, "and about which your husband has been writing me and claiming damages. He said that you were quite badly hurt."

"Wh-a-a-a-t?" exclaimed the astonished lady, then turning on her sheepish husband, "did you write this gentleman and say that I was badly injured, and make a claim for damages?" she asked.

The husband twisted and squirmed and looked at the ceiling, "Ye-e-s," said he, "I thought that you were hurt a good deal worse than you thought you were, and I thought it best."

"You thought it best, the dog's foot! Why, I'm ashamed of you. I was not hurt to speak of at all — just a little abrasion on my knees, and I never went to bed a single minute because of it."

"Well," said Mr. Jones, "then I presume you don't make any claim."

"No, sir. I do not. I would be ashamed of myself to claim damages for such an insignificant thing, and I am ashamed of the doctor for having annoyed you about it If I had known that he was going to do it I would certainly have stopped him. If I had been really injured and the railroad company had been to blame I suppose that I would claim damages as quick as anybody, but I will not make a dishonest claim, nor will I ask for damages when there is nothing due."

"Then you do not object to signing this release," said Mr. Jones.

"No, sir, I don't," and she signed it promptly.

Mr. Jones said that he had no doubt that the doctor spent his time at the office that evening, for, from the war cloud that he could see gathering on the wife's brow, he was sure there would be war.

But, anyway, here was an honest woman and a dishonest man.

It is a rare thing that a woman gets hurt by a corporation that her attorney does not allege injury to the organs of procreation — usually the uterus — no matter, what the character of any other injuries she may have sustained, may be.

They seem to take it for granted that there is no trouble in convincing a jury that a woman's womb has been hurt, simply because she has a womb and that no one else except a woman has.

Case III. — Not long since I was called by telephone by the trial attorney of the Metropolitan Street Railway, of this city, to come to one of the divisions of our Circuit Court to testify as an expert in a case against the Street Railway Company. I asked him what the case was.

"Well," said he, "it is the case of a woman against the Metropolitan and I can't very well give you the details of the case over the telephone. I simply want you to answer some hypothetical questions. Please come as quick as you can, for I wish to put you on the stand as soon as you get here."

I went down. When I got into the Court room he said, "take the witness stand, Dr. King."

I did so. In a hasty glance over the persons sitting inside the bar railing I saw a little, scrawney woman, sitting beside an anti-corporation lawyer and concluded that she must be the plaintiff in the case. After I had been sworn the attorney asked me the following hypothetical question.

"Dr. King, suppose that one year ago, a woman, thirty-four years old, married and the mother of three children and who is again *enciente*, at four months, is riding on a street car, at six o'clock in the afternoon, and that, when she stands up preparatory to getting off, the car gives a sudden jerk and she is thrown forward and is struck on the lower part of the abdomen by the. corner of the seat in front of her, that she suffers greatly, that then she goes home and suffers all night with what seem to be labor pains, and that she has a miscarriage, at four months, at six o'clock the next morning, that she flows a great deal afterward and continues to flow for days and weeks, that two weeks after the accident she sends for a physician; then, when he comes, he finds a part of the afterbirth retained, and that he uses the curette and removes it, and that he has to curette several times afterward, that she flows for four weeks and then ceases and that she then leaves her bed, but is very weak and that she has continued to be weak ever since, and that she has been under the treatment of different physicians, since, but continues to suffer from womb trouble, what would you, from your experience as a physician, say as to whether or not the blow she received by the comer of the car seat was the cause of the miscarriage and of her continued and present trouble?"

"I cannot very well answer that question," I answered. "There are elements or at least there is one element in the question that is not true; it assumes an impossibility."

"We object to the witness criticising the question; let him answer it;" interposed plaintiff's attorney.

"What are your objections to the question, doctor?" asked the Court.

"There is an element in the question which is not true, which cannot be true and hence there is an assumption of an impossibility."

"State the particular element in the question that you regard as being untrue, and your reasons for regarding it as untrue," said the Court.

"Well, the question assumes that she was struck by the comer of the car seat at six o'clock and that twelve hours afterward, she miscarried as a consequence of that blow. That is assuming an impossibility and, in the very nature of things it cannot be true."

"Why not?" asked the street car company's attorney.

"Well," I said, "the womb is composed of a body and a neck, and, in the normal unimpregnated state the neck is as long as or longer than the body. When pregnancy takes place the body of the womb grows larger to accommodate the growing foetus, but the neck remains practically the same until about the seventh month, when it expands and, for the time, becomes a part of the body, as if a gourd handle were expanded and became a part of the body of the gourd. "Now, when a woman miscarries at four months that neck must dilate and, unless it is dilated by the contractions or the physician dilates it, it takes days and days for it to dilate sufficiently to permit the exit of a four months foetus. A woman, under such circumstances, usually goes about and suffers the pains consequent upon the contractions necessary to dilitation and flows for one or two weeks, or even longer, but it cannot occur in twelve hours. That is why I say the question assumes an impossibility."

"Well," said plaintiff's attorney, "suppose that it did occur, then what would you say?"

"I would say that she was getting ready to miscarry before she received the blow, and that the blow only precipitated the miscarriage a little sooner, or acted as an exciting cause, when the predisposing cause was already present"

'The Metropolitan attorney then called other physicians who testified as I did; and yet the jury gave her one thousand dollars.

The conductor and gripman of the car knew nothing of the case. Both testified that the lady had not made complaint nor had she by word or act called their attention to the fact that she had been hurt, nor could either of them remember that there had been such a lurch or jar of their train as to cause anyone to fall or get hurt.

Their attention had not been called to this woman's case, in fact, until suit was brought, which was months afterward.

She received her verdict on her own unsupported testimony (except her physician's testimony) as she stated that she did not know anyone on the car and had not called the attention of any one to the fact that she had received such a blow, although she testified that she was made very sick and blind by the violence of the blow, and could scarcely get home.

It would, as a matter of common fairness, be right that, under such circumstances, a woman, before she could recover damages, should be required to show that she either called the attention of the conductor to the fact that she had been hurt, or that she should have called the attention of some other passengers to the fact.

They will give as a reason why they did not that they were embarrassed and ashamed to call attention to themselves, on account of their delicate condition, yet for the sake of getting some of the street railway corporations money, they will go upon the stand and before men and strangers, the Judge, the attorneys, the jury and the mixed audience, they will talk about their wombs, about being pregnant and flowing and miscarrying, and they will do this with an effrontery that is astonishing.

I surely for one have no sympathy for such pretended modesty, for it is all a pretense and a sham. Such cases are being continually trumped up against street railway corporations and against cities and in cases, too, where the plaintiff had not sustained a fall or blow of any kind, at the hands of the street railways or the city, and they get verdicts and collect thousands and tens of thousands of dollars by such dishonest methods. And yet, our newspapers will continue to harp about train robberies and train robbers, and about "The tall man and the short man" who held up the street railway conductor at the remote end of the line and, at the muzzle of a pistol, made him give up his change.

Why, to my way of thinking, train robbers and "hold up" men are eminently respectable as compared with those who hold up the corporations through fraud, malingering and perjury.

Not long since, in conversation with a lawyer on this subject I expressed the opinion that, in many, very many instances, people brought suit and recovered damages from street railways and from cities, who had not been hurt at all, or if they had been hurt, it had been in some other way and that the idea of collecting damages from the street railway company was an afterthought.

"Why, I know it is an afterthought," said he, "I can give you a case in point:"

"Not long since," said he, "a man whom I know very well came into my office, and after the usual salutations and greetings, I asked after his health."

"Oh, I am pretty well," said he, "except that I am awful sore."

"What made you sore?" I asked.

"Why," said he, "I was going home a few nights ago, and, in my hurry, I cut across some vacant lots. It was quite dark and I was walking pretty fast. In some way I caught my foot and fell and I thought for a while I had just bursted myself wide open. I never had such a fall, and while there are no cuts or visible bruises, I am as sore as if I had been beaten with a club.

"Why, you are foolish," I said to him.

"Why so?" he asked.

"Why don't you claim that you fell on the street, by reason of a bad or defective sidewalk, and then sue the city and collect damages. That is the way to speculate and raise the wind in these days."

"We laughed over the suggestion and I thought no more about it, until two weeks afterwards, I saw in the court house items that a suit had been brought by a prominent corporation lawyer, who employs a "snitch," in the name of my friend and against the city, on account of injuries received by falling on a defective sidewalk, claiming permanent injuries and placing his damages at ten thousand dollars, and he is a pretty reputable man, too," said he.

"No, he is not," I said, "he is at heart a thief and a robber and ought to go to the penitentiary."

"And do you propose to stupidly sit by and see this man rob your city and say not a word?" I asked.

"Why, of course," said he. "It is none of my business."

"Yes, but it is your business," I said.

"You should inform the city counsellor and have him call you as a witness and thus defeat this rascal in his attempted robbery."

"And lose his friendship and his legal business?" said he.

"Oh, no, I am not such a fool as that. I would have had this case, but he knew me well enough to know that I would not take such a case; so he went to the 'snitch' lawyer, but, I will continue to be his attorney in all honest litigation."

And so it goes.

Chapter Eight - Injuries to the Eyes

Case I. — IN 1899 I was directed to assist Judge Elijah Robinson, company's attorney, in bringing out the medical evidence in a case in which a United States mail clerk claimed that he had lost an eye, on account of the carelessness of a Missouri Pacific employee — an agent at a small station on the L. & S. Branch, between Kansas City and Joplin.

I do not give this case for the purpose of showing any malingering or false swearing, for I believe the man was perfectly honest and that he swore to the truth, as he understood the matter, but I give it more for the purpose of showing the curious suits that are brought against a railroad company, and the rare manner in which men may be hurt.

This man brought suit for ten thousand dollars damages. His own testimony and that of the agent constituted about all the evidence except a few oculists for and against the plaintiff, and they did not differ materially, except as to the manner and force with which the mail sack was thrown.

Plaintiff testified that, when the train stopped at the station, he opened the door of the mail car and the agent began to throw in the mail sacks. I do not remember how it happened that there were so many sacks at so small a station, but believe it was where another line crossed the L. & S. and this was a transfer point.

These cloth mail sacks are tied with a small rope, about a quarter of an inch in diameter. Each separate piece of rope has a knot right on the outer end. The rope and the knot are almost as hard as wood.

When the sack is tied and the rope is drawn tight there is about a foot of spare rope with the knot on the outer end. Of course, when a sack is thrown, these little footlong, hard ropes swish and whizz around like so many small whips.

The mail agent said that the railroad agent was throwing the sacks in and he was grabbing and throwing them back as fast as he could. He said that the railroad agent seemed to be in a hurry and was throwing the sacks very rapidly and with great force and violence. As he had thrown one sack back, out of his way, he turned and had stooped forward to pick up another one and, as he did so, the railroad agent, without waiting for him to pick the sack up and get his head out of the way, threw another one with great force and the knot on the rope struck him on the right eye lid, I say "on" the right eye because he was looking down, the lid was partially closed and the knot struck on the lid and not on the naked eye ball.

The eye pained him at once, and it continued to pain him without cessation. He went to an oculist within a few days and had the eye examined. The oculist testified that he found an inflammation of the retina — that is, an inflammation of that part of the posterior and inner part of the globe upon which images of objects are formed. It is made by the spreading out of the optic nerve, after it enters the posterior part of the globe.

A number of oculists testified in the case and the consensus of opinion was that the man was either totally blind, or nearly so, in that eye.

The jury gave him a verdict for ten thousand dollars.

I presume that, in making up its decision the Supreme Court will consider two points and only two, viz: The question of liability and that of contributory negligence, as the plaintiff continued to work when all of the specialists said he should have taken a layoff and given his time solely to the task of saving that eye.

I should have said, in the introduction to this case, that a great many cases of injury to the eye come to the railroad surgeon, and they are almost wholly of two classes — section laborers and machinists.

Section laborers get their eyes hurt quite frequently by a piece of steel flying off the head of a spike maul and striking someone in the eye. Where such a piece of steel does fly off it goes with the velocity and force of a Krag-Jorgenson bullet, and usually penetrates the eye very deeply.

In doing so it traverses all of the media of the eye and, if it be of any size, it is apt to lacerate and wound the different media very badly. A very common result is a dislocation of the crystalline lens into the anterior chamber.

In the shops the machinists often suffer from the same character of accidents. In either case it often sets up a pan-ophthalmitis, or a slow inflammation of the deeper structures of the eye, and it is often the case that the eye must be removed in order to save the other from what it is called "sympathetic inflammation." Indeed, I believe that the better class of oculists are about agreed upon the idea that, when it is found that the different media of the eye have been destroyed, so as to render the eye useless, and if the piece of steel cannot be removed, the proper and wise thing to do is to remove the eye ball at once.

Case II. — Several years ago I was called upon to assist the company's attorney. Judge Elijah Robinson, in the defense of a case in which the plaintiff claimed to have sustained an injury which resulted in the loss of one of his eyes.

Plaintiff had, many years before this, been a switchman in the employment of the Missouri Pacific in Kansas City, and claimed to have been struck in the eye by a large, hot cinder, which was thrown from a smoke stack which had a worn out and defective screen.

Plaintiff did not bring suit until the time limit of three years had been almost exhausted and, after he did bring suit, there were continuances and delays, so that the case came to trial many years after he claimed to have lost his eye.

Plaintiff came into Court with one eye undoubtedly "out." It was a peculiar looking eye, the whole of the cornea being infiltrated so that it was all a milky white in color and gave the eye the appearance of a fried egg, which had been broken up somewhat in being fried!

He was, to all appearances, a very ordinary fellow and it was plain to be seen that he was not an enthusiastic leader in Sunday school work.

When looking at his eye and the general expression of his countenance I could not help thinking of the four men who were playing cards. One of them was a one-eyed man. He had but one eye and the other eye was of the fried egg variety. He had a big moustache, a goodly amount of thick tangled hair and, in all respects, he had a most sinister expression of countenance and his fried egg eye didn't detract any from his dangerous aspect. The chips had been sliding in his direction all evening and it was plain to all that he was getting the best of the game. Finally a fellow named Jim, who had lost heavily, called for ten dollars worth of chips and a new deck of cards.

"Why, Jim," said the man with the fried egg eye, "you don't think nobody's cheatin' nor nothin', do you?"

"No," said Jim with a sigh, for Jim dreaded the one-eyed man —

"I don't accuse nobody of cheatin' nor nothin'" — and pulling out a big revolver and laying it on the table in front of him, "but I've bought some more chips and ast for a new deck; and ef I ketch anybody a stealin' cards or cheatin', I'm goin' to shoot his other eye out!"

The case finally came to trial. The plaintiff took the stand and testified that on a certain evening, in a certain month and year he was doing switching of Missouri Pacific passenger coaches near the union station. There was an engine on one of the tracks all ready to move out. When the engine started the exhaust threw out unusually large cinders — the screen in the smoke stack being old and defective and permitting the exit of much larger cinders than would escape if the screen were as it should be.

One of those hot cinders had been blown "straight down" and struck him in the eye, burning it severely. An inflammation followed and the destruction of the eye, of the loss of sight, caused by the deposit and organization of inflammatory material in the coats of the cornea, causing what is called a leucoma, was the result.

He had had much treatment and had spent a great deal of money, all to no purpose.

There was little other testimony on plaintiff's side of the case, when his attorney announced that he rested.

I was then put on the stand for the defense. The company's attorney asked me a question in which the cinder being "blown down" into plaintiff's eye was used several times. This same expression was used over and over when plaintiff was on the stand.

"The cinder was not blown 'down into plaintiff's eye,'" I said.

"It was not?" asked the attorney, "why not?"

"If you ever observed the smoke and cinders coming out of the smoke stack of an engine, when the engine was exhausting, you saw this:

"The smoke and cinders first went straight upward, then, when the propelling force had been sufficiently overcome by gravity and atmospheric resistance, they curved outward in every direction, unless blown in one direction by a stiff wind — just like the water from a fountain, and for the very same reason. As they curved outward, while the propelling and the resisting forces were contending, they almost came to a standstill; then the cinders descended slowly to the ground on a perpendicular line, while the smoke, being lighter, went elsewhere. Hence the cinder could not have been blown and was not blown down into plaintiff's eye.'"

As we went to lunch the attorney said to me, "I sat there and heard that expression 'blown down into my eye,' repeated over and over and, in my mind's eye, I could see those hot cinders, coming down, on a slight slant and being blown directly into plaintiff's eye; but, when you made the explanation you did, I felt like going out and asking some one to please kick me."

We found an oculist upon whom plaintiff had called, at about the time that he claimed that his eye was injured, with a view to having his eyes examined and treated. The oculist even found his notes in an old case book, in which was the date, plaintiff's name and the diagnosis was "specific purulent ophthalmitis." I have never been able to understand, nor can I now remember how they ever permitted the oculist to testify to what he did. He did not treat the lease, however, but he made a diagnosis, which according to some decisions "was equivalent to making a prescription." In short, a purulent inflammation of the eye from having been poisoned on account of plaintiff's having a loathsome disease at the time, and the scoundrel tried to work off an affliction, which came to him through his own vicious and immoral habits, on the company and to collect large damages on it!

The jury promptly found for the defense. Indeed, I am not sure that the Judge did not take the case away from the jury; or, in other words, order them to find for the defense without leaving their seats.

A rather ludicrous incident occurred while plaintiff was on the stand. The case was being tried before the late Judge John W. Henry. Every one who knew Judge Henry knows what a profound contempt he had for everything small, mean and cowardly.

At a certain point in the examination of plaintiff Judge Henry took a hand and asked, "What do you do?"

"Who, me?" asked plaintiff.

"Yes, what is your occupation?"

"Why, I'm a 'plugger'," answered plaintiff.

"A what?" asked the Judge.

"A 'plugger'," said the plaintiff, as a mean, sickly smile played over his vicious countenance.

"What is a 'plugger'," asked the Judge.

"Why, Judge, don't you know what a 'plugger' is?"

"I certainly do not," answered the Judge.

"Why, you see, Judge, I work for a gambling house in the West bottoms and I go out and meet fellows and get acquainted with them and get them to go in and gamble."

From the expression on Judge Henry's face it was easy to divine what his thoughts were.

Here was a case in which there was an out and out attempt to steal, by false pretenses. This rascal knew that he did not get a cinder in his eye, he knew that the condition which ensued, after the purulent specific inflammation, was due to that specific inflammation and to nothing else. Hence, it was not only a clear case of false pretenses, but there was an attempt to sustain it by perjury.

I cannot help but believe that, had the corporation pursued this man and had taken his case before the grand jury, he could have been punished.

I confess that, while my experience in the last twenty-five years has tended to cause me to lose confidence in humanity generally, yet I have not lost all confidence, and I, therefore, cannot help but feel and hope that, should a proper effort be made, such cases could be punished.

The effort should be made, I believe, in every instance where it can be clearly shown that a plaintiff has committed perjury or any of his witnesses has done so.

If it were done I am quite sure that convictions could be obtained and dishonest persons punished. If this could be done it would, no doubt, have a deterrent effect and would, therefore, tend to prevent others trying to obtain money in this way.

I am quite sure that there would be more horse stealing if there was not a law in existence which punishes such a crime quite severely, and which is enforced, and this I believe to be true regarding every form of felony.

The corporations which are annoyed so much by this constant effort to rob them should wake up, and they should organize a special set of men whose duty it should be to follow up and get those people indicted, tried and punished. A little money spent in this way would be well spent, and if it should become known that all railroad and street railway corporations had started such a crusade it is my opinion that the very announcement of this fact alone would cause a withdrawal of a good many suits for damages.

Chapter Nine - Injury to The Brain

Case I. — A NUMBER of years ago I was directed to assist Assistant Attorney W. A. Johnson of Gamett, in the trial of a case of supposed injury to the brain, at Burlington, Kansas.

The plaintiff was a widow, about thirty-eight years of age and with a history. Her deceased husband had been a physician and had also kept a small drug store at the small town of Leroy, in Coffey County.

After his death the widow continued to run the drug store for some time — doing all the work herself, even acting as prescription clerk.

But the business did not pay and she closed it out. She sued one of our engineers for breach of promise of marriage and got a verdict for nine hundred dollars and ran garnishments on his wages so persistently that he was compelled to leave the employment of the road and seek employment elsewhere, where the widow could not locate him. Failing to raise the wind in this way, the widow got herself hurt.

She claimed that she, together with her sister-in-law, who had a baby with her, was riding on the caboose of a Missouri Pacific freight train, somewhere in Southern Kansas.

The train men were setting in a car. The lady with the baby sat on the side seat, such seats as are found in the ordinary caboose, belonging to a modem freight train. The widow sat on the same seat with her sister-in-law, with her right arm out of the window, clasping the side of the window, so as to hold on. The train was headed north and she was on the east side of the caboose. When the car that was being set in struck the caboose it did so with considerable force. A brakeman, who sat in the cupola said that the first he saw of the widow, after the jar, she was lying on the floor about the middle of the caboose. He climbed down and picked her up and got her on to a seat. She seemed to be unconscious for awhile, and she was bleeding from a slight cut above her right eye. She soon regained consciousness however.

After making demands upon the company for a large amount and failing to realize she brought suit for a large sum and alleged injury to the brain as the basis for her claim for damages.

When the case went to trial, the widow went on the stand in her own behalf. She proved herself to be an adroit and skillful fencer.

She testified that, when the collision came, it was of such great' violence as to tear her arm loose from its hold upon the side of the window and to throw her violently to the middle of the floor, where her head struck upon an iron spittoon, which caused the wound above her right eye.

Both she and her sister-in-law testified that the latter, though she had a baby in her arms and was not holding to anything, was not thrown at all, and, in fact, was not much disturbed by the shock of the collision.

Neither of them could explain why it was that the force of this collision affected the widow so seriously and had so little or no effect on the sister-in-law. The widow even swore that such was the force of the collision it bruised her arm and abraded the skin in tearing it loose from its hold upon the side of the window.

We could never find out nor even conjecture just how she came to be on the caboose floor with a wound upon her face.

That the whole thing was planned beforehand and that the widow herself contributed to her injury we had not the least doubt, but that she should have taken the risk of voluntarily falling out there and striking her head upon the spittoon was almost beyond belief.

She testified that she had headache all the time, that her memory was failing rapidly and that her eyesight had got to be so bad that she could barely read ordinary newspaper print.

Two physicians who examined her, of whom I was one, found nothing; and hence, could testify to nothing. The result of the examination was negative in character.

The train men knew little or nothing, the doctors knew nothing and so, the only testimony given which might influence a jury, was that given by the widow and in the deposition of her sister-in-law.

The case, therefore, looked dangerous; but, fortunately for the railroad company the widow undertook to and did play a trick and was caught.

She had testified, when on the stand, that the pupil of the right eye often dilated suddenly.

In truth it was dilated then, though she said it had not been dilated the day before.

Two physicians, whom she had summoned, testified that this erratic dilatation of the pupil of her eye was indicative of a serious brain lesion.

At the noon recess the landlady of the hotel where we and the widow put up, came to Judge Johnson and told him that she had caught the widow putting something in her right eye that morning, before she went to the court house!

She was using an ordinary dropper and the landlady watched the proceeding for sometime before the widow saw her. She then implored the landlady to say nothing about it, as it might hurt her case, if known.

She said it was just a little eye water which she put in that eye sometimes because the eye gave her much trouble.

The honest landlady was summoned and went on the witness stand and testified to the facts above stated. The widow looked awfully crestfallen and her attorneys, who were chronic anti-corporation lawyers, were furious. They looked as if they could tear the landlady to pieces.

The widow went on the stand again and tried to fix the matter up, but she couldn't do it.

Judge Johnson challenged her to bring her bottle of "eye water" into court and submit it for examination and analysis but she declined.

And yet, and yet the jury gave her a verdict for seventy-five dollars. That made the railroad company pay the costs, anyway. The widow, having run a drug store, was acquainted with the action of many drugs and she was, no doubt, using a solution of the sulphate of atropia in her right eye, when the landlady caught her that morning.

In attending these lawsuits it was often the case that the attorney and I would have to wait a day and sometimes longer before we could go to trial. Some case ahead of us which it had been supposed would last only one day, would develop unusual staying qualities and last two or maybe longer.

I remember that, in waiting for the case just narrated to come up, we had to remain three days.

I had often waited with the attorney for two days, but this was the longest I had ever had to wait.

At such times we most always spent our time in the court house, listening to the trial of cases. We often witnessed some very interesting trials— sometimes civil and often criminal; and, often we heard some things that were very amusing and entertaining.

On the occasion of this three days' wait we heard a trial which was, in some respects, as funny as any farce comedy I ever heard on the stage. I refer particularly to the testimony of one man.

The case had come to the Circuit Court from a Justice's court at a small railroad town in the county and the history of it, in brief, was as follows:

A young man, a saddler by occupation, who lived in this small town, had taken it into his head that he wanted a pair of young horses. To gratify this ambition he had gone to the country one Sunday, about a year previous to this time, to the farm of one Barrett. Barrett had quite a number of young horses, some of them Texans and some native Kansans.

Amongst others, were a number of Kansas yearlings and Texas two-year-olds — all grays; but the Kansas yearlings were as large as and, in some instances larger than the Texas two-year-olds.

This saddler, whom I shall call Mr. Spoons, selected, purchased and paid for a pair of gray Kansas yearlings. He promised to send some one for them on a certain day that week. He did so, but lo, and behold, when his man returned, he brought him a pair of Texas two-year-olds which, on account of their being ponies, were not nearly so valuable as the Kansas yearlings. Spoons was furious. It was near Sunday and, when Sunday came he took his man and went out to Barrett's farm, taking the pair of Texas two-year-olds with him. When they arrived at Barrett's they found no one at home; so he just turned the Texas two-year-olds back into Barrett's pasture and turned out the pair of Kansas yearlings, which he claimed to have purchased, and drove them ta town. It did not take Barrett long, after his return home, to discover that an exchange had been made and he went at once to the little town and demanded of Spoons that he return the Kansas yearlings. This Spoons refused to do. Barrett then went to a Justice of the peace, swore out a warrant and had Spoons, arrested for horse stealing. Things were now becoming interesting and people began to take sides as is their habit in the country.

Spoons had his preliminary hearing and was bound over to await the action of the next grand jury. The grand jury had promptly indicted him for horse stealing and Spoons had had his trial and had been acquitted long ago.

Barrett then replevined the Kansas yearlings and Spoons replevined them back. This had been done about twice cm each side, when the case came to the Circuit Court for a final hearing before a jury. This was the final hearing and Spoons was the man who created the fun. He did not do it intentionally, however. Oh, no, naturally Spoons was as serious as a deacon, but it was Spoons' appearance, his ways and his manner of giving testimony that made the fun.

Spoons was a funny looking man, to begin with. As said before he was a young man — perhaps twenty-eight or thirty. He was tall and slender, had a watermelon shaped head, ears that were large and stood straight out from his head and a rather long and pointed nose, that was simply continuous with his forehead. If you had laid a pencil on Spoons' nose and forehead you would have found that it touched both at every point.

Spoons listened with his mouth, and, when he talked he talked rapidly and it was hard to stop him. In fact it took the attorneys on both sides, the Court and the sheriff all combined to stop him, and then they often found it hard to do it. When Spoons got under way he looked toward the ceiling and his under jaw worked like the walking beam of an East River steamer.

When Spoons was waiting for a question he sat with his head cocked on one side and held his mouth about half open. When the question was finished Spoons started in and then the fun began. Spoons was much inclined to get in matter which the lawyers call "irrelevant, incompetent and immaterial," and when he had got in a lot of this kind of matter, the lawyer on the opposite side would try to stop him, but he couldn't do it. "Hold on! that will do! Stop right there!" but Spoons went right on and did not seem to hear the lawyer at all. Then his own attorney would call on him to stop, but Spoons didn't seem to hear him either. Then the Court took a hand and, failing to command obedience, would command the sheriff to stop him. The sheriff, who was always near the witness box, would step quickly to Spoons' side, lay his hand on his shoulder and say, "Here, young man, when the Judge tells you to stop, you must stop."

Spoons would turn his head to one side and look at the sheriff's hand on his shoulder as if it were a snake, or some animal and would say, "All right." Then he would cock his head on one side, open his mouth, roll his eyes toward the ceiling and await the next question. When the question was finished, he started right in and that walking beam under jaw began to go up and down in perfect rhythm and, invariably it took his own and the opposing lawyers, the Court and finally the sheriff to stop him. He would always give that funny look at the sheriff's hand, as if he thought it something that should be blown or brushed off.

The lawyers, the Court, the Jury, the stenographer and the audience were simply in convulsions. The Court laughed as well as the rest and I thought the stenographer, who was a beautiful young lady, would have to be resuscitated. One question was asked him over and over and he always answered it in the same way. I came to believe that the opposing attorney asked the question so often just to hear Spoons give the answer. It was this: "Mr. Spoons, how did you know that the colts turned out to your man by Mr. Barrett, were not the colts which you selected and purchased on the Sunday previous?"

Spoons would cock his head on one side and answer, "because I was personally acquainted with them colts." And then everybody including the Judge and the jury would break down and laugh.

Taking it all together Spoons was about three-quarters of an hour in getting in his testimony, which, under ordinary circumstances, should have gone in in ten or fifteen minutes.

Spoons won his case, however, for it was apparent to everybody, that a job had been put up on him, and that more persons than Mr. Barrett had been engaged in it In fact they regarded Spoons as being somewhat simple minded and they thought they could fool him as they pleased; but they reckoned without their host, for Spoons was a persistent and hard fighter, and it was evident to all that he was perfectly honest and truthful.

I had a habit of sketching people in the court room on such occasions and, while not an artist, if the person has a peculiar face, and I can get a side view of it, I often get a pretty fair picture.

I got out my little book and pencil as soon as Spoons went on the stand, for I instinctively knew that there was something more than ordinary in that head and face. I caught him with his head cocked on one side, his mouth half open and he looking toward the ceiling. I wrote under it, "because I was personally acquainted with them colts." I sent it from attorney to attorney, to Miss Emma Lane, the stenographer. She bowed her acknowledgements and smiled. Pretty soon I saw a paper making its way toward me, through the hands of the lawyers. Each one who got it would look at it, then at me and smile and then pass the paper on. After awhile it reached me and then it was my time to smile. A long-haired lawyer from Ottawa had sketched me while I was sketching Spoons. I had been sitting in an ordinary Court room chair and leaning back against a column, with my book in front of me and intently engaged in my work. The Ottawa lawyer had caught me just as I was; and it was not only a good picture from the standpoint of the attitude and the pose, but it was a good one of my features. To my dying day I will never get a better picture of myself.

The Ottawa lawyer was an artist. He had written under it, "The sketcher sketched."

I sent it over to the stenographer also. The last time I saw her she told me that she had both of them framed and had them hung in hers and the Judge's room; for she and the Judge afterwards married.

The Judge was an old bachelor and everybody thought that he was incorrigible; but, after having the sweet faced stenographer near him for several years and getting acquainted with her sweet ways and happy disposition, he decided to give it up and so he yielded.

Chapter Ten- Miscellaneous Injuries

Case I. — I GIVE the following case not on account of any particular value it may have, as related to the other cases in this book, but more to show how queer and erratic some people are, and with the kind of people those who are settling personal damage suits are sometimes called upon to deal:

Some years ago the Missouri Pacific road had a little platform built at a sag or depression, in the locality of the Little Blue River between Kansas City and Independence. There was no depot and no agent, as the platform was built merely to accommodate a few families who were settled in the Blue valley at that point; and no trains stopped there except the short train between Kansas City and Independence.

One day, the engine of this train was derailed right at this point. It did not leave the ties and did not turn over, but simply ran along on the ties for some distance and tore the track up to some extent.

There was only one person standing on the platform, waiting for this train, and that was a young married lady who lived in a big house on a hill a quarter of a mile or more from the platform. About the only damage done to the train was that a wire screen door on a baggage car, I believe, was torn oflF and hurled onto this platform. It struck the young woman flatwise over the abdomen and knocked her down. She was picked up and taken to her home where, upon investigation, it was found that there were no cuts or bruises and, in fact, that the young woman was not injured at all, but had simply been shocked and scared a little.

The case was reported, however, and, the general claim agent and I, being in Kansas City about three or four days thereafter, and having a few hours to spare, decided to go out and see her. It is best to see, settle with and take the release of all such cases; for, if not, the party may turn up in Court with a suit for twenty thousand dollars damages and claiming injuries to the spine and may get a verdict for ten thousand. Such persons — people injured no more than this woman was — have been brought into Court in an invalid chair, or on a cot; or, which is often just as effective with the jury, have given a deposition and remained at home in bed, on the ground that their condition is too serious for them to come, or to be brought into Court.

Well, Mr. Jones and I got off at the little platform and climbed up a big hill and soon reached the farm house. It was a large, old-fashioned farm house, in which this young woman and her husband occupied, only two or three rooms; indeed, it looked as if they might be there merely as caretakers. We found both husband and wife at home — the latter being in bed. I don't think that she was playing a part, for they didn't know that we were coming, but I think that she had not yet gotten over her scare.

The husband was a big, stalwart fellow, who looked like a farm hand, and was not highly educated. In other words, "he was one of the people."

In a short conversation with him it was ascertained that the young woman was *enciente* — about three months "gone."

I was permitted to examine her and found absolutely nothing.

Then, efforts at settlement were made between Mr. Jones and the husband. Mr. Jones could not get him to say how much they wanted; but he insisted that the claim agent should say what he was willing to pay. Finally, Mr. Jones offered him twenty-five dollars. We could see in a minute that he was highly indignant. He said he didn't want to talk to people who proposed to treat him in that way, and he got up and walked to the door and looked back at us with a "come-on-and-get-out-of-here" expression on his face and with a significant gesture of his right hand, which seemed as much as to say, "if you fellows don't get out of here, and that mighty quick, I will throw you out," and he could have come near doing it.

141

We went off down the hill, feeling, I imagine, like two burglars who have attempted to blow a safe and the fuse wouldn't work. In short, we felt humiliated. We had never been treated so in all of our experience.

"If the fool had waited, I would have offered him more," said Mr. Jones.

"Well, he wouldn't wait for you to do it, nor tell you what he wanted, what could you do?" I asked.

"Now," said Mr. Jones, "we will have a suit against us for about twenty thousand dollars, and they will allege spinal injury."

"Yes," I said, "and a lot of fool doctors will get on the stand and swear that her spinal cord was injured, notwithstanding the fact that the blow was on the abdomen. They will swear that it can be injured by a blow from the front just as well as one from behind."

We went on, and all the way home, we continued to vent our indignation at the big, double fisted fellow for the arbitrary, high-handed and "get-out-of-here-quick" way in which he treated us.

Mr. Jones was manifestly uneasy about the case, for within a week he wrote up to Sedalia and ordered the division claim agent at that point. Dr. Rogers, to go up and see those people and see if he could not settle with them.

Dr. Rogers went up and settled the case for fifteen dollars!

Of course, Dr. Rogers had the laugh on Mr. Jones and myself. I asked Dr. Rogers, "how did you manage it to settle for so small a sum?" "There was no management about it," said Dr. Rogers, "I simply asked the husband how much he wanted and he said fifteen dollars and I paid it."

It is my recollection that Doctor Rogers was authorized, if the worst came to worst, to pay them a pretty stiff little sum — possibly two, three and maybe five hundred dollars, rather than let them escape.

I have always thought that he must have misunderstood the general claim agent and thought he offered five dollars instead of twenty-five, for it does not look reasonable that he would settle for only fifteen dollars after having been offered twenty-five by another agent, and with one coming so soon afterward upon our heels. He must have known that we were prepared to give more than we had offered, and he would, therefore, have asked for more.

Dr. Rogers said the fellow didn't mention the general claim agent or myself, but completely ignored us. He, evidently, thought that we were a very poor and shabby lot of sheep.

Here was a man who, had he known the kind of instructions that the assistant claim agent had, would have received a sum of money which would have temporarily paralyzed him.

He had, probably, never possessed at one time in all his life, more than twenty or thirty dollars. This kind of people are not speculative as a rule. The poor, the hard working and the ignorant are not speculative, at least not so much so as the fairly well educated, and those who are greedy and grasping and who already possess more or less of this world's goods.

It is strange, and it is an unusual thing for the negroes to bring suit for damages, even when they seem to have good legal claims. Why is this? It is simply due to the fact that they are a race who know but little of the value of money. They have never possessed much money at one time, and they are, above all, the happiest race that we know anything about; and, so far as the matter of committing perjury is concerned, I would trust them to tell the truth and to refrain from fraud, from malingering and from perjury as quick as I would the white man. I belong to those who are supposed in some quarters, to be prejudiced against the negro — which, however, I do not admit I was reared amongst them, and, although I never bought or sold one (of which fact I am both glad and proud), but I have owned them, owned them when they were forced on me, through my marriage, by entailment.

I think that, like most Southern men, I know more about them than do those who make more fuss about their welfare, and who do less to demonstrate their assumed philanthropic ideas in regard to them than I and my people do.

Yet, as said before, the negro is not speculative, and in regard to the matter of playing the hypocritical part of an injured person and of claiming and collecting damages that are dishonest and unfair, I must say that he has his white brother at a great disadvantage.

Mind you, I do not say that the negro is naturally more honest and fair than the white man. Do not misunderstand me; for I do not say this. But, in the matter of claiming what is not due him, on account of a little accident, he holds his white neighbor at a decided disadvantage.

Why is this? Well, it must be as I have already stated; the negro is not and has not been used to possessing or handling large sums of money. He is satisfied with less than his white neighbor. He is neither speculative nor greedy. He is, as a general thing, satisfied if he is supplied with the necessaries of life for the present and a very short while in the future.

Out of a great number of negroes whom I have known to have been injured, I have known only one; who brought suit and fought it to a conclusion, and swore falsely — and she was half white and had a white attorney!

Case II. — I give the following case on account of its unique and humorous elements and to show how easy it is to get along with some people and how hard it is with others, how mean and contemptible some are, and how kind and generous others are.

When some people are hurt on or by a railroad train, they seem to begin, at once, to hate all railroad corporations and railroad men in general, the one by which they have been hurt in particular, and they seem to begin to hate everybody connected with that particular road and to regard them as enemies.

This is a case in point— of the better sort.

We had at one time and for many years, connected with the claim department of the Missouri Pacific, at Atchison, Kansas, a young man named Frank

143

Everest, Who is it, who ever met or saw dear, witty, generous, big hearted Frank Everest, who does not remember him? Frank's father was wealthy, Frank an only son, and the father had given him every advantage, had sent him to college, and had given him an education in law as well, for the father was himself a lawyer; and to put on the cap sheaf had sent Frank on a long tour of Europe and the Continent.

Frank undertook the practice of law, but did not succeed very well, for it is a rare thing that a man so generous and so full of fun, ever succeeds in law or medicine. A few like Sunset Cox and J. Proctor Knott, may do so, but they are endowed with other qualities that help them to success.

Well, Frank quit the law and became an assistant general claim agent at Atchison, and was put in charge of a division, or district.

Frank always had many funny experiences to relate, in connection with his settlement of claims, but I don't think I ever heard him relate another that was quite as unique and funny as this one.

An old, fat gentleman, in Northern Kansas, or Southern Nebraska, was struck at a crossing by a passenger train. He was riding on top of a load of hay at the time, and was thrown some distance. Strange to say, both his wagon and his horses escaped without injury. Prank went to see him within a very few days. Missouri Pacific claim agents do not wait after they are satisfied that an injured person is in condition to talk business.

Frank said he found the old man in bed; for, though not seriously hurt, he was bruised up some — enough, at least, to confine him to his bed a week or two. Frank said he found him to be a big, fat generous natured old fellow and just as full of fun as he could be. Frank had been there only a short time until they were fast friends and were telling each other funny stories. After awhile the subject of a settlement was broached. The old man was ready to settle, said he was glad he was hurt no worse than he was — glad he was not killed, in fact Frank said that when the old gentleman talked of the accident he kept talking of the great distance he was thrown. "Why, Mr. Everest, you ought to have seen how far I was knocked — why I was knocked 'way yonder — at least fifteen feet."

Andy after talking awhile the old man would again come back to the great distance to which he was thrown, and always put it at fifteen feet

"Why, Mr. Everest," he would say, "I didn't know that a man could be knocked so far and not get killed. Now, you may believe me or not, but I tell you I was knocked fully fifteen feet; yes, sir, every foot of it."

Frank said he knew that he could take nearly any liberty with the old gentleman that had fun in it, and that was not rude or vulgar; so he finally said, "Look here, my old friend, you keep talking about having been knocked fifteen feet; now, what do you say to settling by the foot!"

Frank said that the old gentleman was in a roar in a moment.

"Ha! ha! ha! well, that's good! Settle by the foot! Ha! ha! ha! That's just what we'll do — settle by the foot. What will you give me per foot?"

"What do you say to two dollars per foot?" asked Frank.

"Oh! That's not enough," said the old man," "You ought to give me five, at least."

They dickered awhile and finally compromised on three dollars per foot. The check was made out for forty-five dollars, the release was signed and Frank gave the old man his hand in a jolly good-bye.

He said that, as he went away, as far as he could hear the old man's voice he could hear his jolly laughter, and "Oh, my, settled by the foot! don't that beat you? Ha! ha! ha! well, that beats the Jews. Three dollars a foot for being knocked off a hay wagon! ha! ha! ha!"

Now, here was a man who took a sensible, reasonable and common-sense view of the matter. He didn't begin to hate the railroad company and everybody connected with it, on account of an accident which perhaps, no one could avoid, and for which no one was to blame. He was of the kind whom I am always glad to see get something where he is injured and were I doing the settling and paying, I think I would always give such a person more, other things being equal, than I would one of the grasping, greedy grinding malingerers, who begins to stir up his hate as soon as he can do so after an accident, and who does not hesitate to exaggerate his injuries and to tell lies about his aches and pains.

Such a person does not deserve much and yet, they are the ones who get the most. They are the ones whom the claim agents dread and fear more than they do others.

Case III. — On the 29th of June, 1889, there was quite a serious passenger wreck on the Lexington and Southern branch of the Missouri Pacific about six miles north of Nevada, Missouri. It was the Joplin day passenger train which went into the ditch, injuring quite a number of passengers.

I remember the date because the chief surgeon and I and other surgeons who were connected with the hospital department of the road, were in Salt Lake City, Utah, and when we read the news of the wreck in the morning paper, we took the first train for home. The paper had stated that six persons were killed and many seriously wounded; whereas, the facts were that no one was killed and not many injured, and only one or two of them very seriously.

Amongst those who were slightly injured was a little, poorly developed sixteen years old orphan girl, who was going home from Nevada to Arthur or some station near the Osage river to some family with whom she had been staying. When the wreck occurred, she was thrown forward and her forehead struck against the seat in front of her — making a small lump near the hair line. A few days afterward one of our assistant claim agents went out there and gave her twenty-five dollars and took her release, instead of having a curator and guardian appointed for her and then going into Court with a suit for damages, and permitting them to take judgment for the amount agreed upon, which would have been the better plan. However, there was a woman in the neighborhood who took charge of her. This woman was large and masculine in appearance. She had a large nose, a projecting chin and a catfish mouth — in short she had the typical female litigation face. She took charge of the little girl's interests, brought suit very soon afterward and had the settlement set aside. I forget the amount for which she sued, but it was large enough and she, no doubt, had her arrangements for a large slice of the pie. Before bringing suit she went into probate court and had herself appointed curator and guardian of the little girl.

The case finally came to trial. After the jury was impanelled, either two or four of us were appointed to examine the plaintiff. We found nothing which had any relation to the wreck, but we found that the little girl was poorly developed.

She was an orphan and had seen hardships, at a time when a little girl needs the tender love and fostering care of her mother. She had worked in other people's houses, when she should have been playing out in the sunshine and going to school. The result was that the period of adolescence was postponed and her development imperfect.

That was all that we could find; but, unfortunately for the child her imperfect development had no relation to the wreck.

The little plaintiff testified to pains and headaches, to weakness and to many things which one would know that she suffered. Much of her testimony showed long and careful coaching.

The doctors who examined her all swore to about what I have stated above. But the testimony of the plaintiff's experts was too mild to suit her attorneys. They wanted something more radical and reckless, so they had summoned a fellow from Rich Hill, who was known; and in fact, who advertised himself as "The tramp doctor." At the opportune time the tramp doctor was put on the stand.

He was a study. He was a man about thirty-five years of age, was slender, thin and ordinary looking in appearance as to dress and everything else and in everything he filled the bill of "the tramp doctor." He was shabbily dressed, and you could locate his third dorsal vertebra by the buttons on the back of his coat. His pants were large, loose and worn; and, in all respects reminded you of the three cities in France — Toulong, Touloose and Barras!

He was a magnificent specimen of the degenerate. His head was ill shapen and looked like a cushaw that had grown under the fence and got warped. His ears were large and stood straight out from his head and looked like two great fans. His eyes were small and close together, his nose was small and deflected, his teeth crossed and doubled; and, in fact Caesare Lombroso or Max Nordau would have gone into ecstasies over him. The plaintiff's attorneys handled him very gingerly for I think that, after they had seen him, they feared some catastrophe.

After they had gotten through with him the attorney for the defense took him in hand.

"Doctor, you say that you saw and examined this plaintiff?"

"Yes, sir."

"At what college did you graduate?"

"Well, sir, I never graduated at no college."

"Ah, that is unfortunate."

"No, sir, it hain't unfortunate; for I wouldn't give five cents to be a gradjate uv all the medical collies in the New Nited States."

"Why not, doctor?"

"Well, sir, just because I wouldn't I wouldn't give what God a'mighty has put into me, so that I can look into people and see through 'em and see whut's the matter uv 'em and know what'll cure 'em for all the college and book larnin that ever was."

"What did you find to be the matter with the plaintiff, doctor?"

"Well sir, she has 'sposmotic of the overs.'"

"Please tell the jury what 'sposmotic of the overs' is."

"Well, sir, it is when the overs jest draw up and squeeze up and git jest as hard as a rock and jest stay that a'way."

"How large are the overs in their natural state?"

"Well, sir, they are about the size of a hen aig."

"Did you prescribe for the plaintiff, doctor?"

"Yes, sir, I did."

"What did you give her."

"Well, sir, I give her dickatalis.

"Did you give her the tincture or the extract?"

"Well, sir, I give her the extract."

"How much did you give her?"

"Well, sir, I give her a teaspoonful every two hours."

One dose would have been all "the tramp doctor" would have given her. The Coroner and the undertaker would have done the rest.

The doctor was then allowed to go.

I have forgotten what the verdict was, but think it was either one thousand or fifteen hundred dollars. I presume that, perhaps, the case was settled out of Court.

A great deal of mischief is done by would-be disinterested persons, such as the curator and guardian in this case. Without her unwarranted interference there would have been no suit in this case. The little girl had been well paid for the slight bump she had received, and in truth the money she received was a God send to her.

Yet, many will say that the assistant claim agent should have given her more, and I believe that, had I been settling the case, I should have given her as much as one hundred dollars, just to satisfy public opinion (which means a concurrence of the untutored mob) if for no other reason. The introduction upon the witness stand of "the tramp doctor" was a surprise to everybody, for scarcely anyone would believe that an intelligent attorney would put such

147

an ignorant monkey and ass on the witness stand to testify, where education and intelligence are demanded.

Yet, lawyers are quite smart about such things sometimes and know more about what influence such creatures will have upon the average jury than I would.

I have no doubt but what his testimony favorably impressed many of the jurors.

His idea that he was a "natural doctor," that "God A'mighty" had just made him so that he could "just look into people and see into 'em and see what is the matter uv 'em, and know what to give 'em to cure 'em," was an idea that has been quite prevalent in the world at times.

It is on a par with the idea that some men, who are uneducated and ignorant can preach better than an educated man; that God inspires them as to what they shall say and so forth and so forth.

I felt profoundly sorry for the poor neglected and orphaned girl, as we all did, and could I have given her a goodly sum, so as to take her poor, little weak body out of other people's kitchens, without robbing the railroad company, I would have gladly done so.

Case IV. — Not long before I quit the service of the Missouri Pacific Railroad Company, I was asked by Judge Elijah Robinson, the company's attorney to go to a certain boarding house, in this city, and there examine one Mrs. Williams (for the purposes of this narrative that shall be her name) who had a suit pending against the company for a large sum of money. He desired that I examine her with a view to assisting him in the trial of the case, which would be held in about two weeks.

I went to the boarding house and there found Mrs. Williams. She flatly refused to permit me to examine her — although her family physician was present until she had telephoned her attorney. He directed her to permit the examination as it was done by arrangement between himself and Judge Robinson.

I found her to be a woman fifty-five years old, though she looked to be every day of sixty. She was tall, angular, thin and bony. She had high cheek bones, a basilisk eye, a catfish mouth and there were a half dozen fights in every square inch of her face. She had an unusually long neck, and a very large *pomum Adami* which, when she swallowed, made excursions up and down the anterior of her neck, like a small elevator.

She gave me to understand that I was not to hurt her, and if I did the examination would stop right then. She seemed to look upon me, from the beginning, as an enemy, and that she must hold me at a distance and be prepared for a conflict at any time. I spoke to her very kindly and handled her very gently, but kindness and gentleness do not make much impression on such people.

I examined her, but in truth there was little to examine. I found her heart, which was the organ she claimed to have been injured (?) to be somewhat weak, rapid and irregular, her digestion was no doubt, bad, as she was poorly nourished, she was constipated and she said she slept badly, which I have no doubt was true.

She had a very great hatred of the railroad company, which she abused roundly, and she seemed to consider me the paid agent of the corporation in helping it in its nefarious designs.

I reported to Judge Robinson the facts as to what I had and had not ascertained in the examination and warned him that we had a fight on our hands with no mean antagonist — one skilled in warfare, in fact, as that had, from all indications, been her chief occupation in life.

The case came to trial, within the specified time and the plaintiff was on hand, arrayed in all the panoply of "grim visaged of war."

She was the first witness for her side of her case, and these are the facts, or assumed facts which were brought out on direct and cross-examination.

That she was fifty-five years old, had been married twice — the last time to a well-to-do German farmer, who lived near St. Charles, Mo., by whom she had one son — now nine years old — and that she had one daughter by her first husband, that she had been separated from her last husband several years and had since been living most of the time with the daughter, in this city, that she had been sick some, had been in the city hospital twice and, the last time,, had been operated on for haemorrhoids by the city physician, and, since then, had enjoyed excellent health, that during the heated term of 1898, she had gone with her daughter and granddaughter to Colorado and had sojourned for about two months at or near Colorado Springs, that in the very last days of August they had started to return home, and that night, at Pueblo — while the train crew was setting in a coach to relieve the great congestion of the trains, consequent upon the return of tourists — the collision between the car and the chair car, in which she was sitting, was so violent that it threw her against the back of the chair in front of her — which was leaning back and which struck her over the region of the heart

She said that it gave her great pain and that she could scarcely get her breath — having a "smothery" feeling.

She said that she called the attention of the train conductor to her condition and asked him for some whiskey; but he, being busy, referred the matter to the porter who procured it for her.

She said that she had never seen a well day from that time and never expected to again.

Her daughter, who was also a grass widow, and her granddaughter — sixteen years old — both substantially corroborated her story.

The conductor and train crew all testified that they had heard nothing of her being hurt at Pueblo; but the conductor did remember of her complaining of being sick and asking for the whiskey, and the porter testified to the fact of procuring the stimulant for her.

The defense showed that she had been an invalid, for the greater part of her life. The old German farmer stated, in a deposition, that she was always sick and complaining while she lived with him, and he gave a formidable list of physicians who had attended and treated her. He said that she put in her time principally, in raising every variety of cane around the house and quarrelling with the neighbors.

It was shown that she was sick, or complained of being sick, most of the time since she came to Kansas City; but that she grew better, temporarily, after the operation for the removal of the haemorrhoids by the city physician.

Three letters to her son were introduced by the defense. In the first she wrote that she was no better and that, if there was not some change in her condition, she feared that she would die. She said his sister was going to take her to Colorado, to remain during the heated term, and that she hoped that the trip might improve her health; but, if it did not, she did not know what was to become of her.

After having been in Colorado nearly two months, she wrote the little son, on August 24th, that she had been there now nearly two months and was no better, in fact was worse, if anything, than when she came.

She wrote again, on August 28th, and right on the eve of departure for home, that she was still no better, and that she was going home and she feared that she was going to die.

We proved that, when she arrived at the union station in Kansas City on the next night after leaving Pueblo, her son-in-law met them at the station and informed her, in a quiet but firm way, that she could not go to his house, that there was no peace in the house, so long as she was there, that she could go wherever else she might desire; but to his house, never. He told her he would pay her way to any part of the country to which she might decide to go.

After a little consideration she decided to go to some distant relatives in far Southern Texas.

She remained there in the union station about two hours and then took a train for Texas. She rode on that train, without stopping until she reached the city of Waco. There she left the train at midnight and went to a nearby hotel and slept until five o'clock the next morning.

She then took another train and went three hundred miles to the point where her relatives lived. From that place she wrote the general claim agent, making a statement of her injury and demanding substantial damages. The general claim agent made a courteous reply and told her he would investigate the case and would then write her.

He made the investigation; and, found that both the conductor and porter remembered her well, that they remembered the incident of her complaining of being sick and calling for whiskey, but that they did not remember of any complaint being made about her having been hurt. The general claim agent wrote her and refused to make any kind of settlement.

After she had gone to Texas her son-in-law, who was a respected official in Jackson County and had held the same official position for some ten or fifteen years, was shot in his own house. The wound did not prove to be a bad one, but there was a mystery about the manner of its infliction which remains unsolved to this day. He was exceedingly reticent in regard to the matter— did not seem to want to talk about it, in fact.

Soon after this, he sold his residence, which was a very nice one, drew his savings from the bank and disappeared one night and has not been heard from by the general public since, though it is known that he has intimate personal friends who, it is quite well known, have corresponded with him.

He left the furniture, which was quite valuable, to his wife. She was a grass widow when he married her and the sixteen years' old daughter spoken of was hy the first husband. From the first husband she had been divorced. She seemed to be "a chip off the old block," and exhibited in her character and temper strong evidences of hereditary influences. Before the time of the trial she had traded the fine furniture to a boarding house keeper for board for a certain length of time for herself, mother and daughter. The time agreed upon had elapsed and she had refused to further keep her mother, and the lady who kept the boarding house told me that the old lady would starve except for what she had done for her. She said that she had fed the old lady when she had not the means to procure a meal and, at that time, the old lady was doing a little work, in making up beds, dusting furniture and a little light work in the kitchen for her hoard.

At the very time, or up to the time of the trial, the daughter was making strenuous efforts to let her mother into the poor house. The landlady said that, of the two, the mother was very much the most amiable and easier to get along with.

When on the witness stand the plaintiff was asked if her chest turned black and blue at the point where the chair struck her. She answered, with an ominous snap, "I didn't look to see."

With all the evidence in the company's favor, for she made no sort of a case at all, the jury hung.

I do not know what disposition has been made of the case since, nor do I know what has become of the old woman, but presume, from her situation then and the bad state of her health, that she is either in the poor house, or dead. The latter would be infinitely better for her, and for all she is near to for such women can never be at peace with those around and about them. It would seem that such persons must be insane and yet, she was not insane. She seemed to have been born with the very Devil in her, and he kept her busily engaged most of the time.

I think it strongly probable, in fact it is almost certainly true, that she never had any bump at Pueblo at all. And yet, she and her daughter and even her young granddaughter, all got on the stand and swore to a state of things that had no existence, except in their imaginations and their conspiracy. This young girl— only sixteen years old, was put on the stand and swore to a state of things which had no existence at all.

Her little nine-year-old son, in St. Charles County, wrote her, because she was his mother, but his father gave up her letters to be used against her by the defense.

It would seem that any set of honorable men, after having read the three letters to her little son — one before and two after she went away, would have found against her, for her own letters clearly convicted her of perjury. But they did not, which goes to show the prejudice existing in the mind of the average juryman, and that he is always anxious to find against the corporation.

This goes to show the dishonesty in the great majority of men. The learning of this fact, and having it impressed upon my mind, as a fact, gave me the greatest shock of my life.

Case V. A number of years ago— I forget the date, and it does not matter — I was directed by the chief surgeon to go to Council Grove, Kansas, and see and examine two men — an old gentleman and his son-in-law — both of whom had been injured by being knocked from their conveyance, in the M., K. & T. yards in that town, while driving through the yards, on their way home from town.

Arriving in town, I sought our local surgeon, and, finding that he had seen and examined both men at the time of the accident, I secured his services in finding them.

He informed me that, at the time of the accident, both men lived some miles distant in the country, but now the old gentleman was moving into town, where he expected to spend the winter.

We went to the house where it was said the old gentleman was at work, with others, in putting the winter residence in order.

After we had gotten inside we could hear talking and pounding in the cellar. Pretty soon an old gentleman came briskly up the stairs — panting and puffing, as he was carrying a heavy box.

"That is he," said the local surgeon.

The old gentleman was near sixty years of age and seemed quite vigorous and well preserved.

"Why," said I, "you get around quite brisk with your heavy load for an old man."

"Old man!" said he, assuming a look of indignation, "you don't call me old."

"Well, you are not a spring chicken," said I.

"No, that's true," said he, "but you know it's said 'a man is as old as he feels and a woman is as old as she looks,' and, if you go by that rule, I am just as young as I ever was."

"You are still young, then, free from sickness and pain, and all the ills that flesh is heir to?" I said, encouragingly.

"Yes, sir, just as young as ever; never have an ache nor a pain and sleep like a baby."

"Mr. ---, I am Dr. King, assistant chief surgeon of the Missouri Pacific, and I have come to see you and your son-in-law, to examine you on account of the injuries you received in the M., K. & T. yards and for which you have made claim."

Well, I had seen it before. I had seen the change of countenance, the assumed rueful expression, the 'limpy-lame-dog' air, but I don't think that I ever, before or since, saw such an exaggeration of assumed disability as this old rascal exhibited.

He was a typical New Englander and he spoke with the Yankee pronunciation and, in his assumed inability, I think his provincial pronunciation was exaggerated also. He put both hands to the small of his back and backed over to and sat down on a box, and, after some complaint, put his face in his two hands and groaned like a horse. I had to turn my back to keep from laughing in his face.

"Yes, but you said only a few moments ago that you never had an ache nor a pain," said I.

"Yes, I know." said he," but you don't understand. You see I meant natural aches and pains and not aches and pains caused by injury. Of course, everybody that I know and that knows me around here knows that I suffer from them."

"Come, now," I said, "that will not do. Look at the big box you carried upstairs! Why, I could scarcely carry it myself."

"I know," said he, "but it was all I could do to carry it, and it almost killed me. My! how my back hurts! I was promised some help today that didn't come and that's the reason I have to carry such loads."

"And you really think you are permanently injured?" I said.

"Yes, sir, I am. I never expect to see another well day as long as I live. If I could be back where I was before that accident I wouldn't be back —" and so forth. The reader knows the rest of that speech.

I rallied and bantered him and told him that, should he bring suit against the company, my testimony and that of the local surgeon would ruin his case.

"The jury wouldn't believe you," said he.

"They all know me and they know I wouldn't lie about such a thing, but you are a perfect stranger to them."

He was right. He knew the prejudice against the people in the employment of the railroad companies.

We then took a carriage and went three miles to the country to see the son-in-law. When we drove up in front of the house, I could see a man through the window, sitting facing the back of another chair, which he had pulled over with a pillow on it and upon this he rested his head, with his face clasped in his hands.

Then we went in and the local surgeon introduced me. The young man scarcely seemed to comprehend the matter. His eyes were dull, his expression listless, and examination showed a pulse of one hundred and thirty without temperature.

This man had been hurt and he was suffering tortures with his head at that moment He didn't have to put on airs.

I reported the cases according to the above narrated facts. The general claim agent went out in a few days and made settlement of both cases — giving the young man much more than he did his spry and youthful-feeling father-in-law.

He said the old man didn't seem to like me — said I had treated him unfairly, and, if it wasn't for the false position I had put him in and for what he knew my testimony and that of my local surgeon would be, he wouldn't settle with him for any such sum, and "he'd show old Jay Gould whether or not he could hurt people and then not pay them anything."

Addenda

AFTER having written the forgoing and the conclusion — in fact, just before the manuscript had been submitted to the publishers — the newspapers were filled with a sensational story which had its location in Fort Worth, Texas. After all the facts had been revealed, the following proved to be the truth regarding this sensation: A widow, who had at one time been in quite good circumstances, was well educated and had moved in the best society, had finally met with misfortune until she was poor. She had but one child, a son, whom she succeeded in giving a fairly good education, and who was, at the time this story begins, about twenty-two to twenty-four years old. He had, at one time, held a 'fairly good position in the Dallas, Texas, post office, but had lost his position on account of the fact that he had been too busy in using the mails in an effort to make money outside his position. There was nothing seriously wrong or dishonest about what he had been doing, but it was somewhat irregular, enough so at least to cause his discharge. They had moved to Fort Worth and he had secured some kind of a clerical position with the Rock Island Railroad, the duties of which took him about the freight depot and the yards, and he sometimes rode on cars or trains that were being switched from place to place in the yards.

One day, while riding in a box car, the door of which was open, he fell from the door onto the hard cinders in the yards, and this at a time when the cars had been bumped together quite hard, and those who witnessed the apparent accident noticed that he did not arise from the point where he had fallen. When those about the yards went to him they found him in an apparently unconscious condition and they took him to his home and called the family physician. He was also seen by the railroad company's surgeon.

He remained in what seemed to be a condition of imbecility for weeks and months. Many doctors were called — the company even sending to Kansas City for a specialist in order that they might make no mistakes in regard to him. The specialist from Kansas City and other specialists and physicians of eminence saw him, first and last, and, as usual, there was a great diversity of opinion, but, as is also usual in all such cases that have come to my knowledge, the ablest men — those most capable of giving a correct opinion in such cases — agreed that the young man had not sustained any injury worthy of notice, and that he was shamming.

The company, therefore, refused to pay the exorbitant sum which the mother and the attorneys she had employed demanded, and so the mother brought suit in the sum of fifty thousand dollars.

The young man continued to stare and to look foolish, but never spoke a word, unless he did to his mother when no one else was present.

The case finally came to trial and the jury gave a verdict for thirty-five thousand dollars. There was a motion for a rehearing, which was overruled, and an appeal taken.

Just about this time the railroad company's surgeons succeeded, by some kind of representations, in getting the young man into a private hospital be-longing to the company's principal surgeon; and, after getting him there, they put him on the operating table and talked in his presence about trephining the skull — the doctor saying, so that the young man could hear him, that he felt quite sure that the operation would relieve the young man; that his mind would be restored, etc.,. etc. They gave him ether, and when he got to the point where the subject begins to lose mental control and usually exhibits more or less excitement the young man began to struggle and to swear, "like our army in Flanders." "Let me alone, you! Let me alone, I say!" and so forth, and more of the same sort

The doctors then desisted and permitted him to recover from the slight influence of the ether he had taken; and, when he became thoroughly con-scious, he looked at the surgeon and said, "Well, I guess you have caught me."

Just then his mother came in. The doctor said to her: "Mrs. H., I have cured your son. His voice is restored and he can talk as well as anyone." The doctor said that the mother's face took on an expression which it would be hard to describe, but she said not a word.

Just about this time another scene was taking place and being enacted which was much more dramatic than that of the pretence of anaesthetizing the plaintiff, and this scene was being enacted at the court house.

After the railroad company's attorneys had given notice of appeal, an old and eminent lawyer of Fort Worth asked to be sworn and to be permitted to take the stand; After he had taken the stand, he told this most extraordinary story: He said that he had known this young man's mother for a long time.

Several weeks before this young man sustained the fall she came to him, at his office, and presented a hypothetical case to him, of this character: If a young man, working for a railroad company, sustains a fall, and, though not hurt, should put on an appearance of imbecility, should refuse to speak, and should exhibit all the appearances of one whose mind is an entire blank, and should maintain this character, without any change, did he — the attorney — believe that suit could be brought and a large verdict obtained and finally collected. He, thinking, as he said, that she was presenting a merely hypothetical case, answered her — giving the *ifs* and the *ands* and the modifications which would naturally surround and pertain to such a case; but, in the main, he thought a verdict might be obtained with such a case.

Then she threw off the hypothetical cloak and told him frankly that she was thinking of having her son enact such a *role*, and, in case he did so, she desired him, the Colonel, to take the case.

He said that he could scarcely believe that she meant it, but she insisted that she did, and, after having been convinced that she did mean it, he then told her very positively that he would, under no circumstances, have anything to do with such a case, and implored her to drop the whole thing then and there. He told her of what an evil start in life she was giving her young son — her only child — but it did no good.

After having been convinced that the Colonel would not take the case, she then asked him if there were not other lawyers. He answered that there were and mentioned the very firm which eventually brought the suit and conducted it to a verdict for thirty-five thousand dollars. However, those lawyers insisted that she did not come to them until after the young man claimed to have been injured, and that then they never had a hint that the young man was acting a part. The story of the old and most honorable attorney created a profound sensation; the court set aside the verdict of the jury. The widow and her son were arrested, arraigned and afterwards indicted, the attorneys withdrew from the case and even refused to be employed to defend the plaintiff and his mother on the charge of attempt to defraud, and, taking things altogether, the wiley widow and the actor son were left in a bad plight before the community.

The only manhood and decency the young man exhibited in the case was that he vehemently insisted that his mother knew nothing of his attempt to defraud; that he concocted the whole scheme himself, and that his mother believed all along that his case was genuine and that he was really ruined. In short, he tried to save his miserable mother from the reproaches and contempt of the community. But his mother's proposition to the lawyer, even before his attempt to defraud, would contradict this statement.

At last accounts this miserable woman and her son — this woman who had always held an enviable position amongst the people with whom she associated — stood indicted jointly for an attempt to defraud, and, unless the jury refuses to punish anyone for attempting to defraud a railroad company, they will both probably be sent to prison for a term of years.

Very much later than the above two very sensational cases occurred at Kansas City, Mo. In the first one a blacksmith at Brunswick, in Chariton County, Mo., was arrested at the instance of some of the officers of the Metropolitan Street Railway Company for defrauding that company. It seems that a year or more ago the blacksmith had brought suit against this company on account of injuries which he claimed to have sustained at a wreck at the bottom of the incline on the Ninth street line.

This incline was very steep and down the incline cars were taken almost to the union station. Sometimes the cars would get away from the gripman on account of a grip failing to work properly. A number of times there were quite serious wrecks at the bottom of this incline, and there had been a wreck at the time when this Brunswick blacksmith claimed to have been injured; but he had communicated to a man whom he took to be a friend (after he had compromised and had received two thousand dollars from the Street Railroad Company) that he had not been in the wreck — in fact, had not been near there at the time the wreck occurred, and the first idea of making claims on account of injuries said to have been received there was suggested to him by another man.

After having been arrested he confessed the whole thing to the officers and to others, and that confession stood until he saw a lawyer, when he repudiated it and said that he had not made a confession.

Of course, he will go upon the witness stand, when his case comes to trial, and swear that he never made a confession, and he will swear, further, that he was injured as he claimed to have been; and it is strongly probable that the court will rule out his confession which was made after his arrest, because the court will argue, the confession was made when the defendant was "under duress;" but, the one great obstacle in this man's way is that he made this confession to one or more persons before his arrest; in fact, he rather boasted of how he had overcome the Street Railway Company and had made a big "haul" out of them. [1]

Only a few months after this last occurrence another man was arrested in Kansas City, at the instance of the management of the Metropolitan Street Railway Company, who had brought suit (and, I believe, had compromised his case with the Street Railway Company, for a consideration, and who was so tickled over the fact of his smartness that he, too, told a friend that he was not present at the time when he claimed to have been injured).

The officers of the Metropolitan Street Railway Company deserve a medal for their courage in thus bringing to trial two scoundrels who are of the very worst of those who would rob corporations, for, when a man has been in a wreck, we must concede that,, may be, he sustained some injury, but, where a man makes claims for injuries which he claims to have received in a wreck when he was not even present, we are bound to say that he is of the worst.

[1] Since this was written this man was convicted of perjury, in the Kansas City, Kansas, District Court, and is now serving a six years' sentence at Lansing - the first instance of anyone being punished for defrauding a corporation that I ever heard of. All honor to Kansas! Let her have the blue ribbon.

Conclusion

THIS concludes the story of my twenty-five years' of service with the Missouri Pacific Railroad Company, and of my experiences with the sick and wounded employees, and with the malingering, fraudulent and pretending citizens, passengers and others,: who were injured or who claimed to have been injured by the company, or its employees, and of other cases that have come to my knowledge, by reason of my interest in this subject.

It is pertinent to ask the question, right here, why the difference between the sturdy, upright and honest pioneers — the people amongst whom I was reared, and the grasping, pretending and dishonest men and women of the present day? Why the careless indifference of the one, as to money, and what is termed "the good things of this world," and the grasping eagerness to get money, of our modern fellow citizen?

It is a difference in the times, in the value that people set upon money, and the things that it will purchase — not the least of which are, the ease, the comforts, the freedom from care and the ability to go and come at one's own sweet will, and to enjoy all the good things of life, without let or hindrance.

As communities grow older and people are more highly educated, the appetite for enjoyment grows greater — grows to be almost morbid, in fact.

People who do not labor, put in a good deal of time thinking about the gratification of their lower and baser appetites; and, thinking soon blossoms into realization. Men and women seek to do things — and actually do things, the very thought of which would have been revolting to our pioneer ancestors.

The indulgence of the baser appetites degrades people, and as they become more and more degraded, morally, the more readily do they seize upon and indulge in all sorts of conduct which, in the very nature of things, cannot result otherwise than in blunting and stunting all of those higher and nobler qualities and faculties which distinguish men and women in the Better walks of life.

Others, less fortunate — or who think they are less fortunate — seeing the daily conduct of those who have money, time and leisure, grow envious and begin to seek ways and means by which they too may indulge in those things which do not make for their betterment.

They really believe that such things bring happiness; but never were poor fools worse mistaken; for I feel constrained to say, and I wish to emphasize this to you, if you are young, there is no happiness in this life like that which comes from right living; and, when I say "right living," I mean right living in the very highest and best meaning of those words — right living as to honest and fair dealing with your fellow man, right living in being willing to possess that and that alone which is your own, which you have earned, or which has come to you through the honest inheritance of honestly acquired property, and in not coveting your neighbor's ox, nor his ass, nor any thing which is his; right living, more particularly, in curbing those appetites and desires of the animal organism, the indulgence of which leads to the wrecking of both the moral and the physical man and woman.

"Whatsoever ye sow, that shall ye also reap." If we sow righteousness, if we sow moderation in all things, if we sow honesty, then shall we reap happiness — the only happiness which is worthy of being called by that name.

If we sow dishonesty; if we sow covetousness; if we sow bestiality and the indulgence of the baser appetites and desires, then, just so surely, shall we reap bitter unhappiness, in the end. I have stood by the bedside of the poorly educated, honest and hard working — the religious man and woman, who loved their God, and strove to love their neighbor as they loved themselves; and I have seen them die, with that beatific smile, that look of exaltation on the countenance; and I have stood by the bedside of men whose lives had been spent in dishonesty, in covetousness, and in the indulgence of all of those appetites and desires, which inevitably drag down and degrade the human being, and I have witnessed their last end; and I can only say, save me from the tragedy, on the one hand, and, let me die as the good man dies, even though I die in poverty and in ignorance.

Don't understand me to say, or to even believe, that all men and women are bad, for I know that there are good men and women who are falling upward every day. But there is an admixture of the bad everywhere, especially in these modern days, and "a little leaven leaveneth the whole lump;" so that, in time, more and more become bad; and, in the matter of covetousness, in particular, it grows rapidly.

It is not in the nature of the average man and woman to see their neighbors prosper — to see them enjoying all the fine and costly things in dress, in houses, and the lavish expenditure of money for fine furnishings of those houses, without becoming covetousness and desiring to shine also. Hence, men and women seek to obtain money in the easiest way, and in a way that offers the least danger to them, although they may obtain it dishonestly. I know of nothing which appeals to the mind of the average man and woman as to the best method of obtaining what is, to them, a large sum of money, like that of going upon the witness stand and swearing for it. The chance of detection in a fraud of this kind is very slim; and, when a man, or a woman goes on the witness stand and swears falsely as to his or her ailments, and disabilities, there are very few judges who would ever find them guilty of false swearing, no matter how apparent their falsehoods may be to a physician. They know this, hence the alacrity with which they begin and pursue their fraudulent designs.

But, where does the blame lie? At whose door, or doors, does the blame lie for this condition of the public mind, and of public morals, which causes men and women to seek to obtain money by such dishonest methods? Undoubtedly, at the doors of those who are rich, and, who being rich, daily flaunt their finery in the faces of those who are below them in the financial scale.

Since the close of the civil war — about forty-one years — this country has made more than ten thousand millionaires and multi-millionaires, and I do not hesitate to say that at least ninety-five per cent of them have been made by legislation. How? By the granting of monopolies of one kind or another, by the voting of subsidies, in giving away our public domain to great corporations; and, worse still, by failing to throw around the public that protection from grasping monopolies which our national and state law-making bodies could have done, but did not. We have thus, through our national congress, made thousands of millionaires and multi-millionaires, and tens of thousands of others who, though not millionaires, are worth hundreds of thousands, and it is the conduct of many of those people which causes envy and jealousy in the hearts of those less favored, and which causes so many to be willing to perjure themselves, and to wreck their immortal souls, in order to get a little money, with which, if not to put on airs, at least to get more of the comforts of life than they now have, and to make a better appearance in the world than they now make.

I know of no meaner sin, to call it such, than that of those who are favored, by accident or otherwise, to parade their wealth and flaunt their finery in the faces of those who are just as intelligent, just as well educated, and who are just as capable of enjoying themselves, in a legitimate and reasonable way, as themselves, but who, by reason of their poverty, cannot.

If, in the days of the Apostles, to eat meat sometimes caused a brother to offend, and Christians were therefore forbidden to do anything which, by example, might cause others to do wrong, then how much worse is it now, for those who have their tens and hundreds of thousands, and even their millions, to parade their yachts, their costly automobiles, and all the evidences of wealth, which money can buy, before those who are not so well situated in life. I believe in a legitimate enjoyment of all the good things a man may have, that is rightfully and honestly his; but, the vulgar display that is made by those people who have fattened and got rich in ways and by means which, to say the least, are questionable, excites nothing but contempt and disgust. The yacht races and tallyho parades at Newport, the automobile races, the balls and the hundred-thousand-dollar dinners by those who have taken the money out of the pockets of the people, by buying up Congress, State Legislatures and courts, ought to be followed by writs of arrest, quick trials and the penitentiary.

160

The people of great wealth, who permit their wealth to wreck their morals, have many and diverse ways and means by which, through their meetings and assemblages at their favorite resorts, at certain seasons, to indulge in excesses of one kind or another, which are nothing more nor less than orgies, drunken orgies, would perhaps, be a better designation. Many of our own people go abroad for the purpose of learning how persons of their kind in older communities spend their time and their money. England and Prance both have drawing powers, but the former, I believe, gets a majority, and this is true, I am led to believe, because of the fact that the English speak the same language, and of course, the social whirl is smoother and more to their taste, where they do not have to have an interpreter.

In England it is the custom to have "house parties" at certain great houses amongst the aristocracy in the country, where many persons congregate in certain "social seasons," and spend days and weeks drinking, gambling, dancing and eating. No less a person than Miss Marie Corelli, the authoress, says that many of the middle class, in England, now refuse to permit their daughters to act as lady's maids, governesses, or to accept any such positions with many of the so-called "great ladies," because of the bad example that is set before them by those ladies, and of the danger to which they are subjected from the men. And is it any wonder? What tender young girl, who has been carefully reared and well educated, under the auspices of religious parents, and at religious schools, can be brought in contact with such things, without being in danger of utter wreck and ruin of their morals and their lives? How natural it would be for such young girls to feel and to believe that whatever their wealthy and great mistresses indulge in or do must be right.

In this country there are many places at which our very wealthy newly-rich gather, in certain seasons, to indulge in the pleasures of the card table, the yacht and the automobile races, the balls, the dinners and the tallyho parades.

At certain times, when there are to be tallyho parades or yacht races at Newport, Rhode Island, excursion trains and boats are run from many cities to Newport, with reduced rates, in order that the "common herd" may be able to go and see how the par-venue "put on airs." I have seen thousands and tens of thousands gather at Newport, from all over Massachusetts, Rhode Island and other nearby states, and line up forty deep and a half mile long, to see the rich New Yorkers On their tallyhos crack their whips and move off — a dozen or more in line, one after another, around that splendid twelve miles drive around the eastern end of the island of Rhode Island, past the magnificent "cottages" belonging to the millionaires. Just think of a "cottage" with forty or fifty rooms! And then I have seen that vast multitude rush across the open end of the mule shoe and almost fall over each other in order to get to the coming out place, and see the tallyhos when they arrive at the end of the parade. And it is the same with the yacht races, at which the women are the actors. There are thousands of people who are rich, but not so rich as those millionaires, and who cannot get into "the four hundred," who go to those functions and grieve their poor hearts out because of the fact that they are not quite rich enough to be a part of this great display. There are some ways, however, in which they can imitate those rich people, and they do— the men imitate the men in dress, and the women imitate the women in suppressing the finer instincts of motherhood and refusing to bear children, and in having a dog instead. It is actually sickening to read of the dog parties, in which one elegant lady's dog gives a party and cards are issued and other ladies' dogs are invited! Almost every woman must have some little helpless thing to love; and those who refuse to bring children into the world, and do not have them to love and to pet, simply let a dog fill the place which a sweet child should fill. It is a puzzle and a wonder to any right thinking and right feeling human being to understand how a woman — a being claiming to have the feelings and instincts of a woman, and many of them members of fashionable churches, can know that there are thousands of little children without mothers and without homes, or home comforts, that are holding out weak little hands and lifting pale, tender, starving faces and literally begging for some good woman to take them and give them a home and to love them and mother them, and to know that so many of the rich pass by those little ones and take a dog — a nasty, common, woolly dog, or a bulldogs, to their hearts and love and mother them! Bah! Honestly, it is sickening!

And it is just as much of a puzzle and a problem for us to know that there are hundreds and thousands of millionaires and multi-millionaires, who daily see the poverty in the streets of our great cities, where they live and make and spend their millions — who see the hundreds and thousands of poor old men and women, who have failed, from some cause or other, to lay by enough to keep them comfortably in their declining years, and they see the thousands of poor women with the crowds of little, almost starving and freezing children about them, and yet they do nothing, or practically nothing, as compared to what they could and ought to do.

Just think, my kind-hearted readers, what could be done with a little effort. You and I know of half a dozen men in one city who could easily spare from ten to twenty millions, and a great many others who could donate from one to five millions, and dozens of others who could give up hundreds of thousands, without ever missing it, and then think for a moment -what could be done with this vast sum of money! Of the great farms of thousands of acres it would purchase, the magnificent homes that would accommodate from one to ten thousand of aged and indigent men and women and of widows and orphan children.

Now, after all the farms have been purchased, and those great co-operative homes are built, the doors could be opened for the reception of those for whom they have been built. The greater part of the vast sum of money donated could be invested, or put out at interest, and this interest could be used to partly run those homes. Competent superintendents and assistant superintendents could be employed; the larger boys of the orphan class could work on those farms under those superintendents; and such trades as carpentering, blacksmithing, type setting and printing, the tinners, shoemakers, painters, plasterers and brickmakers, and bricklayers might be taught them. Good schools might be maintained, under competent teachers, right in those great houses, for six months in the year; and the girls could be taught millinery, dressmaking, box making, teaching, shorthand and the typewriter, and many of the old men might be employed at such work as they could do, and the old women might also be employed at house cleaning, bed making, cooking, and, in fact, much of the work, inside and out, could be done by such of the inmates, old and young, as could work. Everything in the way of the cereals, vegetables, fruits, melons, and so forth, could be raised, as well as horses, cattle, hogs and sheep; and, in addition to raising those things serviceable in furnishing meats for the home, the boys and girls would be familiarized with the young animals. and I know of nothing which keeps a boy's heart nearer where it should be than handling and loving a young lamb, a pig, a colt or a calf. It is such a life as this that makes great men of those who come from the farm. In addition to giving good homes to thousands and tens of thousands of those who now have no homes, to giving them a plenty of good wholesome food, good warm clothing in winter, and suitable clothing in summer, and good, comfortable beds for old and young — for thousands of those who have nothing better than rags or straw for a bed, the younger could be given a good education, and could assist in making a living for themselves, their mothers, and their little brothers and sisters, in addition to all this,. I say, these young children could be brought up under the influences of the Sunday school and the church, for they could have both right in these homes; and,, instead of the thousands of criminals which come from just such neglected, homeless, naked and starving boys, and, instead of the wayward and lost girls, which come from the neglected, homeless, cloth-less and food-less little girls, could be turned out into the world every year, a number of honest, educated, self-reliant young artisans, and sweet, good, loving. Christian girls, and those boys could work at the trade they had learned in the home, and those girls could teach, work at millinery, dress-making and typewriting, and could make their own living, and contribute their part toward helping forward with every good movement for the world's betterment; and, while the girls would go out and marry and become the lovely centers of admiring groups, the boys would stand as stalwart, intelligent defenders of the great republic.

My God! What can men and women with millions be thinking of? And this great work might be set in motion and carried on near every large city in the Union, and the interest of the endowment fund saved, by the work of the inmates, could be used to buy other land, build other homes and to care for thousands and tens of thousands of the aged and indigent, and of widows and orphans, until, within twenty years, this goodly land of ours would be almost a Paradise on earth. If those who are immensely wealthy would devote their surplus wealth to work like this instead of flaunting their wealth in the faces of the poor, then maybe so many would not be ready to go into court every time they get a little bump or scratch and perjure their immortal souls for a chance to get something for nothing. Those possessing great means would say, no doubt, that this is all "gush" and "rot," and impracticable; or that it would tend to make more paupers, or to make pauperism respectable; but such is not the case. Such a great charity is not only eminently practicable, as any sensible and right-thinking person can see, but it would not tend to create more paupers. On the contrary, every person, male and female, who is capable of working, could be made to work, and to work where their labor would count, and amount to something. Instead of fostering respectable idleness in young boys and girls, every one of them could work; and, while working, would be learning a trade, or a business, which would secure them employment and lay a sure foundation for a respectable living and the leading of a reputable life, after he or she should leave the home. This is not all, — while working, their hearts would be made glad and lighter, by the assurance that, when the days' work is over, they would go to a good, wholesome meal, to an evening in a comfortable, clean room, where they could read good literature, and, at last, old and young could lie down upon a clean, soft bed, with a plenty of warm covering in winter, and instead of such a life increasing pauperism and making it respectable, it would give good, comfortable homes to tens of thousands— old and young — and work, when their work would count for something, not only at the time, but for the young, would lay a sure foundation for their future, and it would lift a load of poverty and want from the hearts of many a poor old man and woman, and they could look forward to having a plenty to eat and a good place to sleep, while they live, and to being put away in a decent way when they should "shuffle off this mortal coil."

I believe that such a work is worthy of the efforts of the very best and noblest men and women that live. And what a consolation to them in seeing so much for good accomplished through their efforts and with the money given by them, as compared with gambling, racing and debauchery by the men, and the indulgence of all the baser appetites of the women, which indulgence is only relieved by the fact that, to pander to the instincts of motherhood, they take to their hearts; their tables and their beds — *a wooly dog!*

www.ingramcontent.com/pod-product-compliance
Lightning Source LLC
Chambersburg PA
CBHW022040190326
41520CB00008B/655